"Because novels and poems name the emotions, putting them into narrative action, literature has always been the home territory of emotion. Now, venturing all the way across the bridge to verbal art from his own discipline of sociology, Mariano Longo shows that a major future assignment of this crossover field will be to specify with stronger theories how emotions are always relationships: social between persons, changeable in historical time. First he offers a critique of the history of sociology, where from circa 1900 to 2019 there has been a steadily growing acceptance that emotions have a rational, historical explanation as part of social change. Next he analyzes a broad international range of literary works to account for the mass-emotion of crowds, the effect of envy on economics and class-relations between the eras of Shakespeare and Trollope, and changes in love (and theories of love) from the Middle Ages to now. Longo doesn't come forward as a literary critic, but he has many habits of attention congenial to the works of imagination under study: he finds crucial turning-point passages to quote, he quotes at sufficient length to exhibit style, and he brings in already-existing literary criticism relevant to the purposes of his innovative theory. So in this well-argued essay, packed with persuasive literary examples, Mariano Longo significantly extends and complicates the sociology of emotions, and of research in emotions generally."

– Donald Wesling, Professor Emeritus of English Literature, University of California, San Diego, USA; author of Joys and Sorrows of Imaginary Persons (On Literary Emotions)

Emotions through Literature

Engaging with the wide sociological literature on emotions, this book explores the social representation of emotions, their management and their effects by making reference to creative sources. With a specific focus on literary narrative, including the works of figures such as Dante, Austen, Manzoni, Tolstoy and Kundera, the author draws out the capacity of literary works to describe and represent both the external aspects of social relations and the inner motivations of the involved actors. An interdisciplinary study that combines sociology, narratology, philosophy, historical analysis and literary criticism, *Emotions through Literature* invites us to re-think the role of emotions in sociological analysis, employing literary narratives to give plausible intellectual responses to the double nature of emotions, their being both individual and social.

Mariano Longo is Full Professor of Sociology at the University of Salento, Italy, and author of *Fiction and Social Reality: Literature and Narratives as Sociological Resources*.

Classical and Contemporary Social Theory

Classical and Contemporary Social Theory publishes rigorous scholarly work that re-discovers the relevance of social theory for contemporary times, demonstrating the enduring importance of theory for modern social issues. The series covers social theory in a broad sense, inviting contributions on both 'classical' and modern theory, thus encompassing sociology, without being confined to a single discipline. As such, work from across the social sciences is welcome, provided that volumes address the social context of particular issues, subjects, or figures and offer new understandings of social reality and the contribution of a theorist or school to our understanding of it.

The series considers significant new appraisals of established thinkers or schools, comparative works or contributions that discuss a particular social issue or phenomenon in relation to the work of specific theorists or theoretical approaches. Contributions are welcome that assess broad strands of thought within certain schools or across the work of a number of thinkers, but always with an eye toward contributing to contemporary understandings of social issues and contexts.

Series Editor
Stjepan G. Mestrovic, Texas A&M University, USA

The Unmasking Style in Social Theory
Peter Baehr

Writing the Body Politic
A John O'Neill Reader
Thomas Kemple and Mark Featherstone

Emotions through Literature
Fictional Narratives, Society and the Emotional Self
Mariano Longo

For more information about this series, please visit:
https://www.routledge.com/sociology/series/ASHSER1383

Emotions through Literature

Fictional Narratives, Society and the
Emotional Self

Mariano Longo

Routledge
Taylor & Francis Group

LONDON AND NEW YORK

First published 2020
by Routledge
2 Park Square, Milton Park, Abingdon, Oxon OX14 4RN

and by Routledge
605 Third Avenue, New York, NY 10017

First issued in paperback 2020

Routledge is an imprint of the Taylor & Francis Group, an informa business

British Library Cataloguing-in-Publication Data
A catalogue record for this book is available from the British Library

Library of Congress Cataloging-in-Publication Data
Names: Longo, Mariano, author.
Title: Emotions through literature: fictional narratives, society and the emotional self / Mariano Longo.
Other titles: Fictional narratives, society and the emotional self
Description: First edition. | Oxon, New York: Routledge, 2019. |
Series: Classical and contemporary social theory | Includes bibliographical references and index.
Identifiers: LCCN 2019014295 (print) | LCCN 2019018330 (ebook) |
ISBN 9780415793384 (hbk)
Subjects: LCSH: Emotions in literature. | Emotions–Social aspects. |
Self-management (Psychology) | Fiction–Social aspects. |
Fiction–History and criticism.
Classification: LCC PN56.E6 L66 2019 (print) | LCC PN56.E6 (ebook) |
DDC 809/.93353–dc23
LC record available at https://lccn.loc.gov/2019014295
LC ebook record available at https://lccn.loc.gov/2019018330

ISBN 13: 978-0-367-72690-4 (pbk)
ISBN 13: 978-0-415-79338-4 (hbk)

Typeset in Times New Roman
by Deanta Global Publishing Services, Chennai, India

To Michele, and his passion for the social

I would like to thank Luca Benvenga, Fabio De Nardis, Elena Laurenzi, Lucia Mancini, Gianpasquale Preite, Ferdinando Spina and Claudia Venuleo for their help and competent reading.

Contents

1   By way of introduction

A sociology of emotions through literature

The very possibility of a sociology of emotions lies not in homologies but in differences. If emotions were experienced and managed in the same way across historical times, cultures and the different strata of the same society, any attempt at a sociology of emotions would be frustrating. In order for a specific sociological interest in emotions to emerge, the idea had to be overcome, according to which emotions are the sole irreflexive output of some interior drive, a mechanical response to the environment directed by our genetic make-up. Approaches which consider emotions as universal, transcultural and homogeneous, based as they are on some essentialist conception of human action, are endowed with a cogent persuasiveness. Essentialism (so one could plausibly call this trend) may be detected in biology, in psychology and even in the social sciences. The specific features of the approach were defined by Charles Darwin (1872) in his *The Expression of Emotions in Man and Animals*, in which he contested the idea of a divine origin of human expression, justified by the resemblance of humans to God, and, in so doing, established a substantial continuity between animal and human emotions. Thus, according to Darwin, emotions and their expression are inborn, part of our inherited qualities:

> That the chief expressive actions, exhibited by man and by the lower animals, are now innate or inherited, that is, have not been learnt by the individual, is admitted by every one. So little has learning or imitation to do with several of them that they are from the earliest days and throughout life quite beyond our control.
>
> (ibid., p. 351)

The evidence of the inborn character of emotions is to be traced, according to Darwin, in the spontaneous (hence non-imitative) capacity of young children to express feelings. One more quotation may explain Darwin's position:

> We may see children, only two or three years old, and even those born blind, blushing from shame; and the naked scalp of a very young infant reddens from passion. Infants scream from pain directly after birth, and all their features then assume the same form as during subsequent years [...] We can

thus also understand the fact that the young and the old of widely different races, both with man and animals, express the same state of mind by the same movements.

(ibid., p. 352)

Learning as an aspect of emotional expression is not utterly denied by Darwin, but it is reduced to a complementary character of hereditariness and is given the ancillary role of training in the appropriate use of innate qualities: "it is remarkable that some [emotions], which are certainly innate, require practice in the individual, before they are performed in a full and perfect manner; for instance, the inheritance of most of weeping and laughing" (ibid.).

Charles Darwin's approach has been highly influential, chiefly in the field of psychology (Ekman, 1984; 1992), even though traces of essentialism may be detected in some sociological treatment of emotions (see *infra*, Chapter 2). This should not surprise, for at least two reasons: the first is the power of Darwin's argument, which destabilized the long-held idea of a peculiar position of man in the universe, producing a paradigmatic change according to which the human being is a product of natural evolution and cannot be utterly distinguished from the rest of nature. The second is due to the apparently incontrovertible character of Darwin's reasoning: after all, it is part of our experience of the world that we all express (and probably feel) emotions in the same way. Yet, if emotions are conceived as innate, the operating space for the development of a sociology of emotions is, by necessity, limited: emotions are pre-given; hence, emotional behaviour appears as the field of investigation of other disciplinary fields, such as psychology. The sociological perspective on emotion must, by necessity, start from a different set of premises. Some 30 years after Charles Darwin had issued his book on the expression of feeling, Charles Horton Cooley published his *Human Nature and Social Order* (1902). The American sociologist and social psychologist owes his fame chiefly to the idea that our self is the product of a looking-glass effect, by which we construct our personality as a reflex of our fellow people's reaction to our conduct. Sociality is relevant for the individual, and this holds as well for the emotional component of the individual's psychology. Cooley does not deny that some human dispositions (e.g. anger and fear) are genetically determined. Nonetheless, although emotions may be inborn as Darwin stated, we learn how to use and manage them properly in the process of our socialization (see *infra*, Chapter 2). The space for a properly sociological investigation of emotions (the complex relation between raw emotionality and its cultural and social definition) is therefore already traced at the beginning of the 20th century. Yet sociology disregarded Cooley's insights and specialized throughout the 20th century chiefly in the analysis of the rational actor, removing emotions as an object of investigation. The actor is a sociological construct intended as being able to interpret action either as a choice among alternatives, or as the adjustment to social norms and values, which need to be cognitively understood before being translated by the social agent into effective action, or, eventually, as an interpretative process of construction of the meaning of the social scene. In this theoretical framework, emotions have at most a residual or marginal role.

The consolidated idea of the inborn character of emotionality accounts both for the marginal role of emotions in classical sociology (where they represented, with relevant exceptions, a collateral topic) and for the substantial exclusion of emotions and emotionality in post-classical sociology (see *infra*, Chapter 2). One had to wait until the late 20th century for an embryonic sociology of emotions to develop. This was due chiefly to the long-lasting search for a theoretical and epistemological autonomous profile for sociology, in which sociologists had applied themselves at least since Durkheim's methodological investigation (Durkheim, 1895). Emotionality was excluded from the field of disciplinary relevant objects, so much so that even individualistic approaches, although conceiving the social actor as the triggering element of social processes, tended to consider the individual as a rational, cogitative, constantly interpreting agent. This sociological conception of the social actor is an evident over-simplification. Indeed, the process by which we understand reality is not exclusively based on intellectual processes, utterly separated from what we feel and perceive. Emotions – so has been stressed by recent accounts (Nussbaum, 2001) – have a relevant function in determining our reasoned reaction to the environment. One of the tasks of the sociology of emotions is actually to avoid an ill-posed separation between the emotive and the cognitive, the instinctual and the rational, the objective and the subjective. In most circumstances, emotions are, in fact, the premise of cognition. As Arlie Hochschild convincingly states, the opinion is diffuse according to which:

> emotion is dangerous in the first place because it distorts perception and leads people to act irrationally which means that all ways of reducing emotion are automatically good. Of course, a person gripped by fear may make mistakes, may find reflection difficult, and may not (as we say) be able to think.
>
> (Hochschild, 1983a, p. 31)

Yet, emotions are essential as a way to find one's bearings:

> But a person totally without emotion has no warning system, no guidelines to the self-relevance of a sight, a memory, or a fantasy. Like one who cannot feel and touches fire, an emotionless person suffers a sense of arbitrariness, which from the point of view of his or her self-interest is irrational. In fact, emotion is a potential avenue to "the reasonable view".
>
> (ibid.)

Emotions are thus essential in our perception, comprehension and assessment of the social world, in so far as we relate to our fellow people chiefly through emotional display. One more quotation from Arlie Hochschild:

> [l]ike hearing or seeing, feeling provides a useful set of clues in figuring out what is real. A show of feeling by someone else is interesting to us precisely

because it may reflect a buried perspective and may offer a clue as to how that person may act.

(ibid., p. 31)

Yet, regardless of the apparent self-evident significance of emotions for our understanding of the social world, sociology has neglected their role, by generally expunging emotionality from the analysis of action and interaction. The awareness of the importance of emotions in our understanding of the world is a later gain, one which general sociology owes to the development of the sociology of emotions. Chapter 2 is devoted to a short review both of the location of emotions within classical and post-classical investigation and of the chief developing trends of the sociology of emotions, since its emergence as a well-defined disciplinary sub-area in the late 1970s. The chapter analyzes the refreshing effect that the novel interest in emotions as a proper sociological topic produced on sociology. Two things may be anticipated here. Sociology needed a theoretical effort, as well as a keen capacity of observation, in order to dismantle the apparently solid relation between our genetic make-up and emotions. The emergence of a branch of the discipline devoted to the topic shows the capacity of sociology to detect new possibilities and take new routes. Moreover, dealing with subject matters which are the specific field of other disciplines (e.g. psychology, neurosciences) implies a strong disciplinary and methodological awareness. Sociologists may deal with emotions, may make reference to interdisciplinary sources, and yet remain aware of the boundaries and possibilities of their discipline.

It is a matter of fact that the way emotions are dealt with within the sociological perspective is specific to the disciplinary methodological and theoretical reference framework. Emotions are part of our perception of other fellow people; they are aroused and managed in social intercourses. Moreover, emotions do not only belong to the micro-situations of face-to-face interaction. They are also relevant for a wide variety of social processes that operate both on the meso-level of social organization and social movements and on the macro-level of social systems (e.g. the political or the economic system). Sociology looks at emotions as both a cause and an effect of social processes (Barbalet, 2004, p. 9). In the first case, an essentialist trend is at work: emotions are conceived as part of a biological and psychological substratum, able to produce or codetermine social phenomena. In the second case, which one could call constructivist, emotions are intended as aspects of a specific culture and social context which determine when, and in which social circumstances, they may be properly manifested and how they should be managed. This second approach is chiefly interested in the multiple forms by which emotions become socially visible and the plurality of ways society comes to term with (hence controls and drives) what one could call the asocial component of emotionality (Hochschild, 1990; Thois, 1990). Thus, emotions are an inescapable component of the social life, and this is reason enough for every society to detect original, distinct ways to tame their potential disruptiveness. It goes without saying that the relevance of emotions for the social sciences has, by necessity, to do with their sociality. A psychologist or a neuroscientist may be interested in the individual or physiological component of emotions; a sociologist may not.

This implies that in the limited perspective of the social sciences, emotions are social regardless of the self-evident fact that they emerge from within. The sociality of emotions does not imply a neat separation of biology or psychology and the social sciences. It implies a change of perspective, a distancing from the object we observe. When objecting to the substantialist idea that society is only an abstraction, since what really exists are the individuals, Simmel (1917) suggested that even individuals are, in principle, aggregates of cells, organs and processes. Thus, the relevant question is not whether society as such exists or not, but what is the perspective an observer has to assume in order to behold social phenomena. Let us read Simmel:

> when we look at human life from a certain distance, we see each individual in his precise differentiation from all others. But if we increase the distance, the single individual disappears, and there emerges, instead, the picture of a "society" with its forms and colors [...] It is certainly no less justified than is the other in which the parts, the individuals, are seen in their differentiation [...] The difference between the two merely consists in the difference between purposes of cognition; and this difference, in turn, corresponds to a difference in distance.
>
> (ibid., p. 8)

Simmel's approach is an elegant critique of any essentialist conception of social phenomena, which felicitously applies to the questions of emotions. "The right to sociological study" – Simmel writes – "thus is not in the least endangered by the circumstance that all real happenings only occur in individuals" (ibid.). Emotions may biologically or neurologically occur in individuals, yet a perspective distancing from the physiological or biological processes may allow an accurate analysis of the relational, communicational, cultural aspects of emotions, which in turn strongly justifies a specifically sociological approach to what people feel and how they manifest what they feel. And a way of distancing from the mere physiological processes is to focus on the culturally determined procedures by which we define and control our emotions, conforming our emotionally driven behaviour to collectively defined standards. Here is a meaningful quotation, taken from Arlie Hochschild:

> If we conceive of feeling not as a periodic abdication to biology but as something we do by attending to inner sensation in a given way, by defining situations in a given way, by managing in given ways, then it becomes plainer just how plastic and susceptible to reshaping techniques a feeling can be. The very act of managing emotion can be seen as part of what the emotion becomes. But this idea gets lost if we assume, as the organismic theorists do, that how we manage or express feeling is extrinsic to emotion. The organismic theorists want to explain how emotion is "motored by

instinct" and so they by-pass the question of how we come to assess, label, and manage emotion.

(Hochschild, 1983a, p. 27)

Another clear-cut description of the relevance of emotions for the social scientists (including sociologists) differentiates the conception of emotions in the social sciences from the idea, so typical of other branches of knowledge, that emotions are raw materials of our individual experience. The description has been proposed by an historian, Barbara Rosenwein, who, in an essay about the complex methodological question of studying emotions historically, writes:

> Although we tend to speak of the emotions of individuals, emotions are above all instruments of sociability. They are not only socially constructed and "sustain and endorse cultural systems," but they also inform human relations at all levels, from intimate talk between husbands and wives to global relations. Expressions of emotions should thus be read as social interactions. The emotional give and take among people form "scripts" that lead to new emotions and readjusted relationship.
>
> (Rosenwein, 2010, pp. 19–20)

This quotation puts emotions in a sociologically appropriate relational dimension. It, moreover, hints at a relevant topic of this monograph: the idea that emotions are based on short, prototypical scripts, for example on sketchy stories of what it means to feel, manifest, observe emotions or be involved in emotional interactions. Any essentialist conception should take into account that even if emotions were the sole manifestations of internal events, scripts (hence narratives) of emotions are necessary to intend properly their meaningful dimension. And even if we assume that our capacity to narrate is innate, actual narratives are always the social output of a cultural construction. In order to come closer to the topic, a short detour is required here.

The question of narrative has been tackled by a wide variety of perspectives. Structuralist semiotics intend narrative as a mode of communication: it is transculturally diffuse, and as a shared structure, it makes the question of translation less problematic than other linguistic patterns (Barthes, 1966). A narrative may be translated into another language with less difficulty than, say, a joke or a metaphor. As the historian Hayden White (1980) writes by making reference to Barthes:

> far from being one code among many that a culture may utilize for endowing experience with meaning, narrative is a metacode, a human universal on the basis of which transcultural messages about the nature of a shared reality can be transmitted.
>
> (ibid., p. 6)

Narrative as a structure is strongly connected with meaning, so that "the absence of narrative capacity or a refusal of narrative indicates an absence or refusal of meaning itself" (ibid.). What White is aiming at is showing the substantial artificiality of historical narratives, their being an instrument by which the disordered events of human vicissitudes are connected in a story, with a beginning and an end, and in so far as they are structured (since they connect events and give them interrelated meanings), they are endowed with a strong explicative value. Yet the artificial construction of historical narratives, being similar to the invention of fictive plots, has always produced embarrassment among the historians, who try to protect their scientific reputation behind the idea of historical evidence. As White argues:

> The historical narrative [...] reveals to us a world that is putatively "finished," done with, over, and yet not dissolved, not falling apart. In this world, reality wears the mask of a meaning, the completeness and fullness of which we can only imagine, never experience. Insofar as historical stories can be completed, can be given narrative closure, can be shown to have had a *plot* all along, they give to reality the odor of the *ideal*. This is why the plot of a historical narrative is always an embarrassment and has to be presented as "found" in the events rather than put there by narrative techniques.
>
> (ibid., p. 24)

White's theses are controversial. What they aim at is to reveal a substantial homology between literary and historical accounts. This is the first argumentative justification for the presence in this book of Chapter 3, expressly devoted to the history (and historiography) of emotions. The materials selected therein are not to be intended as totally exogenous as compared to literary materials. They are conceived instead, as with White, as narratives and, like any narratives, as endowed with both a fictional and a cognitive value. The historical treatment of emotions gives the social scientist a powerful instrument as to the argument of the sociality of affectivity: it shows how emotions are not the timeless expression of interior processes, since the way they are conceived, perceived, neglected or emphasized is a matter of cultural selection in the temporal dimension. Although historians of emotions are still debating on the controversial question of whether emotions change over time, an historical approach to emotions is generally based on the idea that emotions are socially and culturally conditioned (Stearns, 2008, 2014).

The first relevant input social scientists may derive from historians is of a methodological kind. Historians have, by necessity, to deal with the thorny problem of the historical analysis of emotions: how can they study feelings expressed by people who are no longer there? Susan J. Matt (2014) effectively argues that when dealing with emotions, an historian has to learn how to work with the invisible: the subject matter of the history of emotions is people and what they felt. Yet people and their emotions are part of a past which has irremediably gone. This makes the necessity for alternative historical sources (including literature) particularly urgent. The question of the invisibility of emotions is a strong argument in favour of the use of literary sources as tools to approximately accede past emotionality. This book takes this idea seriously when analyzing envy (Chapter 7) and love

(Chapter 8) from a diachronic perspective, adopting literary sources as exemplification of their changing social function and the changing social attitudes towards both these complex emotions. Chapter 3 has another function in the economy of my arguments: sketching the evolution of emotions in Western society, so as to connect the macro-trend of historical processes to the development of individualism as a specifically modern conception of man. The historical perspective will be integrated by making reference to sociological theory, notably Elias' theory of the civilizing process, which represents the most appropriate link between the historical and the sociological perspective in the analysis of emotions.

What history makes evident in the long duration of historical time (e.g. the sociality of emotions, their being subject to cultural changes), ethnography makes explicit in the confrontation among cultures. The reference to ethnographic accounts requires a second detour, before getting to the specific topic of the sociological relevance of the literary treatment of emotions. In a long review article, James A. Russell (1991) has underlined the difficulty in detecting a set of common categories by which different languages and cultures define exactly the same emotions. Ethnographical accounts of emotions in different cultures show the difficulty in realizing a clear-cut translation of terms referring to specific emotions. Even what in our Western culture could be conceived of as basic emotions (e.g. anger or fear) may not have linguistic equivalents in other non-Indo-European languages. Evidence on the existence of a pan-human set of transculturally shared emotions is contrastive. What is by now sure is that different cultures categorize emotions in different ways, and in so doing establish a set of values, expectancies and behavioural practices which are culturally specific. Russell convincingly proposes to link emotions to cognitive scripts, for example a series of events which converge in their definition. He (ibid., p. 442) writes that in order to understand an emotion as such, one has to make reference to a number of events and sub-events that qualify it as an emotion of a specific kind. Jealousy, for example, "implies a surrounding situation, a social relationship involving three people, specific motives, behaviors, and consequences. These implications must be understood to know what the word jealousy means" (ibid.).

Russell's hypothesis implies that categories for emotions are fuzzy rather than clear-cut. They suggest a vast array of shades of meanings, so that some situations are clearly imputable to a specific emotion (e.g. anger or fear), whereas others are much less easily connected to a unique emotion. Moreover, categories tend "to overlap with one another rather than be mutually exclusive" (ibid., p. 443). Thus, the same situation may be categorized as anger or fear or disgust. A script, which is a series of connected events, may, according to Russell, allow us to come to terms with the fuzzy character of emotions, as well as with their universality and cultural variety. The script hypothesis may imply that some components of the script are transcultural (e.g. frowning when disappointed or angry), whereas others are culture-specific (e.g. the causes that may produce disappointment or rage or the behaviour one should adopt when feeling disappointed or angry). Thus, the way emotions emerge, are socially perceived and are individually managed is a matter of cultural and social contexts (ibid., p. 444).

What is relevant in Russell's account is not a definitive solution to the question of the biological universality or the cultural peculiarity of emotions. Russell suggests, in fact, that further research and new methods are needed in order to properly tackle this question. What is relevant here is the idea that the categories for emotions are fuzzy and that emotions assume their cultural meaning within a script, hence an embryonic story, by which we may understand our emotions as well as the behaviour of our fellow people as the expression of specific emotions. Our understanding of emotions is linked to culturally defined stories about the way people feel and act.

Emotions are thus incorporated in cultural stories, which is what makes them understandable and socially meaningful (for a more detailed analysis, see *infra*, Chapter 4). The connection between emotions and narratives allows us to conceive the sociality of our emotional world from an unusual perspective. The relevant question for a sociologist is not only whether or not emotions are socially produced or socially conditioned or socially managed. As social scientists, we have chiefly to ask, so simple as that, whether or not emotions are told and hence are part of a story. Emotions need to be communicated in order to become socially relevant; otherwise, they would remain the unperceivable features of someone else's inner experience (or of someone else's innate make-up). The communication of emotions needs a specific mode, hence a linguistic solution to the question of making the invisible (our inwardness) part of our ordinary speech (Reddy, 1997; 2001. For the treatment of emotives, see *infra*, Chapter 3). Stories make the intransparency of the interior world (or the neuronal impulses) of our fellow people somehow visible and understandable: we tell our dear ones (or our analyst) how we feel, what we feel, how it feels and that too always in the form of a narrative. When emotions are manifested in socially visible behaviours (e.g. a gesture of affection or a burst of anger), they become mutually meaningful because we can figure out a brief narrative of the emotional causes of one's action, or prefigure a brief story of the future consequences of manifested emotions. Thus, we connect inner states of mind to some external actual or future demeanour ("he/she has done that because he/she feels so" – "he/she will do that because he/she is feeling so"). Even the emotions we ourselves feel acquire meaningfulness for us because we may convert, through the use of everyday language, raw feelings, biological processes or neurological impulses into something understandable for us, hence communicable to others. Stories may, moreover, have emotional effects: they may convey appeasement, joy or sorrow; they may be soothing, exciting or upsetting. In such a perspective, the debate on whether emotions are biologically determined or socially constructed shows its irrelevance: emotions may have a biological origin, yet they are social in so far as they are socially meaningful, and they are socially meaningful in so far as they are communicated in the form of a narrative.

Stories and emotions are thus strongly connected, and this is one of the reasons why I have chosen to deal with the sociological aspects of emotions by resorting to literary fiction as sources of data. Elsewhere (Longo, 2015), I have analyzed the strong interrelation between sociology and fictional narratives, trying to theoretically and methodologically justify the somewhat paradoxical use of patently fictive materials as a means to say something scientifically plausible about the social world. When social scientists resort to literary narratives, they have to come to terms with the question of the cognitive value of the fictional materials they select. In the philosophical debate, the question has been discussed from a different perspective: whereas some authors deny that a literary text may give trustful information about reality, others advocate the idea according to which literature may provide new perspectives from which to observe the external world. These authors, by stressing the cognitive value of fictional works, give literature a relevant quality, intending it as a means by which we may learn something unexpected about reality and ourselves (ibid., Chapter 4, *passim*). The acknowledgement of a cognitive value to literature is due chiefly to two main features of the work of letters. First is the complexity of its meanings, some of which are concealed in both the metaphorical structure of literature and in the artificiality of its language and tropes, which allows a multilevel, never-ending interpretative process. A successful novel, a well-conceived play, a piece of poetry never exhaust their interpretative potential, which may be constantly reactivated due to the complexity of the net of meanings they convey: literature is hence an unlimited source of significance (Eco, 1965). Secondly, narratives (including literary ones) have the powerful capacity, which has been masterfully analyzed by Paul Ricoeur (1983), to connect otherwise separated events through the process of plotting (an aspect I have already hinted at by quoting White, 1980), thus constructing homogeneity in facts and events that would remain otherwise separated and unconnected. Both features imply that we may make a sophisticated sense of the world when recurring to literary sources.

One more feature of literary narratives further justifies the use of literary sources for an appropriate sociological treatment of emotions. This feature, which Jeromy Bruner called "the dual landscape" (Bruner, 1990, pp. 51–52), relates to the fact that literary sources may describe and represent both the external aspects of social relations and the inner motivations of the involved actors. A stipulative accord between the author and his readers makes it possible to probe into the interior world of the characters. Thus, we may follow the fictional characters in their complex thoughts; we may experience how they feel; we may detect shades of emotions, contradictions, mixed feelings; we may, moreover, confront inner states of mind with action in the world, thus connecting the *within* and the *without* of the characters' experience. Dorrit Cohn (1978) has exhaustively analyzed the different techniques by which a novelist may give access to the innerness of fictional characters. *Transparent Mind. Narratives Modes for Presenting Consciousness in Fiction* is the title of her monograph on the topic, which clarifies how what is inconceivable in everyday interaction (getting to know what our fellow people think and feel) becomes artfully possible in fictional narrative (for a more detailed analysis of Cohn's argument, see *infra*, Chapter 4). Of course, our fictional knowledge relates to fictional characters, fictional actions and fictional emotions. Cohn is fully aware of the artificiality of fictional minds when she writes: "In depicting the inner life, the novelist is truly a fabricator. Even if he draws on psychological theories and on introspection, he creates what Ortega called 'imaginary psychology [...] the psychology of possible human minds'" (ibid., p. 6). But if we are fully aware of the fictionality of fictional minds, why should we resort to them as sources of information about emotions, the way they are individually experienced and socially managed? This question is the specific topic of Chapter 4, which starts with a brief treatment of the philosophical paradox of fictional emotions. How may we be moved by fictional characters and their vicissitudes, feeling actual emotions for the fictional representations of fictional human beings? The chapter reformulates the philosophical questions about the cognitive value of fictional narratives, by attempting to demonstrate that the complex and meaningful accounts that literary sources give of our emotional world may be of great utility for the social sciences. It should be added *en passant* that it is by now patent that even everyday narratives have a highly artificial character, as they do not simply mirror reality but distort events (no matter whether strategically or not) since, even in the case that they are trustful, they represent reality from a specific, peculiar point of view and according to specific tasks and relevances (Atkinson and Delamont, 2006).

By making reference to philosophical arguments, literary criticism and neurosciences, Chapter 4 suggests a strong interconnection between fictional and everyday emotions. As neuroscientists have demonstrated, when reading fiction and feeling compassion (or fear or excitement) the same parts of our brain are stimulated as when we experience the real thing. At any rate, by justifying the use of fiction for an appropriate sociological analysis of emotions, no naïve overlapping of literary descriptions and sociological arguments is advocated. On the contrary, it should be made clear from the outset that reading fiction sociologically always implies a dramatic reduction of the polysemous complexity of the work of letters, which is now subdued to the narrow argumentative task of sociological analysis. Once the distinction between literary narratives and sociological analysis has been clearly drawn, one may turn to literary fiction as a resource for the social sciences, the sociological interpretation being consciously one among others, yet not an arbitrary one, as it is based on a set of culturally defined ideas (what Umberto Eco [1979] calls our encyclopaedia) as well as on sociological constructs and concepts. The sense of a work of letters is in fact determined not only by the act of writing but also by the act of reading, the interpretation and reinterpretation which allows contrasting or converging readings, including the sociological. Donal Wesling, writing on literary emotions, acutely imputes the richness of the texture of literary works to the role of the interpreter, intended as a co-writer:

Mikhail Bakhtin thought of writing and reading, and of the relation of dialogic partners, as calling forth "the co-creativity of those who understand". The co-creativity of readers exceeds and completes the creativity of the author. However this occurs—this the assignment for research!—literature unifies into whole actions, with bodily details and moral choices, the materials of psychology, politics, history, sociology, philosophy.

(Wesling, 2008, p. 38)

In this specific sense, literary sources give privileged access to the social and interior world, allowing an articulated representation of emotions and appearing to be an appropriate source for sociological analysis. By adopting the appropriateness of literary sources for the social sciences as a guiding light, the second part of this work is devoted to a sociological interpretation of emotions through literary materials. One question has to be hinted at here, related to the sampling processes, before introducing the themes of each chapter. The selection of literary works, assumed as data for the analysis, is both extensive and highly selective. The selectivity is in part arbitrary, as it depends on my literary knowledge and preferences, yet taking into account the aptness of the selected materials as illustration of particular social processes or theories. The closest procedure in more consolidated research methods is the so-called theoretical or purposive sampling, by which cases are chosen due to their eloquence (what they can presumably tell us) in connection to our prefigured cognitive tasks (Mason, 2002, p. 127 ff.).

In the case of Chapter 5 on social action and Chapter 6 on the mob, the intent is to show the potential of literary sources for the sociological analysis of both emotions and action (both individual and collective). Both chapters are constructed on the basis of a highly selective choice of the literary materials: one single novel has been extensively analyzed in Chapter 5 (Philip Roth's *American Pastoral*), whereas Chapter 6 makes reference to two masterpieces of 19th century French and Italian literature (Émile Zola's *Germinal* and Alessandro Manzoni's *I Promessi Sposi*). The rationale guiding the analysis is twofold: on the one hand, literary accounts are adopted as rich texts, able to confirm or confute the assumptions of sociological theories; on the other, they are assumed as quasi-ethnographic setting, with the peculiar quality (which observation of natural setting may not have) of the double description of internal states of mind and of external actions and circumstances. Chapters 7 and 8 are devoted to single emotions (envy in the first case and love in the second), which are analyzed from a diachronic perspective. Here the selection of literary material is wider, in so far as the attempt is to show, treasuring the experience of Norbert Elias, the strong interconnection which links historical change in the way sentiments are felt and acted upon and structural social transformation in the long run.

Chapter 5 attempts to critique an exclusively cognitive theory of action, exemplified by Talcott Parsons' approach. Seymour Levov, the protagonist of Roth's masterpiece (Roth, 1997), is assumed as a particularly fitting example of a well-integrated personality in Parsonian terms. Roth's novel shows how ill-posed is any hyper-simplification of the social actor to the sole cognitive components of his personality. Seymour Levov is hence observed in the process of gradual distancing from the model of the hyper-socialized actor, whose behaviour is motivated by the compliance with social rules and a sympathetic acceptance of norms and shared values. The reader is led to gradually discover that under the apparent normality and conformity of Seymour's demeanour, under the ostensible good sense manifested in his choices, under the banality of a normalized life, the concealed motive guiding his life and determining his action is the sense of loss for his daughter and the nostalgia for a prospected, yet not achieved, future. The future presents itself with the unexpected, odious features of a broken ideal. Seymour's vicissitudes are adopted as illustrations not only of a tragic biography but also as the individual manifestation of the crisis of solid modernity, consequent to the crash of consolidated ways of life, ideals of order and of social upgrading. In the ideological void which issues from the crisis of old values, affectivity emerges as a problem for the individual: Seymour finds hard what once came to him easily, for example conforming his emotions to socially required standards, and is no longer able to adjust what he feels with his actual, required behaviour. By using Roth's novel to show the discrepancy between Seymour's managed and manifest behaviour and his emotional drives, the chapter attempts to demonstrate the relevance of emotions in social action, assuming as reference authors chiefly Ervin Goffman (1959) and Arlie Hochschild (1975, 1983a).

Chapter 6 is about collective behaviour and the role emotions play in the process by which an aggregate of individuals structure complex sets of complex action. The topic allows the analysis of two utterly different conceptions of the individual actor which may coexist in sociological thought, apparently without perceived contradiction. On the one hand, the theoretical model of man, typical of social sciences (the sociological *homunculus* as described by Alfred Schutz [1962]), was constructed by eliding emotions and emotionality as irrelevant features of social action. The output was a somewhat caricatural image of the individual agent, a cogitative individual constantly compelled to choose rationally among alternatives, to interpret the meaning of the social situation in which he happened to be, to activate everyday rationality in order to give substance and consistency to the social world. On the other hand is the conception of the individual in collective contexts by which, once the individual finds himself in socially unstable aggregates, his rationality and interpretative capacities suddenly evaporate, as if he were at the mercy of the madding crowd. Inconsistent as it may seem, two utterly opposed images of the social actor coexisted, the former characterized by a rational, cognitive relation to the social world, whereas the latter conceiving the turmoil of collective activities as capable of transforming the individual into an instinctive, uncontrollable, almost natural being. The prototypical phenomenon in which the semantic of collective behaviour as irrational and irrepressible was located is the raging mob, notably in the analysis of the French social psychologist Gustave Le Bon (1895).

As a reaction to the excessive simplicity of the conception of crowd behaviour as irrational, and in compliance to the general trend towards the elision of emotions from social theory, even collective behaviour (the last stronghold of emotionality in social theory) was subdued to a redefinition, so that collective entities began to be conceived as issuing from the aggregation of the strategically oriented, interpretative, at places rational choices of the individuals involved. By making reference to literary materials, I argue that both contrasting conceptions are naïve. Émile Zola's *Germinal* (1885) is assumed as a clear-cut representation of the crowd as would be later conceived by social thinking. In particular, I stress the wild, bestial, irrational and womanly character of the mob which is a constitutive part of both Zola's narrative and Le Bon's account of the crowd.

Alessandro Manzoni's narrative (1842) of the 17th century bread riot in Milan is assumed as an appropriate material to test the consistency of two theories which attempt to overcome the conception of collective behaviour as irrational. Namely, Manzoni's sophisticated account will be adopted to test Smelser's theory of the added value (Smelser, 1962) and Turner and Killian's theory of the emergent norm (Turner and Killian, 1957). The use of literary sources (Manzoni in particular) shows that no clear-cut distinction between collective behaviour and social action may be drawn: emotions, rationality, strategy, cooperation and conflict are all parts of collective behaviour (as well as of social action), so that it makes little sense to construct a theoretical representation of both the individual and the collective actor which elides or suppresses one of these components.

The last two chapters are attempts in the historical semantics of emotions, as I propose to detect which semantic changes the conceptions of both envy and love have undergone so as to fit with relevant structural mutations which have characterized the evolution of Western society. By adopting this strategy, the macro-historical process of structural transformation may be connected to the micro-, individual component of emotionality. My theoretical models are both Norbert Elias and his processual historical approach to the analysis of social phenomenon (Elias, 1939; 1970) and Niklas Luhmann's account (1980) of semantic changes as strongly interrelated to transformation in the structural components of society over time. A diachronic approach is needed in order to observe macro-phenomena by adopting literary sources. Indeed, in the case of the micro-dimension of the social action or of the meso-level of collective behaviour, one may recur to literary sources as quasi-ethnographic setting, since narrative sources describe actions and interactions which are logically connectible to the phenomena under scrutiny. On the contrary, when one sets out to analyze macro-phenomena of a structural kind, the direct reference to a single text describing structural phenomena is hardly feasible. One may, at the most, make reference to the comments of the novelist on what he considers the characteristics or the causes of a social phenomenon, comments being often part of literary narratives (Berger, 1977). Comments are presented in the form of an argument, often affected by the prejudices of the author, which reduce considerably the added value of literary sources for sociological analysis (e.g. complex meaning, double landscape and representation of concrete interactions). The diachronic approach, on the contrary, gives the observer the opportunity to make reference to multiple literary sources, which are assumed each as an exemplification of one specific stage in a structural process of transformation, so as to observe changes in behaviour and values over time.

Chapter 7 is based on such a diachronic approach, the semantic changes of envy over time being its topic. Envy is analyzed as a hinderer or promoter of social mobility. In simpler societies, envy is highly stigmatized as a sentiment, in so far as it is assumed as a menace to the hierarchical order. The envious are socially stigmatized, so as to reinforce the ideal of the immutability of social order. In the Middle Ages, the envier is conceived as a sinner (envy is, in fact, one of the deadly sins) but also, due to his anti-social attitude, as a negative force able to destroy both the community where he belongs and himself, as he puts himself consciously outside community bonds. This specific feature of envy is analyzed by making reference to the character of Sapia in Dante's *Purgatorio* (ca. 1313) and to the allegorical representation of envy Giotto painted in the Scrovegni Chapel in Padua (ca. 1305) and to the character of Satan in Milton's *Paradise Lost* (1667). By selecting literary works and literary characters from different times and cultural traditions, an attempt is made to show the gradual change in the conception of envy, from a socially disruptive sentiment to a sort of emotional equalizer, stimulating social changes and social equality. Reference is also made to the resistance of social hierarchies against the process of transformation. Shakespeare's Iago (*Othello* [1604]) and Trollope's Longstaffs (*The Way We Live Now* [1870/1941]) are assumed, each with their temporal specificities, as exemplifications of an envious resistance against the changing social order (the envious as *laudatores tempori acti*). Dickens' Uriah Heep (1850/1953) is adopted as the model of the modern envious character who has almost been able to be successful, yet is stopped by still operating social prejudices. Uriah's final defeat is less imputable to the inept David Copperfield than to social conventions and norms, in a society which is not yet ready to consent complete inclusion to those who do not belong to the middle class, even when they demonstrate possession of the required acquired qualities. *Mastro Don Gesualdo* (Verga, 1890), the masterpiece of the Italian novelist Giovanni Verga, and *Passing* (Larsen, 1929/2004), by the Harlem Renaissance novelist Nella Larsen, are assumed as examples of achieved social rise. Yet envy plays a very different role in the rural Sicily of the end of the 19th century described by Verga and the modern New York and Chicago of the early 20th century, which are the environment of the plot in *Passing*. In the first novel, envy is the extreme resistance of an archaic world to the modern role of acquired qualities: envy may no longer impede social upgrading, but it may cause the exclusion from socially meaningful relations of those who have succeeded. In *Passing*, envy is a stimulus for social innovation and for the initiative of the individuals, being moreover able to trigger economic growth by stimulating competition and consumption. All the quoted works of letters have an illustrative role in the chapter, as they make evident the otherwise abstract interrelation between envy and the maintenance of order or its overthrowing.

The approach of Chapter 8 is also historical, as it aims to detect how the semantic of love has been changing, becoming a relevant component firstly in the construction and then in the dissolution of the modern model of the nuclear family. The reference materials are literary, sociological and historical. The semantic evolution of love is traced, starting from the Middle Ages, when love and marriage were neatly distinguished. Women were intended either as a sinful source of temptation or as an ideal to be worshipped, as is particularly evident in the case of the Italian *Dolce Stil Novo*. By making theoretical reference to Niklas Luhmann's *Love as Passion* (1982), literary works have been selected (Richardson's *Pamela* [1740/1955], Austen's *Pride and Prejudice* [1813/1833]) in order to describe the emergence of Romantic Love, based on the right to choose one's life partner regardless of his/her ascribed qualities (e.g. status, class, race). The difficulty in the social acceptance of the new model of love is analyzed

(Tolstoy's *Marital Life* [1859] and *Anna Karenina* [1876]), as well as the evident contradiction, which soon became visible in literary texts, of stable relations based on the unstable sentiment of love (Goethe's *Elective Affinities* [1809]). Open critique to the conventionality of the new conception of love also emerged, leading to gloomy representations of marital love as a strategical distortion of reality (Tolstoy's *The Kreutzer Sonata* [1889]). The modern process of individualization of choices, which characterizes contemporary love, is eventually made the object of my analysis. Anthony Giddens' convincing account of intimacy in late modernity has been selected as the appropriate theoretical background to detect the main features of late-modern love, exemplified by making reference to Milan Kundera's *The Unbearable Lightness of Being* (1984).

As may be evident from the afore-sketched arguments, the scope of this book is ambitious and yet incomplete. It intends neither to give an all-encompassing account of the sociology of emotions through literature nor to analyze the whole of human emotions from a sociological perspective. Its main task is to show the sociality of emotions by making reference to a specific mode of communication (narratives) and by choosing fictional accounts as artificial constructs, supposedly capable of shedding new light on the complex relation of the individual (and his emotionality) and the social structure. Emotions are not to be underestimated. They are a relevant part of our inner experience, but they are also a relevant component of the micro-, meso- and macro-levels of society. They, therefore, affect interaction, social integration, social conflicts and may become instruments of power and social control (Reddy, 2001). The emphasis on emotions in contemporary public discourse, which is so typical of present-day politics, may result in political choices driven by the rational strategy to soothe the electors' fears or to excite their hatred or to consolidate national identities so as to exclude those who do not belong. And in times of emotional bewilderment, new prophets may emerge, as prefigured by Max Weber (1905, p. 124), who are able to use emotional politics as an instrument of power and control. In the following chapters, I will not limit my analysis to the sole relational component of emotions. I will also try, where possible, to make reference to the strong connection among emotions, emotional control and power. In this limited sense, this monograph has a political intent.

The case of Brexit in Great Britain, newly emerging nationalisms in Western countries and anti-immigration policies in Europe and in the USA are examples of the political abuse of negative emotions as a means to get or maintain political power. Each of the afore-mentioned cases would deserve a careful analysis, which is far beyond the scope of this book. Emotions may have positive or negative social consequences; hence, they are neither to be exalted nor diminished. But, as part of our experience of the social world, they have to be included in the sociological analysis of social reality. The main task of the sociology of emotions is actually to provide a rational account of the emotional component of social behaviour, the relevance of emotions for the individual experience of the world and their possible use as instruments of social control. If this task has a plausibility of its own, if it complies with the general objectives of the discipline, one source that the social scientist may make reference to is literature. Literary accounts provide, in fact, rich materials, particularly apt for the sociological treatment of emotions: they enhance our sensibility for the world of human relations; they give us access to the fictional world of the character's inwardness; they show the complex inter-relation between emotions, the flow of consciousness and action, as they allow us to observe quasi-real settings in which the characters interact, driven by com-plex mixes of emotionality and rationality, impulses and strategy. Furthermore, they show us how things work, since literary sources have the relevant quality of describing not theoretical puppets, as social theory often does, but quasi-real characters with a (fictive) psychology, (fictive) motives, (fictive) ideas and (fic-tive) emotions. Putting the adjective fictive in parentheses implies that fictionality is not an aspect to be stressed. And, indeed, the complex, rounded representation of the social and the individual (including the rational and the emotional), which fictional narratives may provide, is reason enough to resort to fictional works as sources of data, regardless of their alleged untruthfulness.

According to Alfred Schutz (1962), the social sciences have to test the ade-quacy of their accounts of social phenomena and social types to the perception of social actors in their everyday activities. In fact, Schutz writes, social scientists work with constructs of the second degree, for example constructs which make reference to the sense that normal individuals, in their everyday lives, give to their social experience. The social scientist refers, for his analyzes, to objects in the world which have already been interpreted by the individual actors. This requires a further methodological effort, which is not required of the natural scientist: the social scientist has to detect the link between the abstract conceptuality of the social sciences and the everyday rationality of the social actor. This interconnec-tion between the world of science and the way common people perceive and inter-pret their experience is called by Schutz the *principle of adequacy* (ibid., p. 44). Connecting science and common sense is not easy, and some critics have stressed that the effort may even be worthless (Giddens, 1976, p. 38); indeed, science and common sense are to be distinguished, in so far as good scientific accounts of social reality often irritate, offend or disappoint the concrete social actors who are involved in the phenomenon under scrutiny. I do not intend to embark here on the complex methodological discussion (which I have already sketched elsewhere [Longo, 2015, p. 134 ff.]) about the plausibility of Schutz's principle of adequacy. What is relevant for my argument is to stress, on the one hand, the necessary distance of sociological accounts from commonsensical interpretations of reality. After all, sociology is at its best when it produces counter-factual explanations of social phenomena, adopting its own jargon and argumentative style. On the other hand, one has to stress the effortless adequacy of fictional accounts of reality to the everyday interpretation of the social actor. Fiction is artificial; yet, by resort-ing to common sense and common understanding, it is able, at its best, to provide fresh, unusual, sometimes upsetting or irritating representations of reality. Even when fictional accounts distort reality (such as in Kafka's *Metamorphosis* or in Cervantes' *Don Quixote*), literature starts from a set of ideas and concepts that the novelist shares with his reading public. This holds true particularly in the case of fictional representations of emotions: the reader may probe into the characters' inner worlds and understand the relation between what a character thinks and feels and what he does. This is possibly due to the artefact of the dual landscape (Bruner, 1990) and to the convention of the transparency of fictional minds (Cohn, 1978). In what follows, I will try my hand at complex literary materials, attempting to make sociological sense of texts endowed with multilevel meanings and which are, at the same time, adequate to common understanding much more than sociological analysis ever will be. In this sense, this monograph is not only the discussion of a topic, it is also a methodological reflection on the unusual, yet analytically fruitful, bond which links sociology and literary accounts of emotions.

2   Sociology and emotions

An overview

1 Emotions as a concealed object

Although emotions have been thematized only recently as a topic of sociological investigation, it is nonetheless difficult to summarize the debate about their role and relevance. Sociology emerged as an autonomous field of investigation by differentiating itself from akin areas, psychology in particular. In its quest for social facts and social causes, sociology considered the psychological components of human action as sociologically irrelevant or, at least, as the output of social phenomena or processes (Durkheim, 1895). The differentiation from psychology had two main consequences for the topic of emotions. On the one hand, emotions were conceived of as the legitimate monopoly of psychology. On the other hand, sociology became gradually affected by cognitivism (Barbalet, 2004), by which the human coefficient, when taken into account, was reduced to mere cognition. Nonetheless, although a specific sub-discipline did not emerge until the 1970s, emotions were not expunged from classical social thought, as they persisted as an unthematized topic. The first section of this chapter is devoted to a reconstruction of the role of emotions in classical social thought. In the second part, I will discuss the return of emotions in sociological analysis, after a period of diffuse inattention, and I will eventually briefly make reference to recent developments in the sub-field of the sociology of emotions.

The founding fathers of sociology hinted at the role of emotions and emotional control for both macro (e.g. social solidarity, the development of capitalism) and micro processes (e.g. the constitution of the self); they also focused their attention on the effects of society on individual conduct (e.g. modernity, urbanism and the mental life), thereby implying a connection between social changes and the affective life of the modern individual. Thus, although the topic of emotions was not autonomous, it formed a conspicuous part of classical social theory. In its unspecialized and somewhat occasional treatment of emotions, classical social theory shows the complexity and relevance of the topic. Indeed, the theoretical and empirical implications of emotions are cross-cutting. They condition human behaviour from within and yet are socially constructed. As Theodor Kemper puts it, they are the output of sociality, as they emerge as a consequence of social situations. Yet they "are also precursors of the social, by virtue of their mobilizing energy and motivation for the accomplishment of major social tasks, not the least of which is social solidarity itself" (Kemper, 2000, p. 772). Moreover, they affect both micro-situations and processes (e.g. the management of emotions, feeling rules or emotional deviance) and are at the same time a relevant component of macro-phenomena, such as social integration or social change.

The emergence of the sociology of emotions as a sub-discipline dates back to the 1970s. The so-called emotional turn (Lemmings and Brooks, 2014, p. 3 ff.) gave the opportunity for the redefinition of well-established sociological approaches, as well as for a refreshed treatment of old themes and the definition of new issues. The diffuse cognitivism, which affected the main theoretical schools in sociology, could be thematized, as it was now evident that emotions could neither be removed from social theory nor imputed to the sole psychological analysis. Emotions had to be studied from a specific sociological perspective, which would represent a gain for both the understanding of emotions and the advancement of the discipline. From now on, social theory assumed emotions as one of its topics. A new research agenda was needed (Kemper, 1990), able to define the theoretical implications of emotions for sociology, as well as specific fields of empirical investigation.

2 Classical thought on emotions

Classical sociologists did not thematize emotions as a specific topic, yet a reading of the works of the founding fathers is of interest for those who deal with emotions from a sociological perspective. In classical sociology, emotions emerge as a collateral topic of arguments and theories, and may therefore shed new light on the mainstream interpretation of early sociologists. Yet it would be naïve to maintain that classical sociologists anticipated the sociology of emotions, which emerged as an autonomous sub-field only in the late 20th century. Although a collateral topic, emotions played nonetheless a relevant role in classical sociological thought (Shilling, 2002).

One of the tasks of early sociology was to make sense of the abrupt social changes which characterized Europe at the threshold of modernity (Longo, 2005). The theme of social order assumed great relevance, as a reaction to the rapid transformations issuing from the processes of modernization (e.g. industrial economy, democratization, vindication of civil and labour rights). In France, society came to be conceived of as a moral fact, able to promote integration and reduce social unrest. In its integrating capacity, society rests chiefly on shared feeling and symbols, which have a relevant emotional component. Society could indeed foster order only in so far as it was able to promote symbols and values which, once interiorized by social actors, converted individual impulses into moral action, for example, "action prompted by feelings and ideas of empathy, altruism and self-sacrifice" (Shilling, 2002, p. 17).

2.1 Émile Durkheim

An example of a reference to emotions as an instrument of integration may be found in the late August Comte, who gave relevance to emotions as tools able to guarantee the integration of humanity, within a new positivist religion, based on human sympathy and universal brotherhood (Nussbaum, 2013, p. 61). Commentators distinguish between two phases of Durkheim's sociological productions, each with a specific conception of emotions and their social function: emotions were at first considered by Durkheim as a potential danger for social integrity, whereas at a later stage they were conceived of as the prerequisite for the maintenance of the social bond (Arppe, 2014, p. 55). Although less extensive in scope, in its second phase Durkheim's treatment of emotions is within a Comtian perspective.

In his first relevant work (*The Division of Labour in Society*, 1893) integration is seen as the mechanical output of societal organization. In modern society organic solidarity is guaranteed solely by the functional interconnections of social roles, with emotions playing an almost irrelevant role. Since 1895, emotions seem to acquire a negative role: in this phase, Durkheim becomes more aware of the relation between emotions and social control. Society is, as it were, constructed against emotions, in the sense that it is possible only if "individual's primary emotions are both controlled and socialized" (Cuin, 2001, p. 91). As is evident in his study on suicide (Durkheim, 1897), order is connected to the control of individual passions, a process which becomes explicit whenever the relaxation of social ties makes the control of the emotional substratum of individuals problematic (Arppe, 2014, p. 100).

At a later stage of his work, Durkheim (1912) became increasingly interested in religion and its integrative function. Within the framework of Durkheim's sociology of religion, emotions are no longer conceived as a menace to the social order, as they are intended as tools to create and reproduce social integration. Collective situations of social effervescence (e.g. rituals), in which a group may recognize itself as a collective unit, are relevant components of the social bond. In their constitutive character, emotions help configure an anonymous horde as a society. At an early stage of social development, which Durkheim exemplifies with Australian totemism, tribal rituals reinforce collective feelings. Collective ceremonies are occasions for early human groups to gather together, adore the totemic being and, as the totem represents society and its unity, reinforce group solidarity (Fisher and Koo Chon, 1989, p. 3; Durkheim 1912, p. 252). Yet the function of collective rituals is not limited to the earlier stages of social development. Collective excitement may "recreate social solidarity and bring about social change" even in modern societies (Fisher and Koo Chon, 1989, p. 3), where social effervescence connected to collective behaviour may steer collective affectivity in the direction either of social stability or of social change (think of a riot or a revolutionary process).

A specific anthropological conception exemplified in the idea of the *homo duplex* is at the core of Durkheim's treatment of emotions. The individual is both natural and social, such that whereas he would tend to expand his needs by avoiding social constraints, society opposes subjective impulses with the strength of its collective ties, in the form of social conventions or religious, moral or juridical norms. This produces a dramatic tension in the individual, torn between the dual aspects of his being human (Durkheim, 1914, p. 151; Longo, 2015, p. 87). The natural component of human nature is characterized by infinite desires, a negative affectivity supported by "the egoistic passions of man" (Arppe, 2014, p. 63). This inner and obscure energy is contrasted by "another sort of affective energy which is fixed, crystallized in a material or symbolic form and which manifests itself in institutions, laws, myths, moral norms" (ibid., p. 79). Once sublimated in social symbols and rules, the amorphous excitement of collective emotions is converted into a socialized kind of sentiment, for example a consciously social affectivity, which is directed to the maintenance of societal ties and exteriorized in collectively shared symbols (ibid., p. 87). Complying with social norms has to do with the sacred character of the social, whose power is lived in an emotional fashion (the respect for certain symbols, for example, but also shame for wrong behaviour, anxiety when we commit a crime or indignation when we witness others doing so). Thus, not only is society constructed on an emotional base, it is kept alive as a sacred external fact thanks to the integrative function of emotions (Cuin, 2001, p. 96).

In contrast to political economy, which reduces the individual to the pursuit of his personal needs and interests, Durkheim considers the individual as a tangled complex of egoism and sociality, corporeity and morality, personal interests and solidarity. The function of society is hence that of elevating the individual: "transporting him into a milieu other than that in which he passes his profane existence, making him live a very different kind of life, higher and more intense" (Durkheim quoted in Arppe, 2014, p. 88). Emotions are sublimated once they are socialized: they lose their negative character and become the fundamental element of social integration, connected to the integrative force of symbols, shared beliefs and socially accepted norms.

2.2 Max Weber

The individual and his action are at the core of Weber's theoretical conception of society. Sociology is, according to Weber's well-known definition, a science: "concerning itself with the interpretive understanding of social action and thereby with a causal explanation of its course and consequences. We shall speak of 'action' insofar as the acting individual attaches a subjective meaning to his behavior" (Weber, 1915, p. 4). The main task of sociology is, therefore, the understanding of the meaning which social actors attach to their actions. By posing sociological analysis on the individual level of action, Weber's overall theoretical approach tends to emphasize the actors' contribution to the construction of macro structures and historical processes: an approach which, being antithetical to Durkheim's, affects Weber's treatment of emotions.

In Weber's treatment of action, a general devaluation of the emotional component may be noticed. Affectual action ("determined by the actor's specific affects and feeling states" (ibid., p. 25)) is Weber's third type in his well-known typology of actions. Weber clearly states that it is difficult to distinguish it from non-meaningfully oriented actions, which take place in the case of "an uncontrolled reaction to some exceptional stimulus" (ibid.). Affectual action shares this borderline character (not yet meaningful or not exactly meaningfully oriented) with traditional behaviour. Traditional behaviour too "is very often a matter of almost automatic reaction to habitual stimuli which guide behavior in a course which has been repeatedly followed" (ibid.). It is also akin to value-rational action, since in both types "the meaning of the action does not lie in the achievement of a result ulterior to it, but in carrying out the specific type of action for its own sake". Only instrumental rational action poses no difficulty as to its meaningfulness: being the output of a careful analysis of the most suitable means to achieve a specific goal, its meaning is easier to understand for an external observer (ibid., p. 26).

Weber thus gives instrumental rationality a prominent position, in so far as it better embodies the characters of meaningfully oriented actions (Cuin, 2001). Weber is yet too strong a social theorist and too good a connoisseur of social life to aspire to a reduction of social action to its rational component. He is, moreover, well aware of the methodological character of his typology, which he intends as a tool to give order to the apparently unordered jumble of human activity. No pure type is to be experienced in actual social processes. Nonetheless, the *zweckrational* type is, according to Weber, more predictable since it is based on a careful choice of means in relation to specific tasks. It also represents, at the level of the individual, a general trend of modern society, that is rationalization.

The interconnection between the individual, his emotions and their control is the premise of Weber's analysis of rationalizing processes. Structural phenomena are thus closely linked to individual conduct and the changing features of social behaviour. This results in a treatment of the macro effects of emotional control, which is particularly evident in Weber's analysis of capitalism. The essential features of Weber's analysis are well known: the Calvinist's methodical conduct anticipates and fosters the specific character of the instrumentally rational action typical of modern capitalism. Methodical conduct is a reaction to the doctrine of predestination, according to which God pre-determines who deserves salvation, the individual being unable to change the inscrutable divine will. The Calvinist anticipates some of the features of the modern individual: a lonely person, responsible for his worldly life, uncertain of his otherworldly destiny, who reacts to uncertainties by adopting compensatory control mechanisms. Control mechanisms are not means through which the Calvinist aspires to gain salvation; they are, on the contrary, instruments through which he attempts to limit his anxiety deriving from the uncertainty of his salvation. His anxiety is correlated to the loneliness deriving from the enormous distance between him and God. Thus, the methodical conduct which the Calvinist adopts, although rationally oriented to the suppression of emotionality and affectivity, originates from the emotional search for an antidote to the anxiety caused by the theological doctrine of predestination:

> In its extreme inhumanity this doctrine must above all have had one consequence for the life of a generation which surrendered to its magnificent

consistency. That was a feeling of unprecedented inner loneliness of the single individual. In what was for the man of the age of the Reformation the most important thing in life, his eternal salvation, he was forced to follow his path alone to meet a destiny which had been decreed for him from eternity. No one could help him. No priest, for the chosen one can understand the word of God only in his own heart.

(Weber, 1915, pp. 60–61)

Since the Calvinist cannot change the divine will either with action or repentance, he strengthens his methodical self-control in the direction of his professional activity, intended now as a vocation (Beruf) or "duties which the Divine Will had imposed upon him" (ibid., p. 44). Profession as a vocation may be connected to the Divine Grace only provided that the wealth which derives from economic activity is not enjoyed in unproductive idleness (ibid., p. 104). The productive employ of wealth (hence the investment of profit for further profit), together with methodical conduct, is the link between the ethics of Calvinism and the spirit of the entrepreneur of modern capitalism. Moreover, if we intend the modern capitalist as a prototype of the individual in modern society, the result is a social actor in which emotionality is put into brackets, as he seems able to rationally act upon the world and interact with his fellow-men.

Jack Barbalet (2000, 2008) has rightly stressed that in the *Protestant Ethic* Weber's suspicion for the irrational side of humanity becomes evident, as well as an implicit appreciation for rationality and its historical consequences. The concept of *Beruf* "provides an account of the mechanisms required to realize in action the quality of rationality" (Barbalet, 2000, p. 330), and this is a prerequisite of methodical conduct. Translated into the language of worldly existence, the Calvinist's methodical control of passions and the removal of the irrational from his behaviour give shape to modern capitalism. Capitalism transplants an ethos into economic activities oriented towards profit. And this is possible thanks to a rational bracketing of emotions and needs (both elements which in Durkheim converge in the figure of the *homo duplex*): the immediate fulfilment of the individual's needs is now replaced by the rational search for a postponed profit.

Regardless of the doubtless admiration for rationality and rationalization, Weber is aware of the negative consequences of both on modern societies. The iron cage as a symbol of modernity shows the dark side of a rationalized and de-emotionalized world (Weber, 1905, p. 124). Thus, emotions are never completely suppressed: they may come back, for example as new charismatic leaders (new prophets), charisma being the emotional component in Weber's conception of power. Emotions are a propulsive element, in so far as they are able to convert routinized traditional actions into something new, thus fostering social change. This is the reason why a complete rationalization of humanity and society is perceived by Weber as the nightmarish aspect of rationalized modernity: a society which has completely suppressed emotions is doomed to stasis (Cuin, 2001, pp. 88–89) and may turn into a nightmare, where spirit and heart are suppressed. Thus, although Max Weber's conception of emotions is to be located within a social theory which undermines the relevance of the emotional side of human action in favour of rationality, Weber's passionate description of the possible consequences of rationalization may not suppress emotions altogether. They are at the root of social phenomena, and indeed: how could the Calvinist's methodical conduct have evolved, had not his personality been marked by an all-encompassing emotion, that is anxiety for salvation (Cuin, 2001, pp. 86–88)?

2.3 Georg Simmel

Society is, according to Simmel, the combined output of social interactions. As compared to the Durkheiman tradition, society is not a *sui generis* reality, imposing itself onto the individual as a fact. On the contrary, it is the product of the actors' reciprocal action, to which Simmel ascribes a constitutive function (Frisby, 2002, Chapter 2, *passim*).[1] Yet society, although constituted within interaction, is able to acquire independence from social actors, transforming the living interaction of people into static forms, once the specific content of experience has been crystallized:

> The large systems and the super-individual organizations – Simmel writes – that customarily come to mind when we think of society, are nothing but immediate interactions that occur among men constantly, every minute, but that have become crystallized as permanent fields, as autonomous phenomena.
> (Simmel, 1917, p. 10)

Although society should not exist as an autonomous reality, as it is the output of mutual influences among social actors, yet social phenomena are able to acquire a reality of their own: "As they crystallize, they attain their own existence and their own laws, and may even confront or oppose spontaneous interaction itself" (ibid.).

It is within the above trivialized theoretical conception that Simmel's approach to emotions has to be framed. Simmel is, among the founding fathers, the only who has thematized emotions and analyzed them within a specifically sociological perspective: from a strictly sociological point of view, emotions are analyzed both as elements triggering interactions and as effects of reciprocal action. Emotion is a psychological drive strongly connected to action. In his essay on love, Simmel is quite clear in this regard: "It is probably possible to regard the impulse for behaviour as the emotional side of the beginning of the behavior itself. The fact that we feel ourselves 'impelled' to perform an action means that the action has already begun" (Simmel, 1919, p. 163). Yet emotions are a relevant component of interaction, and it is in that that they are social.

There are two main features of emotions which Simmel deals with in his works. The first is more explicitly linked to the theoretical relevance of emotions and has to do with "emotions in the context of their reciprocal effects between individuals" (Gerhards, 1986, p. 902). It is hence closely connected to the micro-dimension of affectivity. Operating on the macro level, the second is an aspect of

Simmel's critique of modernity and the effect modern society has upon the quality of social interaction. This second feature of Simmel's analysis of affectivity is associated with Simmel's assessment of contemporary society, especially aimed at detecting the effects that modern social structures have upon individuals, their behaviour and their psychology (Dal Lago, 1994).

Simmel distinguishes between primary and secondary emotions. By primary emotions, he means emotions in so far as they are the triggering element of interaction. Secondary emotions are, on the contrary, to be understood as the product or output of interaction (Gerhards, 1986, p. 903). Even in this second case, emotions may not be understood as the mere output of some social factor since their emergence needs the interpretative role of the individuals involved in the interaction. Social actors as psychic systems are demarcated from the environment in which they are immersed. Environmental *stimuli* become meaningful for the actor only when he evaluates them according to his own categories. Thus, the psychic reaction to the environment is only in part determined by external factors, as it depends chiefly on the individual evaluation. Emotions depend on the process by which psychic identities interplay with and differentiate themselves from the environment. And indeed, they emerge, as Simmel writes, from the "perceived discrepancies between subjective structures of evaluation and social environmental *stimuli*" (Simmel quoted ibid., p. 904). Gratitude, for example, emerges when Alter exceeds in his benevolence towards Ego and Ego evaluates Alter's action as discrepant with his subjective expectations. Shame arises when Ego perceives that his norm transgressing behaviour has been noticed by Alter. The rupture of shared expectations about the appropriate behaviour, as well as the awareness Ego has that he has "failed to act with tact" (ibid., p. 907) generate a feeling of improperness. Jealousy is generated in complex triadic relations and depends on Ego's frustration due to the fact that $Alter_2$ receives attentions from $Alter_1$ (the beloved) which Ego would have for himself. Secondary emotions may have specific social functions, as is the case of gratitude and shame: gratitude is a strong trigger of social cohesion, while shame is an instrument of social order. When shame emerges, in fact, the broken social norms and expectations are re-established, and interaction may thus proceed.

Emotions are, according to Simmel, instruments for social cohesion. In this respect, they are primary, since they may be conceived as *a priori* in the construction of social solidarity. Gerhards (1986) has underlined a close similarity between Simmel's analysis of primary emotions and Durkheim's conception of the role of emotions as tools for social integration. Emotions establish and enhance a sentiment of belonging to a community or social group, support social ties and supplement laws and norms with the irrational component of feelings. In this regard, emotions are not the output of social interaction but are, as it were, the foundation of social bonds. Simmel's critique of modernity is in part connected to the ever less relevance of primary emotions as constitutive elements of social order. In fact, in modern societies, the interconnection among social actors tends to be ever more determined by rational instruments, money in particular, understood as a tool that, although facilitating transaction, tends to eliminate the qualitative elements of emotions from social intercourses. The consequences for the modern individual are the intellectualization of his mental life, a loss of meaning and a predominance of calculus which is by now adapted from the restricted field of natural sciences into the broader sphere of social relations (Simmel, 1903).

3 Early American sociologists on emotions and sentiments

What follows is a brief presentation of four early American sociologists (the fourth, Florian Znaniecki, being an American by adoption) who, in a way which reminds one of European sociologists, dealt with emotions not as their chief object but as a collateral topic. This implies that it would be improper to talk of theirs as a sociology of emotions *ante litteram*. Nonetheless, the selected authors conceived of emotions and sentiments in a properly sociological dimension, as they were imagined not only as relevant elements of the inner life of human beings but as indispensable components of social action and social processes. The relevance given to emotions and sentiment is compatible with the developing American sociological thought, as it was being elaborated between the 19th and the 20th centuries. By synthesizing the thought of one of the earliest American sociologists, namely Lester Frank Ward, Robert Bierstedt underlines that, according to Ward, emotion and not reason is the chief component of human action, hence the element triggering and determining human activity: "Ward – writes Bierstedt – gave the distinction of the *primum mobile* to feelings, not ideas. Men are moved by the power of sentiment, not intellect" (Bierstedt,1981, p. 52). Yet emotions and sentiment are not understood by Ward as a positive social force, as they are potentially anti-social. They have produced a huge amount of evil, which according to the positivist Ward have now to be reduced thanks to intellect and education (ibid., p. 53).

As compared to the gloomy representation proposed by Ward, sociologists such as Cooley, Park, Burgess and Znaniecki analyse the relations between emotions, sentiments and society from a more optimistic point of view. Although they give great relevance to the emotional component of the social actor, they all conceive of emotions as a socialized component of the individual, and in so far as they are socialized, they represent a relevant factor of social stability and integration of the individual in society.

3.1 Charles Horton Cooley

Sociology owes to Charles Horton Cooley the idea that the self is the output of a constant confrontation between the actor and his fellow-people, who reflect the actor's image as a looking-glass. The self is social, in so far as it is the product of three, converging, elements: "the imagination of our appearance to the other person; the imagination of his judgement of that appearance, and some sort of self-feeling, such as pride or mortification" (Cooley, 1902/1922, p. 184). Cooley's conception of society is holistic, a whole in which the individual and the social may not be neatly distinguished but have to be considered as strongly interrelated

(Bierstedt, 198, pp. 92–94). As a corresponding idea of the sociality of the self, Cooley conceives of society as mental, since it emerges from the relations among personal ideas, for example the ideas people have of both real and fictional others. As Cooley writes: "In order to have society it is evidently necessary that persons should get together somewhere; and they get together only as personal ideas in the mind" (Cooley, 1902/1922, p. 119). By stressing the strong interrelation between the individual and society, such a conception locates the question of emotions in a liminal position: not completely individual and not yet social.

In the introduction added to the second edition of his *Human Nature and Social Order*, Cooley (1902/1922) poses the questions of emotions within a discussion on the relevance of both hereditary and the social environment. Self and society are the complex output of the intertwining between what Cooley calls the germ-plasm (e.g. hereditary) and the cultural (language, intercourses, education) (ibid., pp. 4–5) so that it is hard to distinguish what contributes to what. Human behaviour is not predetermined by instinct but is, on the contrary, made possible by what Cooley defines as instinctive emotions. As opposed to instincts among lower animals, instinctive emotions do not produce "fixed modes of behavior" (ibid., p. 29). They are, as it were, genetic prerequisites for plastic actions: "[t]hese instinctive emotions predetermine, not specific actions, but, in a measure, the energy that flows into actions having a certain function with reference to our environment." (ibid., p. 26). Some instinctive dispositions are clearly related to our animal nature (e.g. anger and fear). Yet, simple emotions may not explain human behaviour. As Cooley writes: "all such dispositions [...] are rapidly developed, transformed, and interwoven by social experience, giving rise to a multitude of complex passions and sentiments which [...] change very considerably with changes in the social life that moulds them" (ibid., p. 27).

Thus, the cultural and social context redefines the content of any emotionally determined action by defining "more or less peculiar modes of feeling" (ibid.). This does not imply the irrelevance of emotional dispositions. They in fact produce the vital energy indispensable for human behaviour; yet that emotional energy has to be socially tamed in order to be converted into meaningful actions. In Cooley's words:

> Although instinctive emotion probably enters into everything we do, it enters in such a way that we can rarely or never explain human behavior by it alone. In human life it is not, in any considerable degree, a motive to specific behavior at all, but an impulse whose definite expression depends upon education and social situation. It does not act except through a complex, socially determined organism of thought and sentiment.
>
> (ibid.)

Instinctive emotions are to be refined through social ideas, so as to be converted from raw psychological materials into relevant elements of social organization:

> These ideas that enrich the meaning of the symbol—the resentment or fear, for instance—have all, no doubt, their roots in instinct; we are born with the

crude raw material of such feelings. And it is precisely in the act of communication, in social contact of some sort, that this material grows, that it gets the impulses that give it further definition, refinement, organization. It is by intercourse with others that we expand our inner experience.

(ibid., p. 104)

One of the theoretical consequences of the interconnection between the individual self and society is the idea of a collective consciousness, emerging from communication and cooperation among individual selves. The first chapter of Cooley's second book, *Social Organization. A Study of the Larger Mind* (1910) starts with a clear-cut, axiomatic sentence: "Mind is an organic whole made up of cooperating individuals" (Cooley, 1910, p. 3). This has at least two relevant consequences: the social mind is not an epiphenomenon of individual minds but the output of processes of cooperation, conflict and communication. Moreover, even what has been conceived so far as individual consciousness is an aspect of the social mind, both in the sense that consciousness emerges in the process of social interaction and in the sense that what (and how) we think and feel is socially determined. Indeed, as Cooley writes in a sentence which is proverbial: "Self and society are twin-born, we know one as immediately as we know the other, and the notion of a separate and independent ego is an illusion" (ibid., p. 5).

Against these background assumptions, Cooley's reflection on emotions becomes subtler. He distinguishes between feeling, as an aspect of the individual inner life, and sentiment which is expressly defined as "socialized feeling", that is "feeling which has been raised by thought and intercourse out of its merely instinctive state and become properly human" (ibid., p. 177). Feelings need another feature so as to be converted into sentiments: they have to emerge from the "sympathetic contact with the mind of others" (ibid.). Thus, according to Cooley, "love is a sentiment while lust is not, resentment is, but not rage" (ibid.). A sentiment is a feeling directed towards another actor within social interaction and, in so far as it is socialized, it has a moral value in it. Cooley thus conceives sentiments, as Durkheim and Simmel had already done and Parsons would later do, as means for social integration. Yet social integration in modern societies is possible only as an effect of two trends in the contemporary evolution of sentiments, the second being the more relevant. The first trend is diversification, that is a multiplication of sentiments as an effect of the increasing complexity of social life. The second trend is humanism, "meaning by this a wider reach and application of the sentiments that naturally prevail in the familiar intercourse of primary groups" (ibid.). As a collateral effect of diversification, sentiments tend, according to Cooley, both to get less strong and reach a higher degree of refinement (ibid., p. 178). The artificial system of modern society, by dissolving traditional social bonds, needs some compensatory integrative force, and this is to be found in a sentiment of mutual kindness and brotherhood (ibid., p. 189) which in modern society is expanding from primary groups to the society as a whole. This expansion contributes to a new ideal of moral unity and to the strengthening of the we-feeling as opposed to the I-feeling (ibid., pp. 188–189). In a perspective which seems to anticipate Parsons' conception of the societal community (see *infra*, Chapter 5),

Cooley proposes a theory in which sentiments are understood as means to make integration even in complex societies possible.

As Bierstedt (1981) has rightly stressed, much of Cooley's writings are affected by a naïve optimism and an underlining moralism. His conception of emotions is both refined and naïve: they are conceived as strongly connected to society, in so far as it is through social intercourses and communication that genetic emotional dispositions assume their social meaning. They are, moreover, a means to foster integration, within an unsophisticated conception of civilization which is moulded on the model of American democracy. Yet, his arguments specify the relevance of the social character of emotions, which, thanks to his intuitions on the sociality of the self, are never conceived of as the output of a sole psychological drive but as malleable instincts, made meaningful due to the social context in which they manifest.

3.2 Park and Burgess

In their *Introduction to the Science of Sociology*, Robert E. Park and Ernest W. Burgess (1921) deal with the theme of emotions and sentiments chiefly in Chapter 6, devoted to the analysis of social interaction, and in Chapter 7, which deals with the topic of social forces. By locating the questions of emotions and sentiments in two distinct chapters, Park and Burgess stress the differences between the two concepts: emotions are the simplest component of communication, the one which equates human beings and animals; sentiments are components of social attitudes and in this specific sense are social forces.

Interaction, Park and Burgess write, is the basic stuff of society, such that "the limits of society are coterminous with the limits of interaction" (ibid., p. 341). The concept does not belong to common-sense as it represents "the culmination of long-continued reflection by human beings in their ceaseless effort to resolve the ancient paradox of unity in diversity" (ibid., p. 339). It is sociology which equates interaction with the basic element of society, as "society stated in mechanistic terms reduces to interactions" (ibid., p. 341). The medium of interaction is communication, and it is within the argument on the way communication works that Park and Burgess introduce the analysis of emotions. Communication operates on three distinct levels: "(x) that of the senses; (y) that of the emotions; and (z) that of sentiments and ideas". (ibid., p. 342). Perception through the senses and emotional responses are "the natural forms of communication since they are common to man and to animals" (ibid.). By making reference to Georg Simmel, the authors show how the perceptual component of interaction is of the greatest relevance since it contributes to the formation of personal attitudes. The German sociologist is clear in this regard, as he maintains that individuals perceive their fellow people "through the medium of the senses". Senses enable two important processes: appreciation and comprehension. The first:

> may induce in us affective responses of pleasure or pain, of excitement or calm, of tension or relaxation, produced by the features of a person, or by the

tone of his voice, or by his mere physical presence in the same room. These affective responses, however, do not enable us to understand or to define the other person. Our emotional response to the sense-image of the other leaves his real self outside.

(ibid., p. 356)

On the other hand, comprehension is a process by which the impression we receive through the senses:

becomes the medium for understanding the other. What I see, hear, feel of him is only the bridge over which I reach his real self [...] The speech, quite as much as the appearance, of a person, may be immediately either attractive or repulsive. On the other hand, what he says enables us to understand not only his momentary thoughts but also his inner self.

(ibid., p. 357)

The two processes of appreciation and comprehension, though analytically distinguishable, are yet strongly linked, such that what we experience as emotional impressions become the basis of mutual understanding and moral judgment.

Whereas interactions are conceived of by Park and Burgess as the basic elements of society, a number of trends are detectable in society which are conceivable as forces promoting and fostering social processes. Social forces, as compared to physical forces, are to be located in institutions and organizations, although common sense tends to conceive "individual men and women" as their basic elements (ibid., p. 437). Yet, on closer scrutiny, even individuals are not elementary units: they may change according to their social roles, social circumstances and time. Hence, sociologists seek the elementary units of social forces, Park and Burgess write, not in the individual, "but in his appetites, desires, wishes – the human motives which move him to action" (ibid., p. 437). Seeking a sociological perspective on social forces entails an explicit critique of the conception of individual interests as developed in classical political economy. Social actors are reduced to "an intellectual calculating machine" (ibid., p. 495), balancing costs and benefits, without any reference to sociality as a constitutive element of the individual, his motives and choices. Sociology remedies this over-exemplification, by introducing new social types, more complex than the *homo oeconomicus*, able to take into account the social components of action, including solidarity and social values (ibid., p. 496).

If one denies relevance to the individual and his self-interests as the basic element of social forces, one has to find an appropriate sociological substitute. Park and Burgess detect one candidate in the concept of social attitude. "An attitude is the tendency of the person to react positively or negatively to the total situation. Accordingly, attitudes may be defined as the mobilization of the will of the person" (ibid., p. 438). Thus, attitudes are to be understood as patterns of behaviour, changing in relation to specific situations, which depend on the contrasting tendencies to approach or to withdraw. This two contrasting movements, often operating together, are responsible for a number of social processes, for example the phenomenon of social distance or the phenomenon of hierarchy. Sentiments are relevant elements in the constitution of specific social attitudes. They are not instinctual, as emotions are, but are to be considered as the cultural "organization of the affective and conative life" (ibid., p. 466).

> In the absence of sentiments – write Park and Burgess – our emotional life would be a mere chaos, without order, consistency, or continuity of any kind; and all our social relations and conduct, being based on the emotions and their impulses, would be correspondingly chaotic, unpredictable, and unstable.
>
> (ibid., p. 466)

In line with Park and Burgess, sentiments may be classified according to the generality of their object. The first case is a sentiment directed towards a concrete object (the love of a mother for her child); the intermediate case is a sentiment toward a category (love for children); the third is a sentiment toward an abstract concept (love for virtue) (ibid.). In the passage from the concrete to the abstract, sentiment shows its integrative function, as it is closely connected to moral values. As Cooley had already shown, according to Park and Burgess sentiments locate emotions in a socialized dimension. It is through the conversion of pure impulses into cultural schemes of behaviours that the social actor may volitionally control "the immediate promptings of the emotions" (ibid.). Sentiments have thus a relevant stabilizing function, as they transform the imponderability of human impulses into controllable patterns of attitudes and behaviour.

3.3 Florian Znaniecki

When Znaniecki published *The Laws of Social Psychology* (1925) he had already co-authored the three volumes of *The Polish Peasant in Poland and America* with William I. Thomas (1918, 1919). He was by then an acknowledged sociologist both in Poland, his home country, and in the United Sates, his adoptive fatherland. In the book, which is an attempt to define the field and subject matter of social psychology, an analysis of emotions and sentiments is available, which would be refined in *Social Actions* (Znaniecki, 1936), the monograph published some ten years later. In the earlier book, Znaniecki tries to methodologically define the specific objectives and tasks of social psychology by excluding the topic of "the actual expression of a disposition rooted in the psychical or bio-psychical individual, like the instincts or the will" (Zanniecki, 1925, p. 78). Social psychology has to restrict its field to social actions, that is actions made up both of social acts expressly aimed at influencing other actors and of the response of those people who are the object of the social acts. An action has, first of all, a volitional component, being characterized by the principle of achievement, that is "*social action, once begun, continues to its purposed end, unless there are factors interfering with its continuation*" (ibid., p. 64) (italics in the original). Moreover, it is determined by some impulse to act, which represents the subjective side of the objectively observable activity of the actors. Znaniecki asserts that the subjective component, although undoubtedly an expression of the actor's inner life, is not to be analyzed by the social psychologist as a matter of psychological states. It is relevant in so far as it triggers the action and sustains it according to the principle of achievement.

Volition is not the sole component of action, since it is also affected by sentiments. Even in this case, the social psychologist should not study sentiments as an inner component of the human being. They are, on the contrary, relevant in so far as they trigger specific types of actions. The social psychologist:

> will ask [himself] what kind of a social action any subject tends to perform when "despising" or "admiring", when "angry" or "afraid"; that is, how does he attempt to influence the object of his contempt or admiration, his anger or fear [...]. The important problem is whether these words of common speech stand for definite and elementary practical tendencies; whether in all cases when a subject despises or admires, is angry or afraid, etc., there is a definite inclination to a specific type of social behavior, a uniformity of social purposes. If on investigating the various actions achieved or begun under the influence of contempt, admiration, anger, or fear, respectively, we shall in fact find such a uniformity of social purposes in each case, then we shall decide that these words denote definite social tendencies.
>
> (ibid., p. 73)

Thus, sentiments are analyzed as social tendencies able to set forth specific kind of social actions. They are surely connected with inner states of mind, and in fact Znaniecki criticizes Dewey's conception according to which action should be studied in its course, as an interrelation of objective and subjective aspects, in which psychological states play no role. Yet the social psychologist does not study sentiments as a general psychologist would (hence separated by concrete interaction), but as real components of the action, since they are perceived as real by the individual actor and his social milieu. Common people, in fact, understand anger, contempt, fear and the like as the existing subjective tendencies to be distinguished from the objective conditions in which a social action manifests itself. The individual and his social milieu:

> produce practical values which are practically real in the very measure as actual human behavior takes them into account as facts and adapts itself to them. Contempt and admiration, fear and anger are thus at least as real as other cultural values — myths, legal rules, forms of property, and so on — whose reality consists in their being treated in practice as realities.
>
> (ibid, p. 77)

In the book specifically devoted to the topic of social action, Znaniecki (1936) distances himself from social psychology, social action being now understood as the proper domain of sociological analysis (ibid., p. 3). Action is social in so far as it is addressed to other individuals and, due to its sociality, it is one of the specific applicative fields of sociology. As Bierstedt clarifies, in Znaniecki's view:

> social actions are those actions that deal with human beings, with human beings, furthermore, who are themselves experienced as conscious objects by the authors of the actions. The object of a social action is another individual (or a collectivity) who has a capacity to be influenced by the action. Otherwise the action, even though surrounded and constrained by norms, is not a social action. Social actions are thus actions directed solely to persons (or collectivities) and would seem, therefore, to be always interactions.
>
> (Bierstedt, 1981, p. 214)

It is the relational component of action which makes emotions so relevant for its meaningfulness. Znaniecki makes explicit reference to the matter in Chapter 16 of *Social Action*, devoted to altruism. In paragraph 3, titled *Sharing Attitudes (Sympathetic Communion)*, sentiments are distinguished from emotions. A tendency to act may be potential. In this case it is to be understood as an attitude, for example the attribution of a certain value to other social actors. Emotions emerge in an intermediary stage between the attitude and the concrete action, as an "incipient but arrested activity" (ibid., p. 535) or a "'yearning' for activity" (ibid.). "[T]his yearning – writes Znaniecki – is accompanied by that peculiar, complex, fluid datum of experience which is called 'emotion'" (ibid.). Thus, emotions are, as it were, the premise of action (ibid., p. 536). They are made up of vague organic processes which manifest themselves in bodily changes (e.g. "facial distortion, visceral changes, random movements, gestures, ejaculations" [ibid.]) which are all symbols of the experienced emotions and, as such, may be understood by other social actors as manifestation of the inner states of others.

When an emotion is socialized it becomes a sentiment. As such, it is no longer simply a datum of the inner experience of a social actor, but it is perceived by others as a psychological phenomenon (ibid.). And it is because it can be understood as a psychological component of a certain social situation that it may be experienced and reproduced by other actors. Sharing sentiments is possible within what Znaniecki calls sympathetic communion (to be distinguished from synesthetic communion – sharing experiences – and synergetic communion – sharing active tendencies), by which social actors do not only share the value they attribute to a specific object but also its emotional component. Thus, when I discuss with a friend about painting or politics, writes Znaniecki (ibid., p. 537), if neither of us is emotionally involved, we may achieve mutual information about the value we attribute to a certain painting or political institution. On the other hand, in case our attitude is "emotionalized" ("I am personally enthusiastic about the painting or indignant about the institution" [ibid.]) social sympathy may emerge, as I attune my emotions with my fellow people's. The output is sympathetic communion, a process by which not only axiological evaluations are shared but also the emotional component of social attitude (e.g. sentiments). Sympathetic communion is socially determined, within specific normative frameworks, which anticipates the concept of emotional rules elaborated by contemporary sociology of emotion. Let me quote Znaniecki directly:

> in many societies custom determines the class of people whose sentiments an individual ought to share and who are expected to share his sentiments, also the kind of sentiments that ought to be shared and the occasions for sharing them.
>
> (ibid., p. 539)

Thus, the process of sympathetic communion socializes sentiments, by determining when they may be expressed and in what social occasions they may become motives for mutual sharing.

By discussing emotions and sentiments from a sociological point of view, Znaniecki anticipates a stance of contemporary sociology of emotions. For a social scientist, emotions are relevant components of social action, both individual and collective. This does not account, anyway, for a reduction of the actor to his psychological components. On the contrary, the actor is sociologically relevant only in so far as he acts, and his action, not his innerness, is the object of sociological analysis (Halas, 2010, p. 145).

4 The relevance of emotions in contemporary social theory

The reference to classical sociological thought shows that, although emotions were not the central topic of sociological investigation, they held a relevant position as a collateral theme. In the works of the founding fathers, the reader may find both arguments in favour and against the role of emotions in society. Emotions may be imagined as residual components of social action, perturbing elements of social order or relevant factors of social integration. Regardless of the way emotions are imagined, they have nonetheless a place in the arguments of early sociologists, in some cases anticipating future developments. Post-classical sociology, on the contrary, tends to disregard emotions: modern society is conceived of as a complex system, where the individual may still play a role but more as a cognitive rather than as an emotional unit. Emotions are now imputed to the field of psychology, thus radicalizing a process which, from Durkheim (1895) on, aimed to define sociology as an autonomous field of scientific investigation. Parsons may be considered the main representative of an attitude conceiving emotions as a psychological topic, reducing their sociological relevance to the question of the integration of the individual in the social system. In his writings, emotions are functional to the reproduction of society, both during the process of socialization, made possible by an affectively oriented family (Parsons, 1955), and in the attachment of the individual to the values of his national social community (Parsons, 1991, see also *infra*, Chapter 5). Sociology had to wait until the second half of the 20th century in order to witness a renewed interest in the topic of emotionality, now understood as a theme worth autonomous investigation.

By reconstructing classical sociological approaches to emotions, Chris Shilling writes that the founding fathers adopted either an order theory approach or an interaction approach. In the first case, emotions could be conceived of as essential components of the social structure, in the second as fundamental elements of human interaction (Shilling, 2002). Although many approaches to the sociological study of emotions have been developed, the two opposite poles of structure and action still hold a relevant place in the sociological analysis of emotions. Yet emotions are often used as tools to overcome old-established dichotomies. The distinction has been declined, focusing on such relevant themes as the micro-foundation of order, stratification, norms and rules etc., thus creating a complex set of theories and approaches which qualifies the sociology of emotions as a sub-discipline. Thus, it is by now possible to detect both a number of questions which may be analyzed by making sociological reference to emotions (e.g. emotions and identity, emotions and social order, emotion and inequalities, emotions and social change, just to mention a few) and a number of perspectives (e.g. interactionism, critical theories, exchange theories) which set the theoretical character of the sociological analysis of emotions.

By locating emotions within social thought, the sociology of emotions had the relevant function to dismantle old established concepts and dichotomies. Indeed, the individual had always been a key issue of sociological reasoning, both as the triggering element of the social (methodological individualism) or as a cumbersome presence, to be set in the psychological or biological environment of society (Luhmann, 1984). Even those currents of sociology which, starting from Max Weber, had traditionally posed the subjective meaning of the social action at the core of theoretical thinking, had discredited emotions as a topic for sociological analysis. Weber seemed to prefer the ideal type of *Zweckrationalitaet* to the other types of action (Weber, 1958, p. 6 ff.). Symbolic interactionists traditionally focused their attention on the cognitive processes of understanding shared meanings and values (Blumer, 1969). Even ethnomethodologists, with their stress on everyday rationality, seemed little interested in emotions and their social consequences (Garfinkel, 1967). Emotions, the interest in which was coeval with the emergence of a sociology of the body, brought people back in, yet in ways which were not compatible with the rational premises of exchange theory (Homans, 1964; 1974). Once acquired as a topic for sociological analysis, emotions made it evident that the individual was a physical component of society, with his body and related feelings. It was no longer possible to neatly separate the rational from the emotional component of the social actor: the Cartesian distinction between *res cogitan* and *rex extensa*, which had resulted in the sociological preference for cognition, could now be finally overcome (Burkitt, 1999).

From a methodological point of view, emotions cannot be reduced to a topic, but are to be understood as a perspective from which old themes and ideas can be remoulded. The over-socialized conception of the social actor (Wrong, 1961), which had characterized mainstream sociology, especially in its Parsonsian version, could now give way to a redefinition of the individual, whose action was to be understood as motivated not only by rational choices, but also by bodily impulses and emotions. The capacity of emotions to provide thematic interconnection may be given the merit to stimulate a reformulation of social theoretical thinking. As Williams and Bendelow write:

> emotions lie at the juncture of a number of fundamental dualisms in western thought such as mind/body, nature/culture, public/private. A major strength of the study of emotions lies, therefore, in its ability to transcend many of these former dichotomous ways of thinking, which serve to limit social thought and scientific investigation in unnecessary, self-perpetuating ways.
>
> (Williams and Bendelow, 1998, p. XIII)

The first dichotomy distinguishes between the emotional body and society. The sociology of emotions can hardly avoid the thorny question of the biological and psychological origin of emotions. The definition of the emotional component of social behaviour is often related to pre-existing extra-sociological concepts. The social mechanisms related to micro (e.g. the management of emotions in everyday life [Hochschild, 1998]) and macro aspects of emotions (e.g. social stratification [Hammond, 1983; 1990]) are therefore connected to the biological and psychological roots of human behaviour. If a neat distinction between nature and culture is by now unrealistic, the underlying danger for sociologists is to transfer the responsibility of the sociological definition of emotions to other branches of knowledge. In an essay dating back to the late 1980s, E. Doyle McCarthy (1989) warns against the excessive dependence of sociology of emotions on other approaches. McCarthy protests against a reified conception, according to which emotions are given as if they exist only in the biological or psychological components of human action and are hence sociologically unknowable. By assuming a Durkheimian stance, McCarthy considers emotions as social facts and, as such, they should be explained by making reference to related social facts, not to some biological or psychological substratum. What is evident in McCarthy's arguments is the difficulty of overcoming the dichotomy of emotion/society and, at the same time, keeping a specific sociological attitude towards emotions.

A thematic variation of the body/society dichotomy refers to the rationality of action. Taking emotions into account implies that they are to be considered as relevant aspects of society. Yet emotions are, as it were, radically grounded in the social actor, and this because "the *self*, the individual organism, is the central reference upon which emotions turn" (Bericat 2016, p. 495). This strong interrelation between the individual and his emotional component makes it difficult to expunge the concrete emotional body from the analysis. Sociology has generally focused its attention on cognition (Baldwin, 1988), thus allowing a generalized agreement on the relevance of rationality as a guide for the individual action. The appraisal for rationality had represented a unifying factor for otherwise competing and conflicting sociological perspectives (e.g. functionalism, Weberian individualism, symbolic interactionism, exchange theories and ethnomethodology). Indeed, rationality is never idiosyncratic, in the sense that, in order for individual action to be conceived of as rational, it has to comply with external rationality standards. Thus action has to be analyzed from the standpoint of an external observer, rather than the perspective of the individual actors. Once emotions are conceived of as relevant elements of society, they make the process of elision of the individual and the individual body from social theory more difficult. This implies that the idiosyncratic element of individual choices is now to be included in the analysis, which entails that a neat separation of the individual from society becomes theoretically more difficult to advocate.

A traditional distinction within social theories sets integration theories (notably structural functionalism) against conflict theories (both of Marxian or Weberian origin). Although the distinction has been made less dramatic by recent evolution in sociological theories (e.g. Elias, 1970; Giddens, 1984; Luhmann, 1984; Habermas, 1984, 1987; Collins, 1988), sociologists tend to emphasize either social order or conflict as premises of their theoretical interpretation. Emotions allow social theorists to give new meaning to the Comtian idea according to which society is both statically able to maintain its intrinsic order and dynamically capable of producing social change. Emotions have in fact been used both as analytical tools to analyze conformity and order (Sheff, 2000) and as social mechanisms to explain social unrest and social transformation (Schoeck, 1966; Ben-Ze'ev, 1992; Barbalet, 1992). What is relevant in this regard is the fact that different emotions are reputed to be co-responsible for distinct social phenomena, which may help to get rid of old established disciplinary fences: society is constantly striving for order because it is constantly changing. Emotions may give new theoretical substance to these apparently contrasting processes.

At a more basic level, introducing emotions in sociological analysis may help mitigate the opposition between micro and macro approaches (Kemper, 1990). In their analysis of the relevance of emotional micro-process on a macro-scale, contemporary sociologists reproduce, in some cases unwittingly, the lesson of both European and American classical sociological theory as sketched above. Starting the analysis from the micro level of the relevance of emotions in everyday interactions, one may realize their contribution as to the integration of society as such (Shott, 1979). In this perspective, the cultural component of emotions tends to give social sense to biological or psychological arousal, by channelling it within a set of established expression-rules (Hochschild, 1979). In his theory, Collins (1990) integrates solidarity and conflict, by considering both as emerging in the micro space of interaction from sentiments either directed towards integrative processes or mobilizing people against those who have opposing interests. Hammond (1990), to mention one more example, considers what he calls affective maximization as a logical premise for the existence of social hierarchies, hence of inequalities. Once introduced as elements of sociological analysis, emotions make it evident that the micro–macro link is unavoidable. Emotions are both the expression of a specific culture and are therefore regulated by shared representations and rules. Moreover, they are able to trigger, at the level of micro interactions, social processes which are relevant on the macro-scale. According to Randall Collins, when we transpose macro phenomena on the micro level of social interaction, what we find are emotions: "[w]hat holds a society together – the 'glue' of solidarity – and what mobilizes conflicts – the energy of mobilizing groups – are emotions; so is what uphold stratification – hierarchical feelings, whether dominant, subservient, or resentful" (Collins, 1990, p. 28).

5 Sketching the features of the sociology of emotions

As I will clarify with further details in Chapter 5, the selection of the aspects of the social that are considered relevant within social theory determines what we, as social scientists, may perceive as of sociological importance. Alfred Schutz proposed a process of construction of ideal-types by which the social scientist acquires his knowledge of society. This process has, as one of its premises, the construction of a model of man, a *homunculus* or puppet as Schutz called it, which is "brought into a fictional reciprocal interaction relationship with other similar constructed models" (Dreher, 2011, p. 504). Schutz was aware that, when sociologists try to understand human beings and social interaction, they construct a simplified image of man. He himself had given little importance to emotions in the construction of his own theoretical *homunculus*: what counted was motives, social roles and knowledge, all aspects which are cognitively determined and oriented. As it emerged, sociology of emotions had the relevant merit to conceive of feelings and emotions as important variables. A new awareness developed, according to which the knowledge of social phenomena is not adequate if emotions are excluded from sociological analysis. By bringing emotion back into sociological theory, a double task could be achieved: "studying the social nature of emotions and studying the emotional nature of social reality" (Bericat 2016, p. 495).

An extended reconstruction of the present day's state of the art of the sociology of emotions is far beyond the scope of this chapter. Reconstructions of the different trends in the sociology of emotions are now available (e.g. Bendelow and Williams, 1998, Kemper, 2000; Stets and Turner, 2004; 2014; Bericat, 2016), and some of the approaches will be dealt with in more detail in the following chapters, intended as attempts to explain specific aspects of emotions in social life. What I propose here is a short review of the contribution given to the sociology of emotions by those sociologists who set the discussion in motion, as their specific conception of the relation between emotions and society still affects the contemporary debate.

When sociology of emotions emerged as an autonomous sub-discipline in the 1970s, its development implied a shift from a sociology which put cognition in a prominent place to one which was more interested in those aspects of social life once conceived of as marginal or irrelevant (Kemper, 1990, p. 3). Until the 1970s, the reference to the cognitive component of action seemed, as Kemper writes, more appropriate in order to investigate the features of the new post-industrial era (ibid.). In the 1970s, a new intellectual perspective emerged, linked to a changing cultural and social climate. Social movements, a new interest in the body and sexuality, a diffuse appreciation for differences (ethnic, cultural, gender-related), all converged into a positive evaluation of emotions as specific components of social life. If action had been conceived of as essentially rational by mainstream sociology, now the idea made its way in social theorizing according to which action is not only determined by what people understand or think but also by what they feel (Hochschild, 1990, p. 117).

In 1975 Arlie Russel Hochschild (1975) published her "The Sociology of Feelings and Emotions. Selected Possibilities" which is one of the first attempts to thematize emotions as a specifically sociological topic. Hochschild maintained that emotions have been expunged from sociology due to a generalized cognitive stance in contemporary society, which induced sociologists to expunge emotions as irrelevant for scientific investigation. This has led to an over-cognitive conception of the social actor, which Hochschild exemplifies by making reference to Erving Goffman. By representing people as incessantly evaluating the best strategy to maintain their social image, Goffman hardly took the emotional component of social life into account. A second, opposite trend derives from Freud and his interpretation of the actor as driven by instincts and the subconscious, yet unable to understand the instinctual substratum of his own action. What Hochschild proposes is neither a chiefly cognitive actor nor an unconsciously emotional one, but a sentient individual, able to consciously experience his emotions and act in connection both to rational motives and emotional drives. Hochschild does not intend to substitute the over-cognitive actor *à la* Goffman with a totally emotional social being. On the contrary: the sociality of emotions implies that a social actor has to constantly adjust his behaviour according to specific emotional rules (Hochschild, 1979) and to a specific emotional culture. The relevant question is then how social actors adapt their emotional states (not just their external demeanor) to a set of conventions about the contextual appropriateness of emotions. The individual in social contexts has thus to adjust what he feels according to the specific setting, social interactions and the supposed expectations of other social actors.

The attention for the individual interpretation is at the basis of the symbolic interactionist approach to emotions. In 1979 Susan Shott published a paper on the specific topic of emotions in an interactionist perspective. By making explicit reference to Clifford Geertz, Shott underlined that "[s]ocial norms clearly have substantial impact on the interpretation, expression, and arousal of emotion" (Shott, p. 1319). Emotions are not completely social yet their content is chiefly determined by the way the individual actor interprets himself in connection to other actors, emotional rules and the social context. An indeed, "[i]nternal states and cues, necessary as they are for affective experience, do not in themselves establish feeling, for it is the actor's definitions and interpretations that give physiological states their emotional significance or nonsignificance" (Shott, p. 1323). In compliance with the principles of symbolic interactionism, the actor is understood by Susan Shott as reflexive, that is able to understand other people's reaction to his behaviour, and hence to adjust his conduct to generalized expectancies (Iagulli, 2011, p. 58). This is particularly relevant for what Shott calls role-taking emotions, for example those:

> emotions [which] cannot occur without putting oneself in another's position and taking that person's perspective. Thus, an individual experiencing

a role-taking sentiment (e.g. embarrassment or shame) has first cognitively taken the role of some real or imaginary other or the generalized.

(Shott, 1979, pp. 1323–1324)

In Shott's analysis of role-taking emotions one finds an interactionist treatment of the micro–macro link, since emotions may help guarantee social orders, starting from the control of individual action. Shott distinguishes between reflexive role-taking emotions, "which are directed toward oneself" (ibid., p. 1314), such that the individual may conform his behaviour to socially defined expectations, and empathic role-taking emotions, "which are evoked by mentally placing oneself in another's position and feeling what the other feels or what one would feel in such a position" (ibid.). As reflexive role-taking emotions (shame, embarrassment, guilt, pride, vanity) are connected to social rules and expectations, they are a powerful tool to guarantee, at the micro-level of interaction, social stability and social control. Both negative emotions such as shame (the self behaves as to regain lost social consideration) and positive emotions such as pride (the self tries to keep social approval) are directed to the control of one's behaviour, being the premises for social order as such (Iagulli, 2011, p. 60).

Among the pioneers of the sociology of emotions, Theodore D. Kemper (1978) proposes a different approach, which connects emotions to the structure of society. According to Kemper, who would develop his theory in the course of his career, emotions are determined by two components of the social structure: power and status. Power is defined after Weber as a "dimension of relationship in which [...] benefits are obtained from others who do not confer them willingly" (Kemper, 1978, p. 33). The second dimension of status, on the contrary, is a component of the relationship in which "[t]he benefits and rewards are freely offered without the use of power" (ibid.). In a dyadic relation, both partners enjoy different levels of power and status. The actors may feel that they have claimed or used an excess of power or status or, on the contrary, they may feel that they have insufficient power or receive insufficient status from the partner. When the self is conceived of as responsible, the issuing sentiment is *introjected* or *intropunitive*. In case the partner is conceived of as responsible, the issuing sentiment is *extrojected* and *extropunitive*. By combining the perceived excess or deficit of power and status with the agency (i.e. who is the responsible agent) Kemper proposes a complex typology of emotions. Just to give an example, shame is conceived of as "the emotions experienced when an actor believes that he has claimed and/or received more status than he deserves" (ibid.). When the self is conceived of as the agent, two outputs are possible: the actor will either withdraw from the relation or try to compensate those who, according to him, have given him more status than he deserved. The *extropunitive* version of shame results in the search for the incompetences of other people. Regardless of the complex scheme proposed by Kemper, one point is of relevance, as it would influence the further development of the sociology of emotions. Kemper adheres to the so-called specificity theory of emotions, according to which each emotion has its own specific physiological reference. Kemper sees a strong correlation between his relational model of status and power and the specificity theory. Indeed, Kemper's attempt is predictive as it tries to determine which social situations may produce a specific emotion, and prediction is feasible only if emotions are physiologically specific. In fact, if emotions are left undetermined as to their physiological base (a biological substratum which may assume different social meanings), culture and society may determine how a generic arousal will be interpreted as a socially determined emotion (Shott, 1979). On the contrary, according to Kemper, emotions are strongly connected to biological and psychological processes, the task of the sociology of emotions being the interconnection between social structure (one's position in the power/ status structure) and certain physiologically specific emotions. Emotions are thus conceived as determined by actual features of the social structure, yet they are essentially grounded in human biological and psychological *substrata*.

The aforementioned three shortly synthesized papers, all of them belonging to the pioneering era of the sociology of emotions, already set the two main trends of sociology of emotions up to the present day: the positivist (or organicist) and the constructivist (or culturalist). In a paper published in 1981, Kemper (1981) clarifies what he means by positivist and constructivist approaches. Positivists (including he himself) consider emotions as the output of a biological and psychological substratum which should not be denied, as constructivists do. Positivist approaches are predictive, as they can foresee which emotion will emerge given a specific relational setting, connected to status and power, whereas constructivists are much vaguer, relating emotions to cultural factors, such as emotional rules or the reflexive capacity the actor has to define the situation. Constructivists reacted to the paper, by underlining, first of all, that Kemper proposed an over-simplified conception of their approach (Hunsaker, 1983). And, in fact, constructivism considers emotions as an interpretative reaction to some environmental stimuli (ibid., p. 436). It is even possible to reverse Kemper's account, by maintaining that the physiology of emotions may be determined by some reaction to the environment, thus reasserting the socially constructed status of emotions without denying their connection to physiological processes (ibid., p. 437). The proper definition of an emotion remains vague and unspecified until it has been interpreted as that specific emotion by the individual actors in connection to some reaction to and assessment of the environment.

Arlie Hochschild (1983b) contextualizes Kemper's reconstruction as based chiefly on two assumptions: that social constructivism is not interested in structural aspects connected to emotions and that emotions would derive from feelings rules. The first assumption is confuted by Hochschild by showing that her work on emotional labour clearly refers to structural components of society (companies, the market, economy). Hence, even though her work deals chiefly with emotional management in the micro-dimension of social interaction, the social structure is not expunged but implied. As for the second critique, according to which emotional rules would determine emotions, Hochschild replies that what she actually states is that her approach is about what people reflexively do and think once social factors have induced in them specific primary emotions

(Hochschild, 1983b, p. 434). Thus, constructivism does not deny the connection between physiology and emotionality. Yet, although emotions may be linked to psychological processes, they are interpreted and acted upon differently according to different social and cultural settings.

Much of the sociological approaches to emotions may be still broadly labelled as positivist (or organic) or constructivist, to which Arlie Russel Hochschild (1990) has added a new one, the interactional. Each model gives the social component of emotions a different relevance: organismic considers emotions as aspects of human biology. Thus, the social component interferes only to "*elicit* feeling, and to *regulate* its expression" (Hochschild, 1990, p. 119). Social constructionists give the social the greatest relevance. Emotions are socially defined in the sense that it is the social that sets their meaning and the normative standards that regulate their expression and management. The biological component is reduced to the organic mechanisms which trigger emotions: the way they are conceived and managed is on the contrary completely imputed to the social. The last model which Hochschild mentions (stating it is her own) is the interactional. In this model, emotions, although produced within the biological body, are constantly reinforced, mitigated, reproduced, modified by the social process of interaction (ibid.).

What emerges from this short review is that emotions are both a substantive theme and a theoretical tool by which to redefine traditional sociological approaches: it is an across-the-board topic, which has been analyzed by making reference to different sociological perspectives. Emotions have been studied within different theoretical frameworks, both micro and macro: symbolic interactionism (Hochschild, 1975; Shott, 1979), conflict theory (Collins, 1975; 1988), exchange theory (Lawler and Thye, 1999) and socio-structural approaches (Kemper, 1981; 1990; Barbalet, 1992; 2004). According to some critics (Stets and Turner, 2004, p. 6) sociology has not been able to take advantage of the opportunity emotions represented, so as to define a single sociological approach to the topic. At its best, it has achieved the relevant task of renovating already established theoretical perspectives and at the same time has increased the reputation of the sociological accounts of emotions, even outside the narrow boundaries of our discipline (Stets and Turner, 2014, p. 7). Indeed, one of the features of sociology as such (not some of its sub-fields) is its multi-paradigmatic character (Kuhn, 1962). Sociologists should ask themselves whether a unifying paradigm is what the discipline needs or if its multiparadigmatic character is a signal of its vitality. This is no place to answer this complex theoretical question. What is evident is the variety of the sociological approaches to emotion which have developed since the 1970s and which account for the capacity of sociology to analyze new topics and themes from different theoretical perspectives. Emotion as a topic has been able to revitalize social thinking, to introduce new topics, to redefine the boundaries of our conception of the social actor, to introduce new links among perspectives and new perspectives from which to look at the social.

Note

1 There are many contradictory aspects in Simmel's definition of society. Kurt H. Wolff
   (1950, p. xxviii ff.) in his introduction to *The Sociology of Georg Simmel*, clearly
   shows the co-presence of both an individualistic and a relational conception of society.
   The second anyway seems the one which better defines Simmel's theoretical conception of the social world.

3 Emotions and their history

A sociological perspective

1 Do emotions have a history?

If one assumes an essentialist perspective on emotions, one could legitimately neglect answering the question posed as the title of this section. The essentialist (or positivist or organicist) conception considers emotions as a universal, unchangeable character of human nature. Yet individuals are moulded by social and cultural forces and emotions appear, in this regard, a peculiar case of how even apparently genetic, pre-programmed features of human conduct are conditioned by the social context. At the outset, there is certainly "the same emotional repertoire, derived from genes" (Oatley, 2004, p. 34). Yet genes are flexible, and the way they may condition actual behaviour is deeply determined by the interaction of the subject with his peculiar social world, since "[t]he genetically given cloth is tailored according to cultural ideas and meanings of each particular society" (ibid.). This strong interaction between our genetically determined emotional make-up and our specific social world is probably nowhere so evident as in the historical analysis of emotions, where emotions are by necessity conceived of as mouldable components of human nature, changing as the historical process unfolds. What is relevant for my argument here is that, once one accepts the idea that emotions change over time, one may think about emotions in terms of the cultural and social context in which they are embedded. Of course, the very possibility of conceiving of emotions from an historical perspective, implies that they are not static: a biological or psychological substratum is, therefore, the premise for a variety of different forms emotions may take in different cultural and historical contexts (Rosenwein, 2010, p. 10).

Nonetheless, history as a discipline has only recently begun to pay systematic attention to emotions as a field of investigation. At the core of this shift is a new conception of man, making its way within the methodology of history. Indeed, as a rule, history has generally made reference to the exemplified model of the rational economic actor, whose action is determined by self-interests. Yet a more complex conception has recently gained relevance, in which emotions have a role in determining human motivations and explaining historical phenomena (Matt and Stearns, 2014, p. 2). Although some antecedents of *longue durée* analysis of emotions are available, both in history and in kin-disciplines (notably Johan Huizinga

[1924] and Norbert Elias [1939, 1969]) and although a theoretical reflection on the role of emotion in history is not a total novelty (e.g. Febvre, 1941), yet a systematic historical interest in emotions is quite recent. This new interest is to be connected to the new conception of affectivity developed in the social sciences, by which emotions are no longer conceived of as a universal, genetically determined component of a person's biological make-up, but are rather understood as the output of complex and interconnected processes (social, cultural, psychological), in which time and social change play a relevant role.

The scope of this chapter is not to sketch the complex historical treatment of emotions, selecting from the huge related literature. My purpose is, more modestly, to make reference to long-duration analyzes which may help explicate the transition to modernity and the changes this transition brought about in the conception of the individual and the management of emotions. Another, although less pressing, aim is linked to the methodological challenge that an historical analysis of emotions poses for the social sciences. Indeed, historical inquiry has to come to terms, more than other disciplinary areas, with the methodological question of sources in the study of emotions. Susan J. Matt, as already hinted at in the introduction, speaks of this challenge in terms of the recovery of the invisible (Matt, 2014) by which emotions (a transient and inner phenomenon) are made a legitimate object of historical investigation. The solutions historians and historical sociologists have detected (e.g. the reference to etiquette books, art, literature) are compatible with my attempt (the use of creative sources as appropriate for the sociological analysis of emotions), although posing specific problems to the historians and social scientists alike.

The historiography of emotions and modernity, as Peter N. Stearns (2014) clearly shows, has been caught up between two extremes. On the one hand, the idea has consolidated according to which modernity radically changed people's conception of themselves and their affectivity in the direction of a more sophisticated control of emotions and the "humanization" of social relations. On the other hand, historians of the Middle Ages in particular have demonstrated how emotional control is not a specific feature of modernity, as it was a relevant aspect of social relations even in earlier times. Great historical narratives of change in the conception and management of emotions are obviously unable to describe complex nuances and differences related to specific social groups, classes, emotional communities and places. They tend in fact to represent general processes, often linked to Western countries, neglecting place, time and cultural specificities. Yet, as research in the area of the history of emotions clearly displays, modernity has produced significant changes, for example in the management of family relations, fear, shame and cheerfulness, which make the connection between emotions and modernity still a relevant topic, one which may reinforce interdisciplinary connections between history and the social sciences (ibid.). In this perspective, the contribution of history to the analysis of emotions appears particularly relevant. It is, in fact, "capable of identifying a significant new trend and tracing its evolution; working to determine the relationship between cultural standards (where change can be readily charted) and actual personal emotional experience" (Stearns, 2008, p. 18).

My attempt in this chapter is therefore limited, as I do not intend to reconstruct a complex debate but rather to single out relevant research which represents important steps towards a better understanding of the relations between time, social change and the conception and management of emotions. Some of the authors I make reference to are historians, some sociologists or anthropologists, which makes it clear how the topic of the historical significance of emotions and emotional changes may hardly be confined to the narrow limits of a single discipline. The argument aims to show that emotions are moulded by historical processes and are, at the same time, able to produce historical changes, within a mechanism of retroaction by which linear causality seems to lose plausibility.

2 Norbert Elias and the civilization of manners

Norbert Elias is one of the most original sociologists of the 20th century, able to combine a *longue durée* analysis of social processes and a de-reified, processual approach to social phenomena. His main theoretical preoccupation was to avoid any reduction of social processes to objects and, by remarking the essential connection between the individual and social structures, to reject a hypostatized conception of the social, which according to Elias, characterized contemporary social theory (Elias, 1970). His contribution to the sociology and history of emotion is generally associated with his early works (Elias: 1939, 1969), yet it may hardly be confined to the first part of his intellectual career. In Elias' approach, emotions are always part of a complex pattern, including both instinctual and social components, both on the micro and the macro level, the latter being connected with the individual's management of emotional drives. Emotions are thus intrinsically connected to macro, *longue durée* processes (social, political and economic) which are analyzed as able to affect "the micro level of psychological and emotional orientation" (Van Krieken, 2014, p. 22).

In Norbert Elias' works, emotions and their control are understood chiefly within a diachronic analysis, whose aim is to connect macro-historical changes with the transformation in the management of the body and the expression of feelings and impulses. As modern society gradually evolved, the control of the body and impulses were imputed to the individual, in a shift which may be synthesized as the passage from outer coercion to self-coercion, that is self-discipline. Outer, hetero-directed forms of social control became gradually less relevant, as norms related to the management of bodily functions and emotions tended to be interiorized by social actors, who were now conceived of as responsible for the expression of their feelings. Civilization is, according to Elias, a complex process, integrating both macro-historical phenomena, such as the emergence of courts and the development of nation-states, and the emergence of new forms of affectivity, new rules of conduct (including emotional rules) and a new conception of the self and human psychology. The genetic substratum of drives and feelings is, as it were, newly moulded, the output of this process being the typical structure of the personality of the modern individual. Elias seems convinced that the structure of affects depends on the historical and social context in which sentiments are developed and managed. He thus anticipates the critique according to which he would have attempted to construct a general theory of the historical changes of emotions, on the base of data referring to a specific social and historical context, namely contemporary Western society. In the post-script to the *Process of Civilization* published in 1968, he writes in this regard:

> Nowadays, in thinking and theorizing about the structure of human affects and how they are controlled, we are usually content to use as evidence observations from the more developed societies of the present day. We thus proceed from the tacit assumption that it is possible to construct theories about the affect structures of human beings in general on the basis of studies of people in a specific society that can be observed here and now – our own. However, numerous relatively accessible observations point to the fact that the standard and pattern of affect controls in societies at different stages of development, and even in different strata of the same society, can differ. Whether we are concerned with the development of European countries over centuries, or with the so-called "developing countries" in other parts of the world, we are constantly confronted by observations which give rise to the problem of how and why, in the course of the overall long-term transformations of society […] the affectivity of human behaviour and experience, the control of individual affects by external and self-constraints, and in this sense the structure of all forms of human expression is altered in a particular direction.
>
> (Elias, 1939, p. 449)

The process, as sketched in the long quote from Elias, makes it evident how affectivity is strongly connected to the social context and, within a specific social context, to the location of the individual in the class structure. Elias thus advocates the strong social character of emotions, yet, complying with his processual approach, he does not deny the duality of human nature, its being both biologically defined and socially determined. In a later paper, published in 1987, he comes back to the topic, analyzing the relation between the body as biologically determined and the social conditioning of emotions. The paper shows how the topic of emotions, the body and affectivity has continued to intrigue Elias throughout his career.

If one analyzes emotions from a developmental point of view, Elias writes, one is likely to find himself at a crossroad. On the one hand, the evolutionary conception, by which emotions are conceived of as biological or psychological components of human beings, tends to stress the continuity of emotions between human beings and animals. On the other hand, when one adopts an historical approach, one tends to neglect the natural component of emotions, so as to stress their specifically cultural components. In the field of emotions, the old-fashioned battle between natural and moral sciences is once again re-proposed, although with little gain for an appropriate understanding of emotions and their function in societies.

In the 1987 paper Elias, by restating his anti-reductionist approach, fosters a way of analysis which underlines both what is uniquely human and what human beings have in common with other species (Elias, 1987, p. 341).

The idea of a biologically determined emotional substratum is conceived by Elias as the "image of a split world", in which the natural and the cultural are considered as part of ontologically separated realms. In processual terms, this image has to be substituted by a conception by which the human species represents an evolutionary breakthrough. The breakthrough depends chiefly on the predominance, in human beings, of learned versus unlearned, genetically programmed behaviours. As Elias writes:

> Human beings depend for their orientation in the first place on the learning of a pre-existing social fund of knowledge. Without it they cannot even find their food or distinguish between food that tastes fine but is poisonous, and healthy food that tastes differently. Without acquiring a fairly large social fund of knowledge they cannot survive nor simply become human. They are in fact biologically constituted in a way which makes it possible as well as necessary for them to orientate themselves by means of learned knowledge.
>
> (ibid., pp. 345–346)

This entails that social changes are by necessity culturally determined. In other words, the relevance of learning in human beings implies that societies do change, yet without any connected modification in the genetic make-up of the species (ibid., p. 344). And indeed, the very possibility of history as opposed to natural evolution depends on this specificity of us humans as a species.

Although emotions are no doubt to be understood as biologically preprogrammed mechanisms, they are employed in human relations in highly specific, culturally determined ways. The expression of emotions is a highly sophisticated instrument which allows the simulation of inner states of mind, or the use of originally genetically determined gestures to communicate something different than what was originally intended. Against the idea of culturally indifferent basic emotions (Ekman, 1984; 1992), which is a relevant component of the mainstream psychological analysis of emotionality, Elias stresses the potentially strategic, culturally determined use of emotions in the social scene. He makes reference to the smile as an appropriate example:

> superimposed upon very weak traces of an inborn tendency to give or to receive a smiling signal is, in the present human species, an extensive capacity for utilizing the ancient innate signal more deliberately in connection with a process of learning which may be different in different societies.
>
> (Elias, 1987, p. 359)

A smile may be used to conceal other emotions, to express hesitation, withdrawal, hostility, triumph, thus showing the highly flexible varieties of use in the human species of innate, apparently mechanical reactions. Indeed, emotions may be socially tamed as they are never the sole expression of natural forces. According to Elias, in fact, *"no emotion of a grown up human person is ever an entirely unlearned, genetically fixated reaction pattern"* (ibid., p. 352) (italics in the original).

Emotions are both inborn and socially learned, and their social function may be fully understood only if one is able to connect them to the socially determined mechanism of self-control: "In the case of human beings" – Elias writes – "unlearnt emotional impulses are always related to a person's learned self-regulation, more specifically to learned control of emotions" (ibid., p. 360). Culturally defined mechanisms of control make emotions properly social and historical and are, as Elias states, clear "indications that human beings are by nature constituted for life in the company of others, for life in society" (ibid., p. 361).

The control of affectivity is strongly linked, in Norbert Elias, with the historical process of individualization. The individual is, ever more, intended as an autonomous subject, deeply separated from the social context in which his personality has evolved. This artificial conception leads to what Elias defines as *homo clausus*, that is a subject intended as a monadic entity, separated from his social environment and able to give sense to his action and to reality by pursuing his specific interests and by relying upon his rationality. This conception of humanity is a cultural product, whose roots Elias traces back to the Renaissance:

> That is the core of the structural change and the structural peculiarities of the individual which are reflected in self-perception, from about the Renaissance onward, in the notion of the individual "ego" in its locked case, the "self", divided by an invisible wall from what happens "outside". It is these civilizational self-controls, functioning in part automatically, that are now experienced in individual self-perception as a wall, either between "subject" and "object" or between one's own "self" and other people ("society").
>
> (Elias, 1939, pp. 478–479)

This conception found its way into the sociological conception of the social actor, exemplified in those sociological approaches (notably structural-functionalism) which tend to neglect the interconnection between the individual and his social environment, thus resulting in a hyper-exemplified, often dualistic, representation of the individual actor and the social structure. Let alone these theoretically significant questions, the emergence of a new, properly modern conception of the individual is a pre-condition of the process of civilization. Elias is well aware that, in order to transform outer coercion into self-control, a new conception of the individual is needed, intended as a centre of rational decisions leading to pre-planned and self-controlled actions. In Western modern culture, at least from Descartes on, the individual is not only intended as the maker of his own destiny but even as the ultimate judge of the ontological sense of reality. The modern subject, now conceived as capable of rationally understanding and controlling the external world, has also to exert his control over his body and affectivity (Shilling, 1993, pp. 150–177). Civilization as an historical process is all-encompassing, as it affects ever more aspects of everyday life, weaselling its way into the weaves of social life and influencing the forms of what Goffman called the presentation of the self (Goffman, 1959).

One of the momentous stages of the civilizing process is, according to Elias, to be identified with the passage from Medieval to court society. Although this passage does not represent the zero degree of civilization, it is relevant both on the macro level (since it would foster the development of an autonomous political system) and on the micro level (as it would affect the way people would manage their corporeality and affectivity). In *The Court Society* (1969) and in *The Process of Civilization* (1939) Elias analyzes in detail the development of a deeper sense of shame and a more acute disgust sensitivity, evolving together with increasingly refined behaviours and manners. In his first book (his *Habilitationsschrift*) Elias deals with the topic of court etiquette, while the second relates civilization to the development of the national state and the increasing complexity of European society (Van Krieken, 2014). In both cases, at the core of Elias' approach is a detailed analysis of the social and political function of a stricter control of body and emotions. Hence, according to Elias, it may be possible to analyze, from an historical and processual perspective, the gradual transformations which led to the self-control of bodily functions so typical of Western society. By now, bodily functions, when publicly manifested, became object of social reproach and generalized disgust.

Shame and repugnance tended to replace the concrete fear of physical menaces. Shame in particular is a form of interiorized fear of the judgement of others and, as such, represents a socialized manifestation of the Freudian super-egoical control (Elias, 1939, p. 414 ff.; Scribano and Mattar, 2009, p. 417). The restraint of impulses and drives and the control of bodily functions may be intended, as far as emotions are concerned, as the historical passage from a society dominated by fear and aggression to one where social relations are chiefly regulated by shame, embarrassment and repugnance. In the shift from fear to shame one may detect the strong interconnection between macro-processual phenomena and individual or psychological processes: a new structure of society, based now on social networks and informal control rather than physical force, gradually emerges, which implies the necessity to impute to the individual social actor the management of his body and emotions, transforming outer control into inner coercion. In Elias' words:

> The transformation of interpersonal external compulsion into individual internal compulsion, which now increasingly takes place, leads to a situation in which many affective impulses cannot be lived out as spontaneously as before. The autonomous individual self-controls produced in this way in social life, such "rational thought" or the "moral conscience", now interpose themselves more sternly than ever before between spontaneous and emotional impulses, on the one hand, and the skeletal muscles, on the other, preventing the former with greater severity from directly determining the latter (i.e., action) without the permission of these control mechanisms.
>
> (Elias, 1939, p. 478)

It is court society where this careful control of one's affectivity first appeared. In this social figuration, relations among courtiers are characterized by strict self-control over actions, cautious assessment of alliances and strategies and struggle for the patronage of the sovereign. Social status is no longer due only to family origins: more important than origins now is a careful self-management and acceptance of court etiquette. The search for social distinction is a specific trait of European court society developing in the passage from the Middle Age to the Renaissance and the Baroque period. Courts represent a sort of model, on which social relations in complex societies, characterized by strong interdependence among actors, would later be moulded. The output is a type of society where a strong self-control of impulses and drives is required and where, by adopting well known Freudian terms, the principle of pleasure is replaced by the principle of reality (Tabboni, 1993, p. 115).

A strong rationalization of behaviour emerges in a specific sector of society which is then gradually able to affect the everyday life of ever larger social spheres, eventually including the middle and the lower classes. Elias makes reference to the growing chains of interdependence as a peculiar feature of modernity: as societies become more complex, as new roles and functions emerge, new forms of control of affectivity appear indispensable. In modern Western society the increasing social complexity makes it necessary for the social actors to achieve increasingly complex performances and competences. The model will be able to influence even specialized fields, such as scientific research (now methodologically intended as a strategic activity aimed to achieve new knowledge) and economic action (rationally oriented to the increase of wealth for the actor or for a nation) (ibid., p. 110).

This process may be better understood by adopting an analytical scheme proposed by Chris Shilling (1993, pp. 163–165), according to whom Elias' approach may be synthetically described as the concurrence of three processes: individualization, socialization and rationalization of the body. I have already hinted at the process of individualization, which is the most relevant among the three: indeed, the collateral processes of socialization and rationalization may be triggered only provided that the distinction between the self and the social group is well-established and the control over the body is imputed to the individual. Socialization refers, according to Shilling, to the process by which body functions are concealed, shame and decency increase and a private sphere gradually develops. Moreover, socialization implies that the body becomes "location for the expression of behaviour codes" (ibid., p. 164). The connection between the body and rules of conduct leads to the third aspect as detected by Shillings: the fact that the body is strongly rationalized, since behaviours are strategically oriented to the fulfilment of specific objectives (ibid.).

One of the few sociological references in *The Process of Civilization* is Max Weber. Yet, it should be clear, even from this brief account of Elias' early works, that the explication of the historical processes which led to modernity as proposed by Elias is quite different as compared to Weber's attempt. The first evident difference is as to the historical epoch and the social class which, according to Elias and Weber, were able to trigger the process. The Protestant ethic was essentially bourgeois, as it was centred on a careful control of drives, strategically aimed at the acquisition of capital. Yet, although this aspect is not to be underestimated, the passage from outer coercion to self-control is, according to Elias, to be located in a previous era and in a different social class. The role of aristocracy is of the uppermost importance in Elias' argument, as it set the model of interiorized forms of control of the body, of bodily impulses and emotions that would be later generalized among members of other social classes (Van Krieken, 2014, p. 23). Combining the two processes could give a better chance to understand apparently contradictory aspects of modernity: the rational behaviour oriented to economic gain, so typical of the bourgeoisie ethic, and the quest for reputation and status symbols, apparently inconsistent with economic rationality. The bourgeois and the aristocrat have different interests, which modify the impact of their behaviour on the evolution of emotions in modern society:

> For the bourgeoisie, it was the acquisition of economic capital, so that emotional expression was regulated in terms of longer term financial gains and losses. Time is money, and thus so is time expended ('wasted') on emotional expression which gets in the way of accumulating economic capital. In court society, however, the concern is with the acquisition, accumulation and retention of symbolic capital, making identity and existence deeply representational, depending on constant display, exhibition and on-going performance of one's status.
>
> (ibid., p. 24)

Although Elias' approach was not exempt from critiques (e.g. Duindam, 1995), its sociological and historical relevance has been widely recognized. In the course of his career, Elias refined his original scheme, applying it to specific social contexts such as sport (Elias and Dunning, 1986) or dying (Elias, 1982). He also tried to contest those critiques which attempted to confute his theory of interiorization of the control of body and affectivity as at odds with the general relaxation of mores, so typical of contemporary society. Elias replied by introducing the notion of controlled decontrol of drives, which accounted for the reduction of the sense of shame (typical, for example, of youth movements) as an argument in favour of the consistency of his theory with contemporary trends (Elias and Dunning, 1986). Self-control has been so strongly interiorized, he maintained, that one may now control even his stronger impulses, for example sexual drives in presence of nude bodies. An assessment of Elias' theory is not scheduled here. What is relevant for my argument is a brief attempt at presenting the approach Elias developed as an historically and sociologically convincing explanation of the macro and diachronic implications of self-restraint, intended as a form of interiorized control of one's body and one's emotions. Elias' achievement is relevant, able as it is to combine history, psychology and social theory and, by making reference to a wide variety of sources (including literary ones), it gives a plausible, exhaustive representation of the relation between emotions and social change.

3 William M. Reddy and the navigation of the self

In his historical analysis, William M. Reddy originally combines a theory of speech acts expressing emotions, political control over emotions and political and social changes. The starting point is a complex analysis of the language of emotions, which represents a specific field of communication, based on a paradox: the incommunicable interior states of mind of the individuals find provisional expression and may thus be conveyed to our fellow people. Emotions are part of the personal experience of individuals and, as such, are impossible to penetrate and difficult to make part of mutual communication. Although every language has its specific set of words which are, as it were, specialized to express culturally defined emotions or sentiments, those terms do not have a referent in the world of things but are about peculiar states of mind belonging to the internal experience of those who feel them. This question is relevant for those scholars (social scientists above all) who are interested in the social aspects of emotional life and are worried about the appropriate data to gather and analyze in order to understand emotions in social contexts. Social sciences, including history, have by necessity to make reference to speech acts expressing emotions. Those speech acts are of a specific kind, being neither performative nor constatative (Austin, 1975; Searle, 1989), although having some of the characters of both.

The question of emotional speech acts has been brilliantly analyzed by William M. Reddy in a paper published in 1997. Emotions are expressed through specific speech acts, that he calls emotives. They apparently refer to something external (as constatative acts do), but what they refer to is not part of a shared experience. It is moreover mutable, as it changes by the very act of reference (Reddy, 1997, p. 331). Let me briefly summarize the argument as developed by Reddy. An emotional statement, he writes, is not a description of a state of affairs, a mere report, as Austin thought. On the contrary, it is an attempt the speaker activates in order to share something that, in principle, may not be shared: a state of mind. It is self-evident that such an attempt is of the utmost importance in social life, in the sense that we need to be informed about each other's feelings in order to sustain social interaction. At the same time, talking about emotions may reinforce or weaken them. Emotives, Reddy writes, have "a direct impact on the feelings in question. If asked the question 'Do you feel angry?' a person may genuinely feel more angry in answering yes, less angry in answering no" (ibid.). Therefore, the referential character of emotives is peculiar, in so far as the referent "is not passive in the formulation of the emotive, and it emerges from the act of uttering in a changed state. Emotives are influenced directly by and alter what they 'refer' to" (ibid.). Emotives share this transformational quality with perfomatives, yet emotives change the world in their very peculiar way. In fact, a performative utterance is self-referential (as it is the case of the utterance "I do" during a wedding, where "I do" refers directly to the will of the utterer) and, by making reference to the will of the social actor, may produce a change in the outer world (the utterer's status changes from bridegroom to husband, from bride to wife).

Emotives, rather than having the capacity to change states of the world, change states of affects by the very process of their expression. As compared to constatative speech acts, emotives appear to Reddy as always unable to define their supposed referent. They are, as it were, always tentative translations of "something nonverbal into the verbal domain that could never be called an equivalence or a representation" (ibid., p. 332). No matter whether the utterer is sincere or hypocritical about his emotions, emotives present a "form of failed reference" (ibid.).

A similar problem of translation has been posed by Peter Berger and Thomas Luckmann (1971) when they describe the necessity of adopting our everyday, shared language in order to describe what they call, by making reference to Alfred Schutz, "finite provinces of meaning". According to the two authors:

[t]he common language available to me for the objectification of my experiences is grounded in everyday life and keeps pointing back to it even as I employ it to interpret experiences in finite provinces of meaning. Typically, therefore, I 'distort' the reality of the latter as soon as I begin to use the common language in interpreting them, that is, I 'translate' the non-everyday experiences back into the paramount reality of everyday life.

(ibid., pp. 39–40)

Something of this kind could be stated of emotions: they belong to an order of reality (the inner life of the individual) clearly incomparable with everyday life and yet need a translation, which emotives provide, in order for emotions to become communicable. Let me quote Reddy:

Since I regard any functioning central nervous system as a site of emotional events, I assert that these constructions are elements in emotional management styles, styles of use of emotive utterances. Grief, fear, anger have a reality, even if we cannot, by using such terms as "grief," "fear," or "anger" or their rough equivalents in any language, refer adequately to what is going on emotionally. Words do not "refer" to emotions in this sense. But this is not to say that emotions do not exist or are discursive "constructions." Locating a feeling outside the self or categorizing it as, for example, an illness is a strategy similar to repression, although the feeling may remain in consciousness.

(Reddy, 1997, pp. 335–336)

Emotives are, as it were, stipulative manners to translate states of mind into ordinary language. They do not create the emotion (as radical constructivism would have it) but help locate them in a properly social context. Thus, although emotives may be attributed an "extensive power [...] in a given community to shape members' sense of identity and self-awareness, members' manner of confronting contingencies and routine" (Reddy, 1997, p. 333), Reddy postulates a residuum, a core which may not be further socialized and which accounts both for what is universal in human emotions and for the potential and limits of social forces in shaping it. The possibility for resisting the shaping power of societies and communities resides in the hard core of emotional life. As Reddy writes:

> In any given field context, one would expect to find a wide range of deviations, resistances, and alternative idioms that point to possibilities for change through crisis, dissolution, or adaptation and that offer grounds for drawing conclusions about who has power and who does not.
>
> (ibid.)

In the theoretical balance between human emotions and social control one may locate the possibility for social change, hence for an historically oriented analysis of emotions, which is what Reddy attempts. In his study of France between 1680 and 1848 (*The Navigation of Feelings. A Framework for the History of Emotions*), Reddy analyzes the contribution emotions played for the outburst of the French Revolution and, more generally, for the development of modern society. In the book, Reddy tries his hand at an extensive application of his theory of emotives and their relevance for the analysis of historical changes. Reddy proposes a set of concepts, which include emotions, emotives, emotional freedom, emotional suffering, emotional refuges and emotional regimes, able to qualify a specific social and historical context in relation to the relevance of emotions and emotional control, so as to propose a politically oriented, non-relativist analysis of emotions in society (Reddy, 2001, pp. 131–132).

Thus emotives, endowed as they are with the capacity to express inner states and at the same time to change them, are an instrument of both social stability and, through the definition of alternatives, of social change. As for social control, emotives do not create emotions as much as they "strongly influence individual emotion in a manner that allows for a certain stability and ideological comprehensibility in a community's life" (ibid., p. 334). Social change, on the contrary, may be imputed to "[t]he variation of individual responses (some fitting expectations well, some going all the way to complete deviance)" (ibid.).

The political relevance of emotives is evident, according to Reddy, in connection to what he calls emotional regimes, which he intends as the set of social norms and related sanctions which regulate the expression of emotions in a given society or a given historical period. Each regime has a peculiar relation to emotional liberty, that is the degree of freedom a society guarantees to the expression of emotions. Regardless of the degree of emotional liberty, communities "provide individuals with prescriptions and counsel concerning both the best strategies for pursuing emotional learning and the proper end point or ideal of emotional equilibrium" (ibid., p. 55). And this control of emotions, Reddy states, is an essential aspect of political regimes. Thus, regardless of the huge amount of variations, in order to be successful, all emotional regimes have 1. to provide a coherent set of emotional norms able to give consistency to the individual selves, hence guaranteeing the stability of the community; 2. to construct an emotional community order in the "form of ideals to strive toward and strategies to guide individual effort" (ibid., p. 64). Emotional refuges are the social antidote to emotional regimes. They are to be intended as groups (no matter whether formal or informal) where the individual may relax from emotional control and which may eventually threaten existing emotional regimes (ibid., p. 131).

At least since Norbert Elias' investigation, the new emotional style typical of European courts has been intended as a specific trend in the refinement and control of sentiments and emotions. In Italy, Renaissance courts set the standard of a new kind of *civility* which consisted both in the respect of etiquette and in explicitly manifest subordination to the ruler, which was displayed "with a facade of nonchalance (*disinvoltura*), ease, and grace that symbolized the freedom and self-determination, in the last instance, of the otherwise obedient courtier" (ibid., p. 324). This highly artificial style, which was strengthened in Versailles and in those European courts which assumed Versailles as a model, was gradually replaced by a new emotional style, sentimentalism, which spread particularly among the emerging middle class.

Sentimentalism may be intended as a new way to conceive emotions and human relationships and, as such, was part of a developing emotional regime which would oppose absolutism. Philosophically, the new approach was connected to Shaftesbury's idea that the moral sense was innate and led human conduct through sentiments. When criticizing Locke's radical sensualism, which reduced human consciousness to the sum of the subject's experiences and perceptions, Shaftesbury maintained:

> men were equipped with an "inward eye" that enabled them to perceive the morally good. Moral perceptions became available to the mind via inborn sentiments. Feelings of benevolence, pity, love, and gratitude gave shape to moral judgement and rendered moral action pleasurable.
>
> (Reddy, 2001, pp. 155–156)

Sentimentalism manifested itself in art, notably in the opera and in the novel, and represented a new liberating emotional style, to be opposed both to the strict control of emotions typical of court etiquette and, even more, to social inequality and lack of social justice. Sentiments were to be respected, regardless of the social status to which one belonged. This idea allowed a vast array of new characters to come into the foreground, all vindicating the right of sentiments against the tyranny of socially defined differences. As Reddy writes regarding the new bourgeois novel and the taste of its reading public:

> The emotional suffering of spouses in arranged marriages, the emotional suffering of domestic servants raped with impunity by their masters, of young educated men and women without fortune, of lovers separated by a gulf of wealth or birth, of young women consigned to convents by their parents, of orphans, widows, and aging spinsters – all these political evils were explored and denounced before an expanding and avid reading public.
>
> (ibid., p. 325)

A new kind of authenticity emerged, connected to the idea that sentiments were naturally able to produce moral sense, social justice and social integration. Emotions assumed a politically relevant significance in the process by which new emotional refuges attempted to become emotional regimes. Reddy skilfully shows how this new emotional ideology was in part responsible for the outburst of the French Revolution and, in particular, for its degeneration during the Reign of Terror. The Revolution had been favoured by the idea that natural feelings were naturally good, which implied that political reforms could be achieved by re-establishing a public role for sentiments. This resulted in an oversimplified optimism, according to which "reform seemed to involve the sweeping away of impediments to natural feeling, rather than the establishment of protective norms" (ibid., p. 326). It is no paradox that the Reign of Terror emerged as an emphasis on natural sentiments. Natural sentiments naturally led to "perfect consensus among good citizens" (ibid.), thus any form of dissent was conceived as a deviation from the sharing of a common vision and ideology. In this sense, according to Reddy, the Reign of Terror was "just as much an expression of sentimentalism as were the lachrymose operas of Gluck" (ibid.).

The end of Terror produced a new, unexpected, emotional regime, as senti-mentalism, which had affected the public sphere, (including political speeches) during the revolutionary period, now came to be seen with suspicion, as a residual aspect of the Revolution. The rapid suppression of sentimentalism, at least from the public space, led to a new model of man, influenced by economic theories, rationally oriented to self-interest and acquisition. The new public sphere was male centred, as sentiments were feminized and made private. Emotions were now to be put aside in favour of publicly displayed self-control (ibid., p. 327). Reddy refers to the French *Civic Code* (1804) as the document in which this new ideology assumed its most sophisticated form. The Code is indeed imbued with a new conception of man, striving for his own interests, in a social environment which is no longer conceived of as the place for consensus and integration but as a public arena where conflicting goals may find a way of coexistence. Within the code, equality is devoid of any sentimentalism, as it is now intended as a pre-requisite for the autonomous pursuing of the interests of social actors in the public sphere. Here individuals endowed with natural rights (chiefly the right to prop-erty), may decide to transact business with other individuals, through the contract as their main juridical instrument (Longo, 2001, pp. 191–192). Reddy shows how this image of humanity was soon downscaled: the conception of a rational public man was contrasted with the idea according to which human beings are influ-enced by the environment, passion, physiology and the like (Reddy, 2001, p. 327). Rationality persisted as an instrument of public choices, whereas emotions and sentiments, excluded from the public sphere, re-emerged as expressions of private inwardness.

Reddy's analysis is much more complex than this short abstract may convey. It gives the reader an animated description of the historical period object of his analysis. He recurs to a wide variety of sources, including private letters, official speeches, novels and opera plots, so as to transmit to the reader a vivid account of the relevance of emotions in historical changes. Regardless of his conclusions, which are *per se* interesting, his attempt, which is both theoretical and methodological, is of great relevance in the field of the history of emotions: emotions are, as such, inexpressible, yet they become the object of human communication as emotives, and the way emotions and emotives are controlled and allowed is one of the central element of political power, political control and social change. Emotions are socially and historically relevant because they are converted, within a stipulative simulation, into emotives, so becoming part of our everyday capacity to express the inexpressible, that is what we feel inside. And in so far it is communicable, our inwardness becomes (this is Reddy's chief lesson) both historically, sociologically and politically relevant.

4 Consumerism and emotions

Another field of historical investigation on emotions deals with modern phenomena and the ways emotions have been moulded, redefined, controlled so as to either adapt to or to enhance innovative processes. The American historiography, in particular, has associated the development of specific emotions to macro processes which have had a deep influence on the people's way of living and on the people's choices. A strand of analysis connects a new conception of specific emotions to the development of consumerism and market society. Consumerism is a typically modern phenomenon, which implies a constantly renewed desire for the possession of new goods. As a matter of fact, this new psychological disposition affects social behaviours and may be functional to a growing market economy. Are emotions and emotional control implied in the success of capitalism not only as a system of production but also as a system of consumption? This question has been raised by historians and social scientists, some of whom have given appealing and sophisticated answers.

Colin Campbell's book *The Romantic Ethic and the Spirit of Consumerism* is an attempt to analyze the origin of modern consumerism, connecting it to Romanticism as a radical transformation of culture and social attitudes. The monograph follows the same line as Weber's *The Protestant Ethic and the Spirit of Capitalism* (1905), trying to give a plausible answer to a relevant aspect that Max Weber neglected: the apparent contradiction between the controlled, upstanding and disciplined behaviour so typical of the Protestants and the unrestricted yearning for new goods and experiences so characteristic of consumerism. In Campbell's words:

> What is surprising, however, constituting one of the central conundrums of cultural history, is that the evidence strongly suggests that the consumer revolution was carried through by exactly those sections of English society with the strongest Puritan traditions, that is, the middle or trading classes, together with artisans and sections of the yeomanry. [...] At the same time, it was observed that this demand was for such luxury goods as toys and fashionable clothes, whilst also involving the pleasurable indulgencies of dancing, sport

and novel-reading. In other words, it was exactly that kind of conduct which, it could be assumed, would be most likely to incur disapproval from those with a "Puritan" outlook which formed the very substance of this middle-class consumer revolution.

(Campbell, 1987, p. 31)

The argumentative solution to this contradiction has generally been a neat temporal separation of the two phenomena, in the sense that consumerism was considered as a later development of capitalism, affecting the future offspring of former capitalists. Campbell disagrees with this hypothesis as he tries to show a deep interconnection between Protestantism and Romanticism on the one hand and capitalism and consumerism on the other.

Campbell's argument is complex and well-informed but, for my limited scope, it must be reduced to some fundamental points. The first is about the connection between puritanism and a new conception of the self. Puritanism brought about a new, more sophisticated form of self-control, which accounts, at least in part, for the development of individualism, as a direct relationship between the social actor and the outer world (ibid., pp. 74–75). Paradoxical as it may seem, self-control was the premise for the development of a novel conception of emotions which were no longer conceived as the output of some external event but, on the contrary, as the expression of the inner states of mind of the individual. And indeed:

emotions were re-located 'within' individuals, as states which emanated from some internal source, and although these were not always 'spiritualized', there is a sense in which the disenchantment of the external world required as a parallel process some 'enchantment' of the psychic inner world.

(ibid., p. 73)

Social actors, conceived of now as autonomous individuals, are the indispensable ground for the development of consumerism as a living style. Consumerism is compatible, according to Campbell, with a new form of hedonism, connected to emotional life. As opposed to traditional hedonism, modern hedonism is based on emotions rather than sensation. Traditional hedonism developed when production surpluses allowed the ruling classes to indulge in the satisfaction of their needs far beyond the subsistence level. This permitted that "for the first time the pursuit of pleasure for its own sake rather than its mere appreciation as an adjunct of action pursued for other purposes, takes on the character of a clearly defined and distinct goal of action" (ibid., p. 65). Traditional hedonism has two characteristics: it is connected to the manipulation of external objects which may produce specific sensations and is socially circumscribed, as it is limited to those who have power and who tend to reinforce their power in order to control the external environment in so far as the environment, once controlled, may provide those objects that procure hedonistic sensations (ibid., p. 66). Modern hedonism, on the contrary, is connected to emotions rather than sensations and implies the capacity of the individual to control the stimuli deriving from experience. It is linked more to the imagination than to the immediate pursuit of pleasant sensations and is achieved through the control of inner stimuli and the reference to the imaginative world of the subject.

It is this control over the imaginative world of the individual that links, according to Campbell, Romanticism and modern consumerism. Romanticism as a whole may be, in fact, intended as a highly sophisticated cultural phenomenon locating imagination in a prominent place. In this sense, it clearly contrasted the idea that modernity was based exclusively on utility and rationality, and paved the way for a positive attitude towards fantasy and novelty which Campbell considers a specific feature of modern consumerism:

> Romanticism provided that philosophy of "recreation" necessary for a dynamic consumerism: a philosophy which legitimates the search for pleasure as good in itself and not merely of value because it restores the individual to an optimum efficiency [...]. At the same time, Romanticism has ensured the widespread basic taste for novelty, together with the supply of "original" products, necessary for the modern fashion pattern to operate; something best illustrated by a recognition of the central function which Bohemia fulfils as the social and cultural laboratory for modern society, as crucial in connection with consumption as science and technology is for production. In all these ways, Romanticism has served to provide ethical support for that restless and continuous pattern of consumption which so distinguishes the behaviour of modern man.
>
> (ibid., p. 201)

The new Romantic ethic was to be connected to modern hedonism in order to give consumerism a chance to evolve. Goods are seen as the concrete projection of the individual's fantasies, a sort of translation of the inner world of the consumer's imagination into real objects. Thus, the consumer purchases the good, hoping to actually take possession of his fantasies, only to realize that the good is not able to provide what it promises. The disappointment leads to a new purchase, in a constantly reproducing circle of purchase and disillusion which accounts for the specific character of consumerism, that is "an endless programme of wanting in relation to new goods and services" (ibid., p. 58).

The historian of emotions, Susan Matt (2009), connects modern consumerism to the emergence of a positive conception of the sentiment of envy and the attitude to emulation. Matt's monograph is less theoretically ambitious as compared to Campbell's effort, yet presents a clear-cut, well-informed link between a new attitude towards envy and consumerism in the United States from 1890 to 1930. The hypothesis developed in *Keeping up with the Joneses. Envy in American Consumer Society, 1890–1930* is that a society characterized by greater social mobility, dynamism and proneness to social change is one where envy plays a new, favourable role. As Susan Matt writes in the introduction, her book is about:

> the process by which it became acceptable for middle-class men, women, and children to envy and pursue the possessions of the rich. This transformation

in envy's meaning and legitimacy was significant because it was part of an emerging emotional and behavioral style that supported the expansion of the consumer economy.

(ibid., p. 2)

Although the book focuses its attention on a specific country and a specific period, the thesis may be applied to other similar contexts. The chief idea is, in fact, that the repression of envy is an instrument of social control in societies where social differences are, as it were, established by birth. Such societies are conservative and hierarchical in structure, their economy being aimed at the maintenance of social inequalities (see *infra*, Chapter 7). Mass production implies a more dynamic social structure, in which differences are no longer defined once and for all. This new dynamism is functional for an increase in consumption, whose emotional basis is a new assessment of envy as a sentiment prompting the emulation of the well-to-do. Between 1890 and 1930, a new conception of life was emerging in America, supported by the new secularized culture, in which sociology and social Darwinism played a relevant role. Sociology promoted a lay conception of society, no longer conceived as set once and for all by the divine will of God. Society was changeable, and mutable were also social relations and social hierarchies. Social Darwinism, on its turn, conceived struggle as an ineliminable, positive aspect of social reality, able to foster, through the selection of the fittest, social change and general progress (ibid., pp. 72–73). Whereas the traditional conception of envy used to stress its dangerousness, since it implied a possible challenge to the social order, now envy started to be perceived as a positive factor, since change was no longer conceived as a hazard, but as the progressive improvement of general social and economic conditions:

No longer did envy inevitably lead to hostility and strife; instead, in a world filled with mass-produced goods, it was at the very least a harmless emotion and some believed even a beneficial one. In fact, many commentators concluded that when men and women acted on their envy of the wealthy and emulated upper-class ways of life, they brought about social progress rather than social destruction. When they made luxury purchases, they raised their standard of living and spurred economic growth. In many minds, these benefits seemed to outweigh the social and moral dangers of envy.

(ibid., p. 73)

Susan Matt's successful attempt shows how emotions, rather than be individual manifestations of a personal state of mind, are deeply influenced by social, cultural and economic contexts and are, in their turn, able to affect social development. In the specific case object of her study, a dynamic social structure and economy are conceived as able to foster a novel conception of envy which contributed to the increasing dynamism of capitalism and modern society as a whole (ibid., p. 6). There was a relevant ideological component implied in the process, linked to equality as a value to be socially pursued. In fact, modern societies emphasize equality among individuals as one of the main features of their demo-cratic values. On its turn, by eliminating pre-defined social differences based on the ascriptive characteristics of the individual, equality functions not only as a political and ethical principle but also as a relevant factor in the dynamization of modern societies (Longo, 2018). In the specific context of consumerism, a gap between expected equality and actual disparities produced envy, which could be now intended as a legitimate emotion in so far as it prompted people to strive for a more equal distribution of wealth. In this sense, the emotion of envy was per-ceived as a positive sentiment as it was intended as "a response to the unrealized promise of equality; the emulation it inspired was an imperfect attempt to fulfil that promise" (Matt, 2009, p. 6). Thus, by emphasizing the role of discontent and envy, consumerism brought about an historical and cultural change, able to undermine the traditional social structure and its stability. Envy was no longer conceived of as a sin but as the legitimate emotion for those aspiring to a bet-ter living, so setting the emotional basis of the consumer society, whose chief characteristics are still relevant nowadays, as they "continue to shape consumer behavior in our own time" (ibid., p. 183).

5 A final overview

Writing emotional history is not a simple task. It entails a number of methodo-logical and theoretical questions which have been only quickly hinted at here. Moreover, the historical analysis of emotions may need to focus its attention on such a plurality of phenomena (specific emotional communities, places or histori-cal moments) that it may be particularly difficult to outline clear-cut, unilinear and unidimensional trends. Due both to the ideographic character of historical investigation (Weber, 1946) and the complexity of the topic, multiple histories of emotions have been produced (Rosenwein, 2010) rather than a unitary historiog-raphy. Nonetheless, some trends have been singled out by contemporary histori-cal analysis, chiefly in connection to Western countries and the historical passage to modernity.

The first trend is a transformation in emotional standards located in the 17th and 18th centuries (Stearns, 2008). Historians have chiefly analyzed changes in kinship and in love relations, characterized by the refinement of family ties lead-ing to the modern family based on romantic love (see *infra*, Chapter 9). Parental and conjugal love was encouraged, while anger started to be perceived as a nega-tive feeling within the family (ibid., p. 20). In Western countries, the accepted method of children rearing became gradually characterized by loving persuasion rather than the violent imposition of the will of the father. Arranged marriages began to be perceived as the unjust legacy of a backward past. Marital ties were now conceived as the natural output of love between two partners who had freely chosen one another. Love as the basis of modern families, refinement of man-ners within family ties and the central affective role of the mother are the central elements of the 19th century sociological analysis of nuclear families. Parsons (1949, 1955) in particular conceived the idea of the modern family as a place where relations were based on affectivity and particularism, a sort of protected emotional zone, whose main function was no longer economic (the production of goods) but rather the reproduction and socializations of social values and norms. In the traditional nuclear family as envisaged by Parsons the affective role was assigned to the mother, whereas the father played the role as the male breadwinner (Rodman, 1965). What is here relevant is that those changes were functionally necessary in order to provide members of isolated nuclear families with emotional support, thus contrasting the rationalizing character of modern society.

Another trend which seems to have emerged in Europe since the 18th century was the gradual reduction of fear and anxiety in common people's everyday life. The Middle Ages were in fact characterized by a diffuse sense of anxiety, due to the incapacity of human societies to control natural forces and the pervasiveness of illness, death and violence. In order to cope with fear, religious practices were largely characterized by the presence of magical rituals, in the attempt to control otherwise uncontrollable forces. The 18th century may be considered as a turning point, when:

> [g]rowing confidence about measures that could control the natural and social environment reduced the need for fear-managing rituals, leading to a shift in religious emphasis and a redefinition of fear that [...] would lead ultimately to the 20th-century formulation of fear as an interior emotion focused on inward demons.
>
> (Stearns, 2008, p. 20)

The emergence of new objects of disgust seems to be another relevant change in the 18th century. Here emotions are strongly connected "to altered experiences of the senses" (ibid., p. 21) and seem to have been motivated both by new sanitary and health preoccupations, and by a need for social distinction between those who could indulge in personal hygiene and those who could not.

Historians look at the 19th century as a period in which the trends set in the 18th century were reinforced and spread geographically and socially, thus affecting new social groups. Historical investigation into emotions centred chiefly on the family and romantic love as an object of study. Research shows how maternal love was highly emphasized, so strengthening the trend set in the previous century. Romantic love, on the other hand, took on the features of a lay religion, implying worship and abnegation for the loved one. Moreover, another trend was a stronger condemnation of anger, which tended to be expunged both from the public scene and from family relationships. Finally, the Victorian Age saw a strong gender differentiation of emotions. In particular, negative emotions were perceived as gender-specific, fear and jealously being appropriate for women whereas anger being justifiable for men. In general:

> Victorian emotional patterns thus provided no overall new direction, but they did adjust prior trends to the new sanctity of the family in an industrial world;

to new social class divisions; and to the new need to define emotional distinctions between boys and girls, men and women.

(ibid., p. 24)

A more difficult task is detecting unitary trends in the 20th century history of emotions. This probably is due to the complexity of contemporary society. One strand of analysis follows the track of Elias' civilizing process and has been developed by Dutch historians and sociologists. To those who tried to attack his theory by describing a general relaxation of manners typical of contemporary Western countries, Elias replied, as we have seen above, by introducing the concept of controlled decontrol of emotions. He tested this idea in his monograph on sport (Elias and Dunning 1986), in which he considers modern highly regulated sports as an example of a form of control of excitement. The controlled decontrol of emotions, Elias states, shows the ever deeper interiorization of social coercion by the social actor in contemporary society. As Stearns writes:

> Spontaneity has revived, but within strict (if unacknowledged) limits. The general argument is that most Westerners have learned so well the lessons of restraint of violence and of unwanted sexuality that they can be allowed a good bit of informal emotional idiosyncrasy as part of personal style.
>
> (Stearns, 2008, pp. 24–25)

Thus, a greater relaxation of emotionality does not imply a general tendency towards less controlled management of emotions. On the contrary, it may be the expression of a stronger individualization of emotions, the single actor being imputable not only for what he does but also for what he feels.

Regardless of the quality of specific researches and research traditions, even this brief overview shows how useful an historical approach to emotions may be for an appropriate sociological investigation of emotions. And indeed, some of the topics only sketched in this chapter will be dealt with in greater detail later, within a diachronic approach. History gives interesting cues on the social nature of emotional expression and management; it shows the effects of macro, long-term processes on emotions and the way they are manifested and conceived. It shows, moreover, that sentiments and their transformation may have important effects on macro-phenomena, as they may trigger and support social change.

4   Emotions and literature

1 Literary emotions: are they paradoxical?

When we make reference to art, we are likely to link the product of artistic genius to emotions: art is in fact conceived as able to reproduce and elicit emotions. This matter-of-fact statement seemingly conceals a debated philosophical question, related to the apparent contradiction of an overtly untrue representation of reality which is all the same able to have emotional effects on the reader or the beholder. The so-called paradox of emotions and literature is a specific variation of a long-established philosophical debate on the truth value of literary accounts (for the debate see Longo, 2015, p. 29 ff.). Those who assume a referential attitude consider linguistic accounts as representations of something actually existing somewhere outside the language. When assuming a referential attitude, one is likely to deny any cognitive value to fictional narratives. Literature, in fact, uses the referential resources of ordinary speech, yet without making reference to something actually existing in the outer world (Falk, 1988). Thus, since literary fiction narrates of non-existent facts and events, its cognitive value is at least controversial.

The selfsame referential attitude, connected to the fictional character of literary narratives, substantiates the paradox of emotions and literature. Indeed, how can we be moved by overtly fictional accounts? Or, to quote the title of the essay which reinvigorated the debate on the topic in the 1970s: "How can we be moved by the fate of Anna Karenina?" (Radford; Weston, 1975). The roots of the question may be traced back to the ancient Greek philosophical reflection on art and its effects. Plato attacked poetry as dangerous, in so far as it could stir passions. Aristotle's conception of art as imitation (*mimesis*) gave art the relevant task to simulate action and life, and in that the philosopher located the possibility for art to move the audience (Holland, 2004, p. 395).

In its more recent formulation, the question assumes the features of a logical paradox. Gregory Currie (1990, p. 187) makes reference to three mutually contradictory propositions which substantiate the paradox. The paradox is strongly rooted in a referential conception of language and representation and derives its consistency from a highly cognitive interpretation of emotions, according to which the reader or beholder should believe in the actuality of what he is experiencing.

Let me briefly reproduce the propositions which constitute the paradox: 1) in order to be emotionally involved, one has to believe that the situation which is causing one to move really exists; 2) one does not believe that fictional events or characters really exist; 3) yet it is a common experience to be moved by fictional characters and situations. In order to make the propositions logically coherent, one has to consider one of them as inconsistent and, according to the proposition which is suppressed, one finds different logical solutions to the paradox of fiction.

The essay by Colin Radford, which started the discussion, shows an evident referential attitude. Radford considers belief in the existence of an object as an essential condition of our emotional involvement. This implies that our being moved by fictional characters is patently irrational. In fact, we should either admit that fictional characters do exist, thus denying proposition 2), or that we may be emotionally involved in fictional events or characters, thus denying proposition 1). The undeniable fact that we are moved by fictional characters and situations, although we are aware of their fictionality, entails that fictional emotions are, according to Radford, "irrational, incoherent and inconsistent" (Radford, 1977, p. 78). Radford's position has not changed over the years and still in 2001 he writes:

> But how can we enjoy these fears or sorrows that can be so unendurable? Because we know that they are induced by fictions […]. The pertinent question is: Knowing that, how can we be moved or frightened? And the answer is: Because we are irrational, and it is because we know that they are induced by and directed towards fictions we can luxuriate in them.
>
> (Radford, 2001, p. 620)

Radford's solution has been contested from different standpoints. One option is to consider fictional narratives as fictional worlds, and fictional emotions as justified by a make-believe game. What is denied in this perspective is the idea that fictional emotions are real emotions. On the contrary, they are emotions of a fictional kind, that is quasi-emotions. In Walton's version (1978) we experience fiction make-believedly, in the same way children pretend that what happens in a game is real. In this pretence-game, we are implicitly aware that what is described in a novel or what we are watching in a movie is part of a narrative, hence fictitious, yet we actually experience emotions which, in so far as they are related to fictional realities, are defined by Walton as quasi-emotions. Quasi-emotions emerge as a response to fictional situations and hence are causally determined by patently untrue experiences, which makes the referential attitude no longer relevant. Quasi-emotions are elicited by actions, situations or characters which, rather than being untrue, are true only in the circumscribed reality of fictional worlds (ibid., p. 10). Thus, the reader's trustful attitude towards the work of narratives does not emerge, as Samuel Coleridge (1817, p. 174) maintained, from a deliberate suspension of disbelief; it is, on the contrary, connected to a make-believe game, a sort of diminished, simulated form of belief.

The make-believe theory modifies proposition 3) as it states that it is possible to be moved by something we only make-believe to be true but only in the form of quasi-emotions, to be distinguished from the real ones. The approach is based on a strong cognitivism, although of a different kind as compared with Radford's. In the case of fictional emotions, in fact, the propositional attitude "make-believe" replaces the propositional attitude "believe". Reading fiction does not entail that we consider fictional reports as truth. Reading fiction is, on the contrary, based on a make-believe game by which "[t]he reader makes believe that he is reading an account of known fact, and adopts an attitude of make-believe toward the propositions of the story. He does not believe the story, he makes believe it" (Currie, 1990, p. 196).

Let me quickly specify the distinction between believe and make-believe in connection to Currie's argument. According to Currie, emotions emerge from three interrelated elements: a belief in some outer situation; expectations as to its evolution and the feeling emerging from the actual outcomes (ibid., p. 192). Thus, we have to believe that a specific situation is true, desire that it evolves in a certain way and feel certain feelings according to the fact that belief and desire harmonize or do not. In Currie's theory of emotions, a propositional attitude towards the truth of our experience is at any rate necessary. In order for an emotion to issue, it is necessary that the experiencing subject believes that what he is experiencing is true. For example, fear would be pathological if connected to imagined events or harmless objects. The connection of emotions to a propositional attitude (I believe that this situation, object, context is true) makes the question of our emotional response to fiction apparently unsolvable. It would be logically inconceivable, in fact, to have emotions for fictional characters since emotions may emerge only in case we believe in the prepositions which describe a specific situation (ibid., p. 187).

The solution proposed by Currie is neither to deny the actual fact that we are moved by fiction nor to conceive, as Radford does, some sort of rational inconsistency in our experience of fictional emotions. On the contrary, he substitutes the attitude of belief with "an attitude of make-believe towards the propositions of the story" (ibid., p. 196). As Walton before him, Currie considers quasi-emotions the emotional output of narratives. Indeed, we do experience quasi-emotions when reading about the destiny of Anna Karenina, yet we are aware that Anna is a fictional character and our quasi-emotions towards her are determined by our make-believe that the story told by Tolstoy is true. This means that we are not actually emotionally involved by fictional events or characters but we take part in a representative game. The theory is cognitivist, in so far as, as Currie puts it "emotion requires belief" (ibid., p. 182). But since "the reader of fiction does not have the beliefs required for emotion" (ibid.) it is necessary to reformulate the belief theory as a theory of make-believe. By make-believing, we simulate the belief in the reality of an utterly different, separated world, that is the fictional world of narrative and art. Peter Lamarque clearly synthesizes this approach, by making reference to Kendall Walton. According to Lamarque, Walton's "ingenious suggestion is that when we appear to be psychologically affected by fictional characters this takes place not across worlds but in a fictional world. We are not really afraid or moved, but only fictionally so" (Lamarque, 1981, p. 292). If the world of fiction and the real world are neatly separated, one has to explain why we nonetheless are empathetically moved by fictional characters. The solution is quasi-emotions: "The physical symptoms of our emotions, the clammy palms and prickly eyes, indicate merely a 'quasi' emotion in this world. For Walton, to interact in any way with a fictional character we must 'enter' a fictional world" (ibid.). Separating the fictional world from the real one entails that fictional emotions are reduced to a diminished kind of emotions (quasi-emotions), which are not to be confused with "actual" emotions as they emerge in a game of pretence which makes us provisionally believe in the truth of fiction (Tullman, 2012).

Thought theory, often exemplified in reference to Lamarque (1981) and Carrol (1990), put into question proposition 1). In order for us to be moved or scared by fictional accounts, we do not need to believe in the actual existence of fictional referents. It suffices to have some sort of mental representations (thoughts) which may produce the corresponding emotions. Here follows Peter Lamarque's clear-cut formulation of the problem with the suggestion of a possible solution:

> How can fictional characters enter our world? What is it in our world that we respond to when we fear Othello and pity Desdemona? My suggestion, which I shall work out in detail, is that fictional characters enter our world in the mundane guise of descriptions (or strictly the senses of descriptions) and become the objects of our emotional responses as mental representations or, as I shall call them, thought-contents characterized by those descriptions. Simply put, the fear and pity we feel for fictions are in fact directed at thoughts in our minds.
>
> (Lamarque, 1981, p. 293)

As compared to the make-believe theory, according to the thought theory it is not necessary to identify a specific process by which fictional emotions emerge. Indeed, we can experience emotions about the content of our thoughts, regardless of whether our thoughts make reference to something actual or not. Lamarque distinguishes between being afraid *of* and being afraid *by*: we may be afraid *of* Martians as a thought object, although we may not be afraid *by* them, as they do not actually exist. But suppose someone is afraid *of* Martians, although aware that they do not exist. In this case, he is afraid *by* the thought (i.e. the representation of) Martians. It is the representation of the object, not the object itself, which produces fear, and this is assumed by Lamarque as the premise to understand fictional emotions. By stressing the independence between thought and belief, Lamarque writes:

> We can be frightened by the thought of something without believing that there is anything real corresponding to the content of the thought. At most we

must simply believe that the thought is frightening. And that belief raises no paradox in relation to our other beliefs about fiction.

(ibid., p. 294)

Thought theory hence states that no neat distinction between fictional and "actual" emotions may be detected. Since we are emotionally involved by thoughts rather than beliefs, we may legitimately fear Frankenstein or be moved by Anna Karenina, without believing that both are real. Emotions are still intentional (since they are directed to – are about – our thought content) but they no longer need to be intentionally connected to non-fictional objects or situations in order to be considered rational (as opposed to Radford's version) or actual (as opposed to quasi-emotions). What probably lacks in the different versions of thought theory is the possibility to explain not only complex emotions (pride, envy) but also more basic ones (fear, anger) which are connected to bodily change and sudden reactions to the environment rather than thoughts. At any rate, by removing the connection between emotions and belief, thought theory may be understood as a step forward towards a less referential conception of fictional emotions (Tullmann, 2012), which may now be conceived as the product not of a presumed assertiveness of fictional sentences but of their capacity to construct networks of meanings and references within the narrative (Lamarque, 1981, 195 ff.).

Other theories have been developed (for a complete review see Levinson, 2006, p. 38 ff.), none able to solve the paradox once and for all. In spite of the many attempts, in fact, the logical paradox persists. Tullmann and Buckwalter (2014) impute this lack of plausible solutions to the way philosophers have understood the verb "exist" in connection to fictional entities. The seeming irrationality of fictional emotions depends on the fact that they are caused by imaginary events or situations. Literary emotions have indeed two specific features. The first is that, when reading a book or watching a film, we are aware of their fictional character: a fictional narrative is hardly confused with reality. One of the oldest formulations is that, as Coleridge put it, the reader has to willingly suspend his disbelief in what he is reading. A further feature, defined by Immanuel Kant as *Interesselosigkeit* (indifference), entails that we do not have any active attitude towards the work of art. Indeed, the object of art is to be contemplated, not to be acted upon (Holland, 2004, p. 398). This means, in plain words, that we may be moved by the fate of Anna Karenina, but we are neither willing nor able to do anything to prevent her suicide. The weakness of the paradox resides in the sharp distinction between facts and fiction, "real" and "fictive" stimuli. Since fictional emotions are characterized by Kant's *Interesselosigkeit*, and since they derive from non-concrete, imaginary *stimuli*, hence they are to be considered as irrational (Radford) or quasi-emotions (Walton). Yet, we know that fictional characters and events do produce emotions, and they do so regardless of any formulation conceived as paradoxical. This implies that emotions may be independent of any "assertive belief concerning the object, situation or state of affairs" (Tullmann and Buckwalter, 2014, p. 788).

The paradox may be easily dismissed if one makes reference to new research on the functioning of our brain. Holland (2004) writes that emotions "originate in regions of the brain earlier evolutionarily and physically below and within the frontal lobes" (ibid., p. 406). That selfsame area of our brain is involved in producing "real emotions towards unreal fictions" (ibid.). Nonetheless, we are aware of the fictional nature of our fictional emotions, and that accounts for our inaction: from a neurological point of view, "the prefrontal cortex's systems for action, is at rest, because we know (perhaps in our dorsolateral frontal lobes) that we are not supposed to act in response to the fiction we are reading or the drama we are watching" (ibid.). Yet, regardless of our awareness and inaction, there is nothing irrational or inconsistent in fictional emotions: they are the same emotions we would experience in real life, facing situations or events similar to those we are watching or reading about. A further quotation from Holland:

> neuropsychologists do generally agree that we respond, in works of literature, at least, with emotions appropriate to basic human situations, situations that one would expect to arouse pleasure or fear or grief or lust or disgust. These responses [...] are not particular to literature; we are simply feeling the emotions appropriate to a situation, be it in life or in art.
>
> (ibid., p. 404)

Experimental findings have shown that people tend to react in a less intense way to narratives they know are fictional. Psychologists suppose that there is some form of emotional regulation (Sperduti et al., 2016, p. 57) which accounts for the lesser intensity of emotional response to fiction. It is a form of cognitive appraisal of the fictionality of, for example, a narrative, which implies some sort of cognitive reduction of the emotional intensity. Yet people respond emotionally to fictional accounts especially in cases of self-engagement, that is when what is presented in the fictional report may be reconnected to actual (often sorrowful) personal experiences (ibid., p. 58). Fictional emotions may be even understood as simulations: they are useful means by which we may train in actual emotions, simulating both what we feel and the social and personal context in which it is appropriate to feel that specific kind of emotions (Oatley, 2011, p. 17).

Research in the field of neuroscience gives a scientific basis to the simple idea that, more than a philosophical paradox, the relation between fiction and emotions is part of our daily experience. Of course, fiction has to be artfully constructed in such a way as to produce emotions. When unsuccessful, a tearjerker or a horror movie are not only unable to produce either sorrow or terror, they are also ridiculous. On the contrary, successful narratives, as prefigured by Hume in relation to tragedies, may combine the appropriate emotion (for example the painful experience of being moved to tears) with the pleasure deriving from our exposure to the artistic construction of the work of art (Yanal, 1991). Thus, the question is not why we are moved by Anna Karenina, but how. Literary emotions are literary constructions, artefacts as envisaged by one of the greatest theoretician of narratives, Paul Ricoeur who, in connection to Greek drama, wrote that "the spectator's emotional response is constructed in the drama, in the quality of the destructive or painful incidents suffered by the characters themselves" (Ricoeur, 1984, p. 43).

2 Literary narratives and emotions

It is by now patent that the so-called paradox of fiction leads into a philosophical cul-de-sac. It is therefore necessary to explore the relation between fiction and emotions from alternative standpoints. One is suggested by Richard Moran (1994). His argument starts from the idea that non-fictional imaginative thoughts, for example related to the past or to the future, may elicit emotions. I may, for example, nostalgically regret something that did not happen in the past. The non-factual character of what Moran calls modal facts (facts expressed using modal verbs, for example I could have, I shall have) (ibid., p. 78) does not imply that we perceive emotions which have been elicited in such a way as paradoxical. What is peculiar in fictional emotions is that they are caused not simply by some propositional requirement, which could make the paradox still plausible, but by the artistry of the fictional narration which accounts for the specificity of fictional emotions. Thus, fictional emotions may be seen not as the output of some make-believe game but as the specific characters of emotionally well-constructed pieces of narratives.

The shift Moran proposes is interesting. In fact, the paradox of fiction is related to the idea that emotions *must be* caused by some actual fact, event, circumstance. Fictional emotions are thus always explained as in relation to non-fictional emotions. Instead, the question may be reworded as follows: how is it possible to feel moved by unreal characters or events, real emotions for actual people and incidents being the yardstick (ibid., p. 82)? As Moran writes:

> This naturally encourages the idea that it is the sense of fictionality that needs to be overcome, or diminished, or distracted from, if we are to make sense of such responses [fictional emotions]. And this, in turn, encourages the idea that artificiality, the assertion of the status of the work as artifact, or the elaboration of conspicuous features that play no role in the construction of fictional truth, must detract from emotional engagement in thus detracting from the coherence of the fictional world depicted.
>
> (ibid.)

The stance Moran assumes is similar to Ricoeur's. The French philosopher does not understand the work of art either as a representational duplication of reality or as an utterly separated fictional world. By overcoming any naïve conception of mimesis, Ricoeur stresses the capacity of the work of art to retro-act on our experience of reality not because it is true, or truthful, but just because of its artfulness, which accounts for the capacity of literary fiction to tell us something unexpected about the world of human interactions (Ricoeur, 1984, pp. 61–99). According to Moran, it is in the artificiality of the language of art that its capacity to move the reader or the beholder resides:

> For it would appear to be the very features of the work that do indeed detract from the realistic presentation of the fictional world that actually enhance,

and don't inhibit, the intensity and richness of one's emotional involvement with it. We know that Starry Night would not really be more emotionally engaging if Van Gogh had calmed down and left out all that overwrought brush work. And the highly artificial, figurative, self-conscious language spoken, for example, by Macbeth does not interfere with our ability to be gripped by the play and his situation [...] The very expressive qualities that disrupt any sense of a fictional world are in fact central for our psychological participation with artworks.

(Moran, 1994, p. 83)

Moran shows that it is actually what makes a piece of fiction less adequate for representative truth that enhances its emotional power (ibid., p. 84). Thus, fictional emotions are generated by the very artificiality of the literary speech, for example "figurations, allusion, rhythm, repetition, assonance, dissonance" (ibid.), and it is this artificiality, and not some simulation of the ordinary speech or attitude (make-believe), which accounts for fictional emotions (ibid., pp. 85–86). By creating its own way to emotions, literature is able to show us something about our real feelings, their proper manifestation and their appropriate causes. In Moran's words: "[t]he realm of our emotional responses provides one of the clearer cases in which imagination is not so much a peering into some other world, as a way of relating to this one" (ibid., p. 106).

Donald Wesling (2008, p. 14) gives literature a fundamental role in understanding emotions, setting a close relation between literary emotions and everyday emotions: both are based on a process of interpretations (reading, in Wesling's wording) as both "involve interpreting signs and gestures (albeit of a different kind)" (ibid.). Indeed, literature gives a huge repertoire of what Wesling properly names "emotions in action" (ibid., p. 15), that is the vivid representations of actions inspired, motivated, determined by the emotional component of the human psyche. And this is no surprise, if we understand narratives as a powerful instrument by which we give sense to human life (ibid., p. 16). Thus, there is no paradox in emotions elicited by literary narratives. Stories, although fictional, "contain some version of the world as we value it", hence they give us a cognitive access to our social habits and cultural values (ibid., p. 118). By telling stories or listening to them, we do not only receive information about the world, we also rehearse, as it were, our emotional competence, since we "recognize, practice, multiply, and control our emotional states, and we need to make surmises about how others feel, too. Storytelling is the most complete re-enactment we know of emotion's social and reciprocal nature" (ibid., p. 16).

Although both based on the interpretation of signs, literary emotions and everyday emotions are not the same. In fact, literary works do not simply reproduce emotions, they represent them within the artificiality of stylistic devices. It is the very writing of literature (characterized as it is by tropes and artifice) that allows the transformation of ordinary emotions into literary ones (ibid., p. 118). In this sense, literary emotions are understood by Wesling as estrangement emotions: they do not simply reproduce what we feel as actual individuals but give a new, unusual perspective on the way we feel and emotionally interact with others. Estrangement is indeed, according to the Russian Formalist Shklovsky, a specific feature of the artistic reception. The function of art is not to get us acquainted with the unfamiliar but, on the contrary "to de-familiarize what's become automatic, forcing us to notice" (ibid., p. 37). Thus, estrangement emotions, that is emotions produced through the artifice of literature, allow the reader to see human feelings from a new, unusual perspective.

From his specific perspective as a literary critic, Donald Wesling is interested in the way literature conveys emotions (ibid., p. 27). And it is actually the conventionality of literary writings that accounts for their reality effect. Authors may recur to a series of rhetorical means in order to elicit emotions in the readers:

> visual and auditory imagery, especially images of the body and the human face, the human voice; personal pronouns and their way of identifying ownership of experiences and of speech; names of emotions as claims that such states are present and experienced; surprise-startle-interruption; changes in the images and the utterances along a plotted path.
>
> (ibid., p. 38)

Yet literary devices are not enough in order to understand literary emotions. In fact, although they are able to de-naturalize the perspective from which we understand our feeling, they are, at the same time, based on a set of values and ideas which are generally shared by the author and his contemporaries. This means that literary emotions have to be contextualized, connecting the work of letters to what Raymond Williams (1977) used to call the structure of feelings. In the interplay between literary critique and historical reading a new awareness may emerge, connected to the overcoming of strict cognitivism. And in this sense, the literary work may represent a useful support for the study of human emotions, including the sociological perspective.

3 An unusual transparency

A structural feature of literary narratives – which distinguishes fiction from everyday narratives – is responsible for the close connection between literature and emotions. One of the reasons why literature may reproduce and elicit emotions is that the narrator may probe into the characters' inner lives, reproducing their thoughts and feelings. This capacity of literary narratives is the subject matter of Dorrit Cohn's beautiful book *Transparent Minds. Narrative Methods for Presenting Consciousness in Fiction* (1978). Cohn's thesis is that literary narratives conventionally transform the opaqueness of the human mind into artificial transparency. The pretended openness of the human mind is a unique feature of fictional techniques. In Cohn's wording: "narrative fiction is the only literary genre, as well as the only kind of narrative, in which the untold thoughts, feelings, perception of a person other than the speaker can be portrayed" (Cohn, 1978, p. 7). Thoughts and feeling, cognition and emotions are, thus, conventionally available to the reader who may penetrate into the consciousness of other (although fictive) people. Cohn analyzes different techniques by which minds (including thoughts and feelings) become conventionally transparent in fictional narratives. The more conventional form is the so-called omniscient narrator, who uses his own discourse in order to portrait the inner life of a character. Cohn (ibid., p. 10), speaks, in this regard, of psycho-narration. Quoted monologue is the Modernist form of presentation of the self in fictional narratives. In this case, the flow of the character's consciousness is in the foreground, including its illogicalities, contradictions, inconsistencies. Narrated monologue (what French critiques call *style indirect libre*) is the third technical option. In this case, the narrator reproduces the character's inner life, in the form of a reported speech. Generally speaking, in the development of Western fiction one may notice a trend towards a greater attention paid to inner cognitive and emotional processes: from the discrete avoidance of interference with the inner state of consciousness in early modern fiction (Cohn quotes, as appropriate instances, Henry Fielding or William Thackeray), to the explicit manifestation of characters' thoughts and emotional states inaugurated by Modernism.

Literary narrative has the specific capacity to show what (fictive) people think and feel. Yet, regardless of this quality, which links directly literary fiction to the representation and the elicitation of feelings, the question of literary emotions has been chiefly discussed in the form of a paradox. Indeed, whereas the cognitive value of narratives (including literary narratives) has been widely explored (Longo, 2015, Chapter 2, *passim*), the question of literary emotions has remained in the background. Yet literary narratives are particularly fit to reproduce and elicit emotions. They are in fact characterized by what Jerome Bruner called a dual landscape (Bruner, 1990, pp. 51–52). Fictional narratives may represent not only the external landscape made of physical objects and social relations. They may also describe the interior landscape of the characters' feelings, thoughts and motivations. Thus, what would be rejected as unnatural in everyday speech (Cohn's mind transparency, that is the direct access to the interior complexity of the actors) is assumed as normal in literary narratives. The dual landscape of fiction implies that "events and actions in a putative 'real world' occur concurrently with mental events in the consciousness of the protagonists" (ibid., p. 51). The relevance of literary narratives for the study of emotions is to be imputed to the dual capacity of fiction to represent what happens both outside and inside the characters' interior world. Incidents may be narrated, social interactions may be described, as well as the effects they produce both cognitively and emotionally in the interior world of the fictional characters. This is nothing natural: indeed, the issuing reality effect is to be imputed to the sole artificiality of the literary speech. As Dorrit Cohn writes, "the special likelifeness of narrative fiction [...] depends on what reader and writer know least in life: how another mind thinks, another body feels" (Cohn, 1978, p. 6–7).

4 What is specific in literary emotions?

Literary emotions are similar to and yet different from everyday emotions. And it is by making reference to both similarities and differences that the proper value of fictional emotions may be assessed. Literary narratives have been often qualified as particularly fit to represent emotions and what is involved in feeling them. Peter Goldie wittily writes in this regard:

> If you ask me to say what the feelings are like when one is feeling disgusted or jealous or angry or in love, I refuse to answer: if you have experienced the emotion, then you know very well what these sorts of feeling can be like, and you do not need me to tell you; if you have not experienced the emotion and want to get at least some idea of what it feels like, then […] I suggest you read a good novel.
>
> (Goldie, 2000, p. 19)

So, reading a novel is a way to access emotions and understand them. But why?

Neuroscience has shown the deep interconnection between communication and action. When we hear or read about an action, two areas of our brain are activated: the former being related to communication and understanding and the other being the same which would be activated in case we ourselves would perform the action. As Keith Oatley puts it: "Recognition of an action in the imagination when we hear or read about it involves brain systems responsible for initiating that action" (Oatley, 2011, p. 20). This neuronal process, which is now interpreted by neuroscientists as the output of the activity of the so-called mirror-neurons, had been already envisaged by Cooley who thought of emotions as based on our observing ourselves as in a looking-glass, consisting of the reaction other people have to our action (Cooley, 1902/1922, p. 184).

Mirroring is part of our everyday experience. When we see someone smile or frown, we tend to smile or frown back. This holds too when we read or hear about situations able to elicit emotions. Most parts of our emotions are consequences of our relational life, which means they require empathy, that is the capacity to relate other people's emotions to our previous experiences (Oatley, 2011, p. 113). Empathy may be based on a simple reaction to other people's expressiveness, as when we react to a facial expression. It may also depend on more complex processes, for example imaginative empathy:

> The process has two parts. One part is that, by simulation within ourselves we infer what emotion the other person is feeling and we impute it to that person. The second part, which occurs at the same time, is that, because of the simulation, we feel a corresponding emotion in our self.
>
> (ibid., p. 114)

Of course, it is imaginative empathy which is involved when we are moved by fiction: we construct a mental model of the character, his personality and motives, on the basis of the narrative skills of the author and our capacity to put fictional "events together, constructing them into something meaningful to ourselves, and experiencing the resulting emotions" (ibid., p. 112). Thus, literary emotions are of a peculiar kind. They allow us to identify with the characters and their plans, they let us experience sympathy for the vicissitudes of the protagonists, they may even have a therapeutic function, allowing us to revive incidents in our life that we may have removed from conscious memory. Moreover, thanks to the craft of art, they can de-naturalize our emotional experiences, giving us the opportunity to see things from a new perspective.

The distinction between literary and everyday emotion is one of the topics of traditional Indian poetic theory (ibid., p. 72) which distinguishes between the aesthetic sentiments (*rasa*) and everyday emotions (*bhāva*). In other words, the aesthetic sentiment of love is what the audience experiences when attending a love-drama. The fictional emotion (*rasa*) is strongly connected to the correlated everyday emotion (*bhāva*), in particular through the past memories of the audience related to the specific sentiment represented in the literary work. Without reference to direct memory (or some form of shared awareness) one could not otherwise understand what is going on onstage. Yet the aesthetic sentiment has its own features, since it is produced as an output of the artificiality of the poetic language (Hogan, 2003, p. 47 ff.).

The literary features of aesthetic emotions are clear in ancient Indian poetics: *rasa* is based on an empathetic understanding of what is going on in the story, without any practical or relational aim. This means that *rasas* are to be understood as the empathic version of an emotion:

> When the hero is faced with a dragon, we do not fear the dragon, experiencing the *bhāva* or emotion itself, and therefore running from the theater. Rather, we fear for the hero. We feel something clearly related to fear, but not identical with fear: We feel empathic fear, which is to say, the 'terrible' rasa.
>
> (ibid., p. 81)

Of course, *rasa* is connected to *bhāva*, since the emotional power of literary work is related to its capacity to elicit emotions by evoking personal memories. Only in so far as the memories of the reader are congruent with the content of a literary text, are they able to trigger his emotional response to the fictional representation (ibid., p. 75). Yet this response is specifically based on the text, whose aesthetic quality is responsible for producing empathic *rasas*:

> rasas are evoked in a reader by words, sentences, topics, and soon, presented in a literary work. This is, of course, in part the result of literal meanings. But it is also, and crucially, a function of the clouds of nondenumerable, nonsubstitutable, nonpropositional suggestions that surround these texts.
>
> (ibid., p. 51)

The artificiality of literary language accounts for a relevant process, which is specific of literary emotions: we, as readers, recognize them, connecting them to our former experiences and memories. Yet, by reading literary fiction, we do not only acknowledge emotions, we understand them (as well as our past emotional experience) from a new perspective. Literary emotions, in fact, allow us to de-naturalize what we know about feelings, so that we may reinterpret them. As Keith Oatley effectively puts it:

> our enjoyment of a fictional story derives first from recognizing patterns of emotions that we have experienced ourselves (in life or literature) in a new context. We project ourselves imaginatively into this context, and experience the emotions in a way that enables us to understand them more deeply, and in the process perhaps to make some changes in ourselves.
>
> (Oatley, 2011, p. 124)

Thus, literary emotions simulate, reproduce, reactivate everyday emotions by recurring to means which are properly literary. This is probably the reason why we perceive them not only as a mere representation of everyday emotions. In Indic literary theory, a *rasa* gives a specific flavour to a work of letter (e.g. the comic, the tragic, the heroic), thus locating it within a specific literary genre. Literary emotions are thus experienced by the reader (or the audience) through the filter of literary craftsmanship. This allows a certain detachment between the individual and the literary emotion (*rasa*) he is experiencing, a detachment which is rarely achieved in case of everyday emotions. We may therefore understand literary emotions better than our everyday emotions, since we are less involved in the situation. By narrating emotions through the resources of literary narrative, they are likely to be understood not as the immediate output of individual sensibility but as more general, human or universal qualities. When reading a good piece of fiction, the vicissitudes of the protagonists are, in fact, not only conceived as specific, individual cases but often as examples of what might happen to us all. Literature indeed gives us the possibility to understand what is peculiar in our culturally defined perception of the world, starting from the cases as narrated.

In order to understand this specific quality of literature, I will make a quick reference to the Marxist art critic György Lukács. Art (and literature among the arts) represents, according to Lukács, a specific form of knowing which may be distinguished from the imperfect and episodic cognition of everyday life, as well as from the more precise but abstract knowledge guaranteed by theory and science. Art (including literature) happens to have another function as compared to science and everyday cognition: it neither attempts to reach universal generalizations nor confines itself to the reproduction of singular cases. Thus, the mimetic capacity of art is neither reducible to the reproduction of singular events or characters, nor elevated to the detection of general laws, the cognitive task of art being to depict (often unwittingly) the peculiar features of a determined social context.

In its quest for the general, science builds a gap between scientific knowledge and common sense, as singular aspects of reality and their relations have to be subsumed under universal laws in order to become meaningful (Lukács, 1971, p. 145 ff.). Art, on the contrary, achieves a knowledge of the world in which the phenomenon and its universal meaning coexist (ibid., p. 236). This unity of the phenomenon and its essence, which is a peculiar character of the work of art, is guaranteed by the specific means of the artistic production which, unlike science, does not reproduce reality through formal concepts but through images: thanks to images, art may show the peculiarity of an epoch or a context and, in so doing, artistic cognition overcomes the fracture between the essence and the phenomenon, so typical of modern science, so as to preserve both the peculiarity of the perceivable phenomenon and its related universal value (ibid., p. 187; Perus, 1976, p. 116). Transposed to our specific topic, Lukács' approach may be a useful tool to understand the role of literary fiction in our understanding of emotions in context: literary fiction represents emotions neither as the output of biological, psychological or sociological causes (as science would do), nor as the episodic expression of the outburst of feeling (as is typical of common sense). Emotions are portrayed in the very context of their fictional manifestation and, although they are part of a narration, they do not refer only to a specific character or a specific episode, as they may give the reader clues about typical characters and typical circumstances. Thus, art (narrative art in particular) may be imputed the capacity to reproduce examples of emotions and their effects on unique fictional characters. At the same time, fictional narratives may show the social, historical, general relevance of emotions and, at their best, the universality of the human condition.

5 The narrative character of emotions

Narratives are relevant in order to understand emotions. Emotions, in their turn, are endowed with a narrative structure. In our everyday experience, we recognize emotions in so far as we locate them within a narrative structure, a script, which makes our emotional reaction culturally appropriate (Oatley, 2011, p. 114). If we assumed that emotions were genetically predefined basic elements of human behaviour, the relation between emotions and narratives would appear as little relevant. On the contrary, although it is undeniable that emotions have a neuronal component, they acquire meaning within a culturally defined set of contextual references. Emotions are in part determined by the functioning of the human nervous system. Yet they are often meaningful elements of the action of individual agents, in connection with other individual agents.

Let's take as an example basic emotions: they evolved as a form of adaptation of superior animals (including humans) to the environment. They are, in this regard, pre-propositional, in the sense that they emerge unconsciously as a reaction to some environmental change. According to Oatley and Johnson-Laird (1987, p. 33): "there is a small number of basic emotion modes which occur universally in the human species. Each has a characteristic phenomenological tone – though no meaning as such, as each is based on a non-propositional signal". These basic emotions (one plausible list being happiness, sadness, fear, anger and disgust) are understood by psychologists as ways to coordinate different modes of the brain. The cognitive system adopts a specific emotion as an assessment of the outputs of an action plan, for example the evaluation of what has been achieved in comparison to what was expected (ibid., p. 35). In this sense, basic emotions, which emerge as a pre-prepositional aspect of our reaction to the environment, become part of a cognitive evaluation of the outputs, hence part of a propositional (linguistic) process of definition of the meaning of a specific situation. Raw emotions are, indeed, meaningless as they acquire meaning within a cognitive process of evaluation (ibid., p. 34). The cognitive element is even more evident when emotions are the outcome of a process of interaction. In this case, the final result is not to be imputed to the sole agent, as it emerges in a process of cooperation (or conflict) in which two or more actors are involved. Thus, interaction bestows basic emotions with a cultural meaning shared by the agents, which makes them mutually understandable (ibid., p. 41 ff.).

The cultural meanings of emotions are defined through a narrative structure. Said otherwise, we understand the social and cultural sense of an emotion in so far as we connect a specific emotion with some culturally determined narrative patterns. Therefore, we understand the appropriateness of our and other people's emotional reaction to a specific situation (e.g. a funeral, a wedding or a party) because we have assimilated their culturally specific narrative pattern. The idea of a narrative structure of the cultural and social component of emotions has had a wide echo. Ronald de Sousa (1987) has been one of the first to hint at the narrativeness of emotions. According to de Sousa, emotions are not just felt, they are learned in connection to a dramatic structure: "The names of emotions do not refer to some simple experience; rather, they get their meaning from their relation to a situation type, a kind of original drama that defines the roles, feelings, and reactions characteristic of that emotion" (ibid., p. XVI). This dramatic structure is called by de Sousa a paradigm scenario, a sort of culturally defined model against which we acknowledge and evaluate actual emotions in actual situations.

A paradigm scenario is made up of two elements:

> a situation type providing the characteristic objects of the specific "emotion-type" and then a normal, appropriate reaction to the situation type, a set of responses which are both biologically and culturally determined. The situation type and the appropriate way to respond to it are learned during our socialization, are reinforced by the specific culture to which one belongs and in literate cultures are eventually supplemented and refined by literature.
>
> (ibid., p. 188)

The quotation from Ronald de Sousa stresses the fact that a clear-cut, definitive separation between everyday emotions and their literary representation is undue: indeed, literary narratives find a ready-made prototypical emotional structure, which may be stressed, supported and reinforced thanks to literary craftsmanship. By underlining the narrative structure of emotions, one may gain in accuracy, in so far as emotions are multifaceted phenomena, better describable as part of a story. Emotions in fact are not static, biological or psychological statuses: they are, on the contrary, dynamic and complex processes, and such complexity is better portrayed within a narrative (Goldie, 2000, pp. 145–147).

Peter Goldie is one of those who have stressed the articulated characters of emotions and their connection to narratives. Emotion are in fact "typically complex, episodic, dynamic, and structured" (ibid., p. 12). Emotions are complex (in so far as they involve psychological and bodily changes, cognition and feelings). They are episodic (since they emerge in connection to specific events) and dynamic (because they change over time). An emotion is, moreover, narratively structured:

> emotion is structured in that it constitutes part of a narrative—roughly, an unfolding sequence of actions and events, thoughts and feelings—in which the emotion itself is embedded. The different elements of the emotion are conceived of by us as all being part of the same emotion, in spite of its complex, episodic, and dynamic features. The actions which we do out of an emotion, and the various ways of expressing an emotion, are also seen as part of the same narrative, but not themselves as part of the emotion itself.
>
> (ibid., p. 13)

Thus, the narrative structure of emotions gives coherence and unity to their complex nature, connecting emotions (what we feel inside) with action (the outward manifestation of emotions) (ibid., p. 144). We recognize emotions because we have assimilated the paradigmatic narrative structures in which the complex character of emotions is, as it were, culturally synthesized. Paradigmatic narratives combine cognition (paradigmatic thoughts), motivation, bodily changes, expressions and actions. In other words, they allow us to recognize specific emotions and the appropriate reactions (both individual and social) connected to them (ibid., p. 33). Moreover, paradigmatic narratives have both an introspective and a social function: they help the individual to recognize the emotions he himself is feeling (so that he may choose to perform in accordance to or in disagreement with the paradigm) and to interpret the emotions emerging in the behaviour of his fellow people (he acknowledges a certain emotion in other people as he is acquainted with its corresponding narrative structure) (Snævarr, 2010, p. 324). Thus we know that someone is jealous (or angry or happy) because we may connect the related emotions to a culturally defined narrative model (what it is like to be jealous, or angry or happy), as well as to our personal experience (i.e. to our history of jealousy, anger or happiness) (Goldie, 2000, p. 144).

The narrative component of emotions has been stressed by the philosopher Martha Nussbaum, within the framework of a neo-Stoic theory. Although emotions are often represented as belonging to the deeper, non-cognitive aspect of the human mind, Nussbaum relates them to a cognitive process of evaluation. We evaluate the external world and we judge the relevance of some of the objects therein as relevant for us and our well-being. Emotions would emerge – this according to the approach developed by Greek stoicism – when we cognitively assess our "neediness and lack of self-sufficiency" (Nussbaum, 2001, p. 22). The cognitive approach to emotions, as proposed by Martha Nussbaum, is intended chiefly to confute a diffuse conception of emotions understood as irrational impulses, pushing people as a sort of uncontrolled energy (ibid., p. 23). The narrative structure of emotions is referred to by Nussbaum as an argument in support of her cognitive, neo-Stoic approach. Nussbaum does not deny the bodily component of emotions, their being rooted in some not totally controllable aspect of the human mind. Yet emotions are always about an object (my fear, my happiness, my love are never unrelated). They are, hence, intentional, in the sense that the object is interpreted by the individual who experiences a specific emotion. Thus, emotions are able to move and push individuals but always as a consequence of the individuals' cognitive evaluation of the relevance of a specific object for their well-being. Nussbaum exemplifies this with the story of her grief for the loss of her mother: pain is here the consequence of the awareness of the loss of a valuable person, hence of a cognitive assessment.

By narrating an emotion, we put different elements together: the object which elicits the emotion, the value one connects to the object, the specific phenomenological aspect of the emotion, our reaction to it, and so on. Narratives of emotions make thus the connection between the cognitive awareness and the bodily, mechanical component of emotions clearer. As Nussbaum writes:

> If emotions involve judgements about the salience for our well-being of uncontrolled external objects [...] we will need to be able to imagine those attachments, their delight and their terror, their intense and even obsessive focusing on their object, if we are ever to talk well about love, or fear, or anger.
>
> (ibid., p. 2)

We need, hence, a narrative structure enabling us to understand the complex relation between the individual, the external world, his expectancies and emotions. Narrative are conceived as relevant in order to give sense to our emotions and the history with the relational object which has produced them. Children, for example, use stories (narratives) to give proper sense to their relationship with relevant others and their environment (ibid., p. 237). Literary narratives, in particular, are evoked by Martha Nussbaum as crafty, artful and structured representations of emotions, able as they are to catch in a sophisticated way the complex interplay among emotions, valuable objects, cognition and the personal history of the individual (Nussbaum, 2001, p. 2 ff.; 236 ff, 470 ff.).

6 Narratives of emotions and literary emotions

Narratives are indispensable for understanding emotions, since emotions are narratively understood and made sense of. They are deeply embedded in a narrative structure. On the other hand, emotions are a constitutive part of narratives: in everyday narratives we often deal with our feelings, whereas literary narratives are hardly thinkable without any reference to emotions. When we try to understand empathetically what emotion another person is feeling, we do not simply apply a term referring to emotions (e.g. joy, resentment, anger) to a specific attitude or behaviour. Indeed, we cannot feel what others are feeling, thus the only way to probe into someone else's experience is by talking to him, and, even so, we hardly understand his actual feelings or internal states. In order to come to terms with this constitutive, internal, character of emotions, we have to relate them to some concrete situation which we have already experienced. Thus, when attempting to identify a specific emotion, we make reference to a standard situation in which that peculiar emotion may emerge (being sad is for example associated with standard situations such as the loss of a loved one) (Hogan, 2011, p. 82). Emotions are understandable only when we have some narrative representation of the way they may emerge in specific situations. This entails that emotions are both embedded in narratives and able to produce and sustain narratives. Micro narratives define emotions (for example being jealous) and then may be further specified in connection to the situation (being jealous of a partner) or some characteristics of the persons involved (a young woman, a former partner, etc.).

According to Patrick Colm Hogan, the relation between narratives and emotions is so tight, that emotions are "at the root of the narrative patterns" (Hogan, 2011a, p. 9). Indeed, from Aristotle on, emotions are understood as a constitutive part of a story. In order to catch the attention of the readers, a story has to narrate a fracture in the taken for granted, by which order is broken and re-established (Longo, 2015, p. 16). The tension which the broken order generates is by necessity connected to emotions. Yet, narratology (with some rare exceptions, e.g. Greimas and Fontanille, 1991) has only recently attempted to understand the deep structural relation held by narratives and emotions (Hogan, 2011a, p. 10 ff.).

This may surprise, if we think that the intrinsic narrative structure of emotions makes the interconnection between literary narratives and emotions ever stronger. This interconnection is probably more clearly evident in romantic comedy and epic. Both genres are cross-culturally present in every known literary culture and may be understood as extensions of the micro-narratives which define the corresponding emotional states (Hogan, 2011b, p. 118). The structural character of these prototypical, cross-cultural narratives is to be found, according to Patrick Colm Hogan, in their emotional component. Both in romantic comedies and epics, the plot moves in the direction of the achievement of happiness (in the form of the happy union of the lovers or the eventual victory of the hero). The eventual joy of the protagonists of romantic plots is the result of a series of emotionally loaded vicissitudes. In tragedies the happy ending is substituted by final diffuse sorrow, as the result expected for the protagonists by the readers or the beholders is eventually subverted. Literary emotions are thus a constitutive part of literary narratives, able to involve and move the reader but also to lead him through the plot, allowing him to make sense of it.

What we make sense of by reading fiction is our understanding of the individual and his relation with the social. Emotions, in fact, emerge in a process of evaluation of the environment. If we accept the idea psychologists and neuroscientists have developed according to which emotions are evolutionary resources for adapting to the environment, in the case of humans, our environment being chiefly social, emotions are to be understood as forms of adaptation to our sociality. And since our environment is mostly social, our emotions are generally elicited by social situations. Moreover, emotions are culturally conditioned, in the sense that society defines which emotion is appropriate to which social situations and which reactions may or may not be made public (Hochshild, 1979).

As narratives (including literary narratives) describe actions, they have to do with the social. They not only depict actors who act over time, it is also through narration that we make action understandable. In this sense, narratives have a powerful explanatory capacity (Longo, 2015, p. 28). As Carr (2008, pp. 19–20) wrote, if we want to make sense of an unusual behaviour, we need to tell a story about it. Thus, if we assume that action and interaction are relevant components of both emotions and narratives, it is evident that narratives (including literary narratives) contain a wide repertoire of action and emotions and are hence a relevant resource to understand the social and psychological aspects of our emotional life. It goes without saying that fictional narratives, being more structured and sophisticated, do this better than everyday narratives. One may even state that literary narratives, being able to describe the complex structure of emotions, are better suited then other texts if we want to understand the place of affectivity in our and other people's lives (Nussbaum, 2001, p. 2).

Since emotions are culturally embedded, they need to be propositionally defined in order for them to become socially relevant, and one of the most effective ways to define emotions and their cultural relevance is through literary sources. We can therefore resort to literature as a wide repertoire of emotions, hence as a relevant source of data about our emotional life (Hogan, 2003, pp. 1–2). We may learn about "emotional reactions to literary works – the sorrow, anger, mirth felt and expressed by readers – [which] clearly tell us something about what moves people in a particular culture, what touches them emotionally" (ibid., p. 2). Thus, literary works represent an important set of data regarding what is considered emotionally relevant in a specific social context. Moreover, literary fiction builds up a stock of narrative prototypes (or paradigm narratives) of what is culturally implied in a specific emotion. From literary sources, we may learn what is appropriate in love or jealousy, for example (Hogan, 2003, p. 240). Literary works may even provide us with patterns of "prototypical eliciting conditions" of specific emotions as well as of goals and projects related to them (ibid., p. 244). Indeed, we need to make sense of our raw emotions which are meaningless outside a narrative reference scheme. Fiction reinforces our understanding of emotions (both ours and our fellow people's) by providing a variety of causes, conditions, values, adjustments, justifications, reactions connected to a particular emotion. The available interpretative models give us the chance to interpret a raw feeling (is what I feel friendship or love?) and to give sense to it. We do not just interpret feelings, since the very interpretative process alters "our experience of the feeling itself" (ibid., p. 248).

Keith Oatley (2011) proposes a convincing metaphor in order to explain the function of literary narratives in our understanding of emotions. As a pilot learns to fly by using a flight simulator, so we learn about ours and our fellow people's emotions through literature. A simulator cannot substitute the real experience, yet it is indispensable since: "[l]earning in an actual airplane is essential, but a good deal of the time aloft nothing much happens. In a simulator you confront a wider range of experiences and try out in safety how to respond to critical situations" (ibid., p. 158). As we may transfer the skills we learn by using the flight simulator to actual flying, so we might transfer the social and emotional skills we have learnt by reading literary fiction to our actual life. Convincing as this metaphor may sound, there must be more than simple simulation. It is the same Keith Oatley who gives us further clues. As compared to everyday narratives of feelings, literary narratives do not only reproduce and reinforce our conception of emotions, they may even propose new perspectives or points of view from which to understand our feelings: "Art enables us to experience some emotions in contexts that we would not ordinarily encounter, and to think of ourselves in ways that usually we do not" (ibid., p. 117). Moreover, art objectifies human feelings, by transposing them into a sophisticated narrative scheme and by doing so, it enables "a growth of feeling and consciousness [...] both in the author and in the person who engages with the created artwork" (ibid., p. 132). Hence literary fiction is not only a "guided dream, or simulation" (ibid., p. 158). It is also a way to recreate our conception of ourselves, of our emotions and of our relational world. In other words, art, literary fiction in particular, may at its best "bring us closer to truths of our human condition" (ibid., p. 156). Thus, regardless of the philosophical problem of the truth of literature (Longo, 2015), regardless of the somewhat artificial paradox of fiction and emotions, literary narratives seem to be fundamental resources in grasping the complexity of lived emotions, both in their individual, social and cultural dimensions.

Experimental psychology has demonstrated that reading fiction enhances one's understanding of the social (of social relations in particular) and of our fellow people's inner worlds. Extensive readers of fiction seem better able than non-readers in understanding both the emotional states of others and their own. Literary fiction endows us with the appropriate vocabulary to express the subtlety of human emotionality, so as both to probe into our emotional world and to empathetically understand the emotional complexity of the people we experience. This should not surprise. In fact: "[f]iction is principally about the problems of selves navigating in the social world [...] Readers of fiction tend to become more expert at making models of others and themselves, and at navigating the social world" (Oatley, 2011, p. 160). This is due to a specific feature of the literary treatment of emotions: its capacity to give hypothetical accounts of fictive emotionality which comply with our everyday experience of emotions. Not the cold description a sociologist, a psychologist or a neuroscientist could produce, but rich, articulated, meaningful accounts of emotions in action. Here follows a beautiful quotation from Donald Wesling, which expresses in a language more elegant than mine what I intend:

> If I am right, literature—storytelling—might bring some dimensions that neuroscience, psychology, philosophy, and sociology cannot usually give to emotion study. Literary thinking has always been good at interpreting emotion states that have already been coded into sequential writing. More consciously now, literary thinking might bring increased attention to the emotional lives

of imaginary persons, to mixed and hypothetical emotion states, to intensity of emotion states, to historicity and the social nature of emotion states.

(Wesling, 2008, pp. 17–18)

Given this richness and complexity, literary sources appear to be particularly adept material for the sociology of emotions. They are both insightful texts through which a sociologist may train his sensibility for the social world and its nuances and an appropriate source of data to study emotions in society. The following chapters are tentative analyses of the complex relations between emotions and society, using literary sources not only as empirical materials but also as theoretical accounts, able as they are to shed new light and point to innovative directions.

5   Action, emotions and emotional control

A reading of Philip Roth's *American Pastoral*

1 Puppets, actors or humans? Luigi Pirandello, Alfred Schutz and the sociological *homunculus*

Six Characters in Search of an Author is a drama, written in 1921 by the Italian playwright and Nobel laureate Luigi Pirandello (1937). In the play, six incomplete theatre characters burst into a theatre, interrupt a rehearsal and ask the director to let them complete their interrelated, unfinished stories. The theatre piece represents the climax of Pirandello's production, as it proposes his usual themes (multiple identities, the convergence between the theatre and reality, the need for social acknowledgement in order to construct one's self) within a neurotic setting in which the characters insist on being made autonomous, so that they may themselves represent their authentic stories. It is, as it were, the protest of the characters for the deviating, potentially untruthful representation that theatre gives of the complexity of their biographies, the motives and sentiment underlining their action. The characters are eventually able to fulfil their story, which is driven to a tragic finale where theatre and reality seem to intermingle. The characters are now responsible for their lives, so what happens on the scene may be imputed to them alone. Luigi Pirandello's play is a theatrical reflection on the betrayal of the characters' complexity, brought about by the playwright and the actors. It is affected by the philosophical arguments which inform Pirandello's work, chiefly related to the possibility of a true expression of one's personality in the social setting. It poses, moreover, the relevant question of the relationship between the complexity of reality and the reduced complexity of any form of representation.

Influenced by Georg Simmel, Pirandello stresses, from his peculiar vantage point, the irresolvable contrast between life and form (Ceserani, 2007), hence the fact that the lived experience of each of us is bound to be impoverished once it is expressed through whatever formal language one may select. Knowledge is impossible without a reduction of reality to the available concepts (be they the ones used in everyday life or in scientific investigations). Yet, social scientists should be aware that what they select as theoretically relevant is bound to determine what they can actually perceive (and hence investigate).

Alfred Schutz has dealt with these fundamental themes in his masterful methodological paper *Common Sense and Scientific Interpretation of Human Action*

(Schutz, 1962). The main purpose of the paper is to connect sociological concepts to the concepts used by social actors in their normal intercourses, since any scientific interpretation of human action has to be grounded in the commonsensical interpretation of everyday life. By making reference to authors such as Whitehead, Husserl, Dewey and William James, Alfred Schutz stresses that we always perceive reality by means of constructs, hence abstractions which help us select what is relevant for our specific purposes (be they practical or scientific). As Schutz puts it: "Strictly speaking, there are no such things as facts, pure and simple. Any facts are from the outset facts selected from a universal context by the activities of our mind. They are, therefore, always interpreted facts" (ibid., p. 5).

Schutz' main task is to show how specific the object of the social sciences is, which implies the necessity for the social scientist of a keen methodological awareness. What is relevant here is the way Schutz qualifies the sociological construct of the social actor. Whereas we perceive people in our face-to-face interaction on the basis of the others' living presence, the social scientist constructs methodological puppets by selecting those aspects which are relevant for his specific cognitive purposes. They are artificial entities, devoid of a biography and of a historically locatable identity.

> He has created these puppets or homunculi – writes Schutz – to manipulate them for his purpose. A merely specious consciousness is imputed to them by the scientist, which is constructed in such a way that its presupposed stock of knowledge at hand (including the ascribed set of invariant motives) would make actions originating from it subjectively understandable, provided that these actions were performed by real actors within the social world.
>
> (Schutz, 1962, p. 41)

As a matter of facts, any theoretical representation of the actor is a reduction of his complexity. What Schutz is exhorting social scientists to do, is not to confuse our thought construct with reality, since the *homunculus* lives, as it were, only to solve specific intellectual puzzles:

> The homunculus was not born, he does not grow up, and he will not die. He has no hopes and no fears; he does not know anxiety as the chief motive of all his deeds. He is not free in the sense that his acting could transgress the limits his creator, the social scientist, has predetermined.
>
> (ibid.)

The *homunculus* has no reality except that bestowed on him by the social scientist. He is an unfinished character in a more radical sense than Pirandello's, since he is a complex set of generalizations (generalized motives, generalized tasks, etc.), with only artificial references to everyday life. Schutz' *homunculus* would be hardly thinkable as protesting (like Pirandello's characters) against his unfinishedness: he has no story to accomplish. Schutz' lesson is about the necessarily reductive character of social sciences and of knowledge as such. But it is also about the methodological relevance of our selection: our representation of reality depends on which generalizations we will eventually select. The selected generalizations will hence define what of reality we will take into account and, possibly more important, what we will neglect.

2 The sociological puppet and emotions

Schutz' argument implies that the way a social scientist defines his *homunculus* (the actor as a theoretical concept and a methodological tool) will determine what elements of social action will be selected as sociologically relevant. In post-classical social theory, the actor is, as it were, reduced to his cognitive competences: the actor is either conceived as able to conform to a normative world made up of rules and values (Parsons, 1951), or to calculate costs and benefits, choosing among different courses of action (Homans, 1974), or to interpret, within an incessant process of reflexivity, his action in relation to others' actions or expectations (Blumer, 1969). The output is the unrealistic representation of a constantly cogitative actor, whose action is cognitively (thus never emotionally or irreflexively) determined. This model of actor, as John D. Baldwin ironically writes, "appears to reflect and cogitate incessantly, continually constructing and reconstructing his or her world of experience" (Baldwin, 1988: 35). As a matter of facts, much of our action is irreflexive, being both habitual (hence mechanical or routinary) or emotional (thus the expression of internal feelings). Neglecting the emotional component in the sociological model of action impedes an accurate observation both of the emotional component of human behaviour and the intrinsic sociality of human emotions.

The sociality of emotions is not to be related exclusively either to the influence of the cultural context, which defines emotions and their contents, or to the normative framework, which specifies when the expression of emotions is socially appropriate. The connection is deeper, in the sense that, as Ian Burkitt has clearly stated "acting out the emotions [...] *are* the emotions themselves" (Burkitt, 1997, p. 41). It would be misleading to consider emotions as a psychological substratum, existing independently of the actions where it manifests. On the contrary, "the emotion is the action itself and is governed by the relationship in which it occurs" (ibid.). What Burkitt proposes is a non-reductionist conception of emotions: they are not totally rooted in discourses (as structuralists would have); they are not completely physiologically driven or socially determined but they are, as it were, complexes of discourse, physiology and sociality which emerge in social relations (ibid., p. 42). This implies by necessity that emotions are embodied: instead of separating the biological and the social component, Burkitt proposes to consider emotions as socially relevant in so far as they are expressed through bodily activities which are intrinsically social.

The sociality of emotions implies that they may be understood as dispositions: "One could say that a culture provide for people an *emotional habitus*, with a language and set of practices which outline ways of speaking about emotions and of acting about and upon bodily feelings within everyday life" (ibid., p. 43). Socialization implies that the individual actors learn how to act in relation to the socially defined *emotional habitus* and thus "develop emotional dispositions that can be expressed in certain contexts throughout a person's life. Emotions are hence both cognitive and pre-cognitive: they involve culturally informed interpretations, but are also bodily dispositions instilled through social practices" (ibid.). What is interesting in Burkitt's relational conception of emotion is that emotions are neither the cause nor the consequence of action. They are a relevant component of action itself. As Burkitt puts it:

> emotions need not be reduced either to inner organic nor psychological processes, but encompasses both these things within the context of everyday life. Individuals do have a psychological and physiological life, but this is fragmentary and intermittent, and is held together in a meaningful way only in the 'weave of behaviours' that composes the practices of social life.
>
> (ibid., p. 44)

Burkitt's general idea is clear: emotions are meaningful in so far as they are part of our everyday practices. The reverse is also plausible, as most of our action can be understood only as co-determined by our lived, emotional experience. From a theoretical standpoint, by occulting this double interconnection, the theory of action has constructed a completely rational methodological *homunculus*, in which emotions hardly play any role. In so doing, social theory tends to neglect the possibility of analyzing emotions as one of the relevant components of social action.

3 Talcott Parsons through Philip Roth's *American Pastoral*

In Chapters 7 and 8, I will make reference to literary works as illustrative of macro social processes, related to the changing conception of envy and love. My attempt there will be to show how emotions and sentiments change over time, hence in connection to changing social relations and social structure. In this chapter and in the following one, I employ literary works as illustrative of social theories rather than social phenomena. This is one of the ways sociologists may make reference to literary works, so as to enhance or modify or confirm their theoretical insights. Sociologists have in fact tested their theories against the quasi-real set of literary narratives, which are generally endowed with a dense and thoughtful representation of human action (Longo, 2015).

What I propose here is a sociological interpretation of Philip Roth's masterpiece, *American Pastoral* (1997). The novel is a retrospective analysis of the broken American Dream, here incarnated by Seymour Levov, a successful American Jew born in Newark in the late 1920s and known as the Swede for his fair complexion. Philip Roth's *alter-ego*, Nathan Zuckerman, is the perplexed observer and the narrator of Seymour's epopee. As a boy, the narrator, he himself a Jew and a classmate of the Swede's younger brother, has admired Seymour for his ability in all sports, chiefly baseball. Seymour has renounced his career as a sports-hero in order to take over his father's glove factory, thus successfully perpetuating his family's business. When both are late in their lives, the Swede asks Nathan to meet, so that the latter may help him write a memory of his dead father. When having dinner together, the portrait Seymour gives of himself is that of an extremely self-content, unquestioning, successful American. He is still a handsome man, in spite of his age, thus the narrator may recognize the hero of his youth, yet a sense of malaise takes over Nathan as the dinner proceeds:

> The Swede, some six or seven years my senior, was close to seventy, and yet he was no less splendid-looking for the crevices at the corners of his eyes and, beneath the promontory of cheekbones, a little more hollowing out than classic standards of ruggedness required. I chalked up the gauntness to a regimen of serious jogging or tennis, until near the end of the meal I found out that he'd had prostate surgery during the winter and was only beginning to regain the weight he'd lost. I don't know if it was learning that he'd suffered an affliction or his confessing to one that most surprised me. I even wondered if it might not be his recent experience of the surgery and its after-effects that was feeding my sense of someone who was not mentally sound.
>
> (Roth, 1997, p. 22)

What surprises the narrator is the self-content superficiality of Seymour's presentation of himself and his biography: a successful career, three boys from his second marriage, all of them complying with the American model of sound rectitude, he expressing only platitudes about contemporary America and showing no perceivable critical sense whatsoever:

> I was impressed, as the meal wore on, by how assured he seemed of everything commonplace he said, and how everything he said was suffused by his good nature. I kept waiting for him to lay bare something more than this pointed unobjectionableness, but all that rose to the surface was more surface. What he has instead of a being, I thought, is blandness – the guy's radiant with it. He has devised for himself an incognito, and the incognito has become him.
>
> (ibid.)

Due to this radical hyper-conformism, the doubt emerges gradually both in the narrator and in the reader that the Swede may be not completely sane:

> Several times during the meal I didn't think I was going to make it, didn't think I'd get to dessert if he was going to keep praising his family and praising his family […] until I began to wonder if it wasn't that he was incognito but that he was mad.
>
> (ibid.)

Seymour's hyper-normal demeanour during the dinner with Nathan is an unsuccessful attempt to avoid losing face (Goffman, 1959). As the novel proceeds, we will in fact apprehend that the self-content image of his self is just a mask behind which the Swede tries to conceal his actual despair. Surface acting (Hochschild, 1983a, p. 33) is what the Swede is performing, that is a kind of behaviour in which a social actor dissimulates emotions (in Seymour's case satisfaction and self-content), without attempting to feel them. The dissimulation is so extreme that it appears not credible (as Roth writes, "all that rose to the surface was more surface"). Nathan has the impression that Seymour has managed to control his reactions to the world so carefully that the mask has replaced the self, having eventually become what qualifies Seymour as a whole (once again a brief quotation: "He has devised for himself an incognito, and the incognito has become him"). In other words, Seymour's outer representation is a mock-reduction of the complexity of the social actor, one with which a social theorist might be content but not a novelist. And indeed, *American Pastoral* may be understood as a quest for Seymour's lost (or concealed) complex identity. The reader is induced to overcome his first impression, transforming the *homunculus* of the Swede's self-portrait into Seymour Levov, the proper literary character of a contemporary American tragedy.

The exterior representation which people seem to have of the Swede, supported by his social demeanour and surface acting, reminds one of Talcott Parsons' conception of the integration between the individual and the social system. The similitude is hardly conceivable as either conscious or accidental, in the sense that Philip Roth was probably able to translate into literary terms a conception of conformity and compliance with shared social norms and values which, during the 1950s and the 1960s, found an appropriate sociological representation in the sophisticated (and at places naïve) sociological approach known as structural-functionalism.

In Parsons' view, on the micro-level, the integration of the social system is guaranteed in so far as the individual actors transform the requirements of system integration into motives guiding their action. Thus, action is regarded as an element potentially fostering or menacing social order. The question of order is particularly difficult to solve if one regards differentiation (hence a typical feature of modern society) and integration as opposed poles. Within such a perspective, it is plausible to ask: how is it possible to keep the social system integrated if contemporary society is growing increasingly more complex and differentiated? Differentiation implies a collateral process of decomposition, of lack of order, of loss of former balance (Schimank, 1999, p. 49). According to Parsons, at the system level, a new balance is guaranteed by the development of specific social systems, each having a specific integrative function. The AGIL model, applied to society as a system, gives to each social sub-system a unique and indispensable function (Adaptation for economics; Goals attainment for the polity; Integration and social control for law and the societal community; Latency for family, socialization, religion) (Parsons and Smelser, 1956). On the individual scale, differentiation produces a plurality of social roles, hence different functions and social stratification.

In principle, the individual actor has to act in favour of system integration, regardless of the fact that, by acting according to shared values and norms, he may perpetuate his low location in the system of stratification, i.e. social inequalities

According to Parsons, the inclusion of every citizen in the social system and the possibility of social upgrading, guaranteed to all in modern societies, are reason enough for individual actors to accept the system of actual inequalities. By introducing the pattern variables, intended as models of action orienting social roles, Parsons proposed a conception of modernity as characterized by acquired skills, as opposed to ascribed qualities. In what Parsons calls the *universalistic model of realization*, the individual may accept the logic of social differences since they are no longer based on the old social distinctions of ranks and birth. One is what he/she becomes thanks to the professional role and the realization of individual tasks, within a functional differentiation of work, whose primary basis " [...] is the imperative of free mobility within the occupational system" (Parsons 1951, p. 187). Thus, "stratification in terms of an open class system seems to be inherent in [modern] society" (ibid., p. 188). If the structure of society is open, characterized by a system of inequalities whose main character is the rationality linked to individual realization, the integrative processes may no longer be based on the particularistic values of small communities. Solidarity is by now an affective tie to the nation as a whole, to be understood as the widest social community.

In the exterior presentation of his self, the Swede is the perfect embodiment of the universalistic model of realization: his father has been able to make his way due to his ability as a glove manufacturer. The Swede has kept and enlarged his father's activity, has married Dawn, a *shiksa*, that is a Catholic girl of Irish origins and a former Miss New Jersey, has moved from Newark to an elegant suburban area, living now in an ancient stone house. He is included within the American societal community, since he has interiorized shared values and has conformed his actions to what is collectively valued as normal and right. His conformism applies not only to action but also to the display of emotions in action. He is able to manage his emotions and feeling, spontaneously avoiding what has been effectively called emotional deviance (Thois, 1990).

Seymour's life not only conforms to shared norms, it is also committed to the realization of shared values. Commitment, as Parsons (1991) writes in a posthumously published working paper on the American value system, is the individual, motivational, component of value:

> From the point of view of the units of a system, hence at some level of the motivation of individuals, values imply what may be called commitment. This it is which relates the normative aspect of expectations to the interplay of performances and sanctions. A set of values are "conceptions of the desirable" to the implementation of which, within limits of objective possibility, the relevant unit of an action system, or the system itself, may be regarded as committed. This aspect of the problem defines the dimension of "conformity and deviance" in the structure of action systems.
>
> (ibid., p. 40)

The level of commitment is, as it were, an indicator of the level of conformity in social action. Seymour Levov is strongly committed, hence his behaviour conforms to the set of normative expectations which makes up the coeval formal and informal normative code. Commitment to the values of the American societal community is particularly evident in Seymour's heroic decision to join the Marines, no matter if the war ends before he may leave for the front:

> The day after graduating Weequahic in June '45, the Swede had joined the Marine Corps, eager to be in on the fighting that ended the war. It was rumored that his parents were beside themselves and did everything to talk him out of the marines and get him into the navy. Even if he surmounted the notorious Marine Corps anti-Semitism, did he imagine himself surviving the invasion of Japan? But the Swede would not be dissuaded from meeting the manly, patriotic challenge – secretly set for himself just after Pearl Harbor – of going off to fight as one of the toughest of the tough should the country still be at war when he graduated high school.
>
> (Roth, 1997, p. 14)

Seymour's commitment to the nation is mediated by his role as a citizen, that is the individual component of nationality. As a citizen, he is ready to put his life at risk, hence he deserves inclusion and protection, regardless of his ethnicity. The compatibility of Seymour's outer personality with Parsons' conception of social inclusion is striking: since Parsons transfers solidarity from particularistic social settings (community, ethnic groups, etc.) to the nation, he may conceive the individual not in connection to his (or her) ascribed social characteristics, or his original social group, but as a citizen. The concept of the nation is connected to the idea of citizenship, to be understood as the new basis for social inclusion, regardless of ascribed qualities, and able to define "belonging in universalistic terms" (Parsons 1966, p. 188).

Citizenship and the values which it fosters become the ideological tie guaranteeing integration of social actors with different ethnic, cultural and religious origins, who hold different social statuses and play different social roles. The inclusiveness of the process is perceived as a necessity of modern society: indeed, according to Parsons, modern society is too complex as to imagine a unitary, common set of shared values as the premise for social integration. Modern society, and American society in particular, is the output of the intertwining of different ethnic groups, with particularistic cultural values, languages, religious practices, etc. Nonetheless, the nation-state is able to produce social inclusion and integration, provided that society furnishes its members a common cultural denominator (Parsons talks of a societal community, so connecting two terms – society and community – which since Tönnies had been understood as dichotomous) according to which they may feel part of a common social context, regardless of ethnic and cultural differences. Actually, the problem Parsons attempts to solve is connected both with the increased pluralisms of values and cultures which modernity brings about and with the specific structure of the American nation. Most

European national states emerged from historical processes by which, neglecting cultural differences, one could imagine an ethnic coherent substratum as the ideological basis of citizenship and the constitution of a unitary state. In the USA, differences cannot be simply elided or denied: they are culturally and socially too evident. Thus, in order to foster the inclusiveness of the nation, one has to select an artificial common set of values (a community within a pluralistic society) so as to guarantee all citizens (including Catholics, Jews, Black Americans) political and social inclusion.

Seymour Levov has personally experienced the passage from belonging to a narrow, culturally uniform community to the possibility of belonging to a wider societal community. National values represent for him not only a cultural, but also an affective tie, since they have been interiorized as a relevant aspect of his personal identity:

> All the pleasures of his younger years were American pleasures, all that success and happiness had been American [...] The loneliness he would feel as a man without all his American feelings. The longing he would feel if he had to live in another country. Yes, everything that gave meaning to his accomplishments had been American. Everything he loved was here.
>
> (Roth, 1997, p. 213)

He had married a Catholic girl of Irish origins, thus contrasting the narrow, ethnically defined will of his father – according to which he should have married a Jewish girl – in favour of the superior values of equality and integration:

> What was impractical and ill-advised to his father was an act of bravery to him. Next to marrying Dawn Dwyer, buying that house and the hundred acres and moving out to Old Rimrock was the most daring thing he had ever done. What was Mars to his father was America to him – he was settling Revolutionary New Jersey as if for the first time. Out in Old Rimrock, all of America lay at their door. That was an idea he loved. Jewish resentment, Irish resentment – the hell with it.
>
> (Roth, 1997, p. 310)

These values were able to convert the particularism of ethical and cultural differences into minor distinction, which could no longer prevent social relationships among members of different groups. When he moves with his family to Rimrock, a white Anglo-Saxon suburb, he has to overcome his wife's resistance, motivated by her fear of being excluded on the basis of her ethnicity and Catholic faith. In his naïve social optimism, Seymour is the fictional embodiment of Parsons' conception of inclusion:

> If she could marry a Jew, she could surely be a friendly neighbor to a Protestant – sure as hell could if her husband could. The Protestants are just another denomination. Maybe they were rare where she grew up – they were

rare where he grew up too – but they happen not to be rare in America. Let's face it, they are America. But if you do not assert the superiority of the Catholic way the way your mother does, and I do not assert the superiority of the Jewish way the way my father does, I'm sure we'll find plenty of people out here who won't assert the superiority of the Protestant way the way their fathers and mothers did. Nobody dominates anybody anymore […] [P]eople can live in harmony, all sorts of people side by side no matter what their origins. This is a new generation and there is no need for that resentment stuff from anybody, them or us.

(ibid., p. 311)

What is evident in the theoretical model proposed by Parsons (synthesized here and made less abstract by making reference to Philip Roth's masterpiece) is the interconnection of individual action and collective tasks within a national state able to guarantee integration through social inclusion and the sharing of a set of common values. Parsons' theoretical description works as a plausible representation of industrial post-war modernity, in so far as it presupposes an alliance between Fordism as a production mode, the state as an effective way to produce and implement political decisions and the individual actor, willing to manifest his loyalty to the values of national belonging, formal equality and merit in exchange for the security of social inclusion (Harvey, 1990). Actually, it is the state as an organization of the political system, which in solid modernity promoted and fostered inclusion (Stichweh, 1998), by preserving substantial differences as functional to system integration. The social system needs social differentiation (hence inequalities) in order to work properly. Yet, since equality is a basic philosophical, political and juridical principle of modern democratic societies, one needs to find a functional equivalent to equality, so as to justify the persistence of actual social differences. Equal opportunity and merit are plausible substitutes, which may legitimate social differences, especially in periods of rapid economic growth, when everybody may take advantage of the increasing chances. It is the case of the post-war Newark Jewish neighbourhood as described by Roth, where the future is a time of great expectations:

Despite the undercurrent of anxiety a sense communicated daily that hardship was a persistent menace that only persistent diligence could hope to keep at bay; despite a generalized mistrust of the Gentile world; despite the fear of being battered that clung to many families because of the Depression – ours was not a neighborhood steeped in darkness. The place was bright with industriousness. There was a big belief in life and we were steered relentlessly in the direction of success: a better existence was going to be ours. The goal was to have goals, the aim to have aims. […] A whole community perpetually imploring us not to be immoderate and screw up, imploring us to grasp opportunity, exploit our advantages, remember what matters.

(Roth, 1997, p. 40)

Social stratification is, as it were, the by-product of an ascendant process, by which those who deserve it, may climb. In Parsonsian terms, stratification may not be eliminated. Yet, Parsons distinguishes himself from the notorious presentation of social inequality by Davis and Moore (1945) since he is convinced that the sole social function of inequality (a fair distribution of wealth, prestige and power related to the relevance of the roles one plays in society) is by itself unable to legitimate social differences. Inequalities must be connected to some sort of moral evaluation (merit in particular) in order to be socially plausible. Social stratification is regarded by Parsons "as the differential ranks of the human individual who compose a given social system and their treatment as superior or inferior relative to one another in certain socially important respects" (Parsons, 1940, p. 841).

This aspect is relevant for a system-oriented conception of social action: in the ordered, rational world which Parsons describes theoretically and in which the Swede lives fictionally, individuals are morally bound to act according to their ranking, which implies that a well-integrated personality, by complying with values and tasks set by the social system, is the indispensable premise of social order (Parsons, 1970, Chapter 4, *passim*). The integrative aspect of personality furnishes the social system a tame actor, who is likely to accept the logic of social differences, hence the differentiated possibility, according to one's ranking, to accede to socially valuable rewards (wealth, power and so on). As Parsons states, institutionalized commitment has to be converted into internalized motives for conforming social behaviour.

> Looked at in social system terms, the level of commitment is what I have often referred to as "institutionalization"; the cognate conception in personality terms is "internalization". The relation between the two is the primary focus of the problem of integration of social systems.
>
> (Parsons, 1991, p. 40)

If all works properly, the social actions of those who have different locations in the system of social stratification are likely to integrate due to the individual acceptance of roles and social differences. In Parsons' words:

> Through the differentiation of roles there is a differentiation of goals which are morally approved for different individuals. But, so as society is morally and hence institutionally integrated, they are all governed by the same generalized pattern.
>
> (Parsons, 1940, p. 846)

Thus, according to Parsons, stratification has a relevant function in defining what each social actor is allowed or forbidden. And in fact, "[a]ction in a social system should, to a large extent, be oriented to the scale of stratification" (ibid., p. 847). A moral collocation of the individuals in the structure of stratification has not only to do with the functional acceptance of one's role, it has to do also with the hedonistic pleasure deriving from the compliance with the social expectations connected to the role.

> The normal actor – Parsons writes – is, to a degree, an integrated personality. In general, the things he values morally are also the things he "desires" as sources of hedonic satisfaction or objects of his affection. To be sure, there are, concretely, often serious conflicts in this respect, but they must be regarded as instances of "deviation" from the integrated type.
>
> (ibid., p. 845)

The Swede is the prototype of Parsons' integrated personality. He accepts his privileged role in the system of stratification, as he perceives it as the deserved output of his achievements, hence of merit in a society constructed as an open system. His self-content as an American, an entrepreneur, a husband, a father derives from the hedonistic pleasure to contemplate the substantial fairness of the social system. In this phase of his fictional life, Seymour needs no effort to conform his external behaviour to his emotional states. He may easily manage to control his emotions, so that they appear to him and his fellow people as adequate to social normative standards and expectations. What Arlie Hochshild (1983a) calls deep acting (the successful effort to conform inner emotions to what is socially acceptable in the specific social circumstance) is unnecessary at this stage of Seymour's life: the Swede is in fact always, apparently effortlessly, emotionally and socially adequate.

Here follows how Seymour's brother describes the attachment of the Swede to his country and its values. Seymour overlaps with his country, living in it as "inside his own skin":

> Got to be a United States Marine. Got to wear the emblem with the anchor and the globe. "No pitcher in there, Ee-oh, poke it outta here, Ee-oh—" Got to be Ee-oh to guys from Maine, New Hampshire, Louisiana, Virginia, Mississippi, Ohio – guys without an education from all over America calling me Ee-oh and nothing more. Just plain Ee-oh to them. Loved that. Discharged June 2, 1947. Got to marry a beautiful girl named Dwyer. Got to run a business my father built, a man whose own father couldn't speak English. Got to live in the prettiest spot in the world [...] [H]e lived in America the way he lived inside his own skin.
>
> (Roth, 1997, p. 213)

Yet the balance between what the system requires and what the individuals are ready to renounce is not stable. The system may show evidence of its crises once stratification is perceived as unfair. In this case, different values and diverse conceptions of the world may confront and clash, without coming to a compromise within the national societal community. Poverty, labour exploitation, unfair distribution of wealth are not part of the morally constructed equilibrium of the Swede's world. Yet they abruptly enter his world in the violent confrontation with his teenager daughter. Here is a passage of conversation *#1 about New York*, where Seymour asks his daughter Meredith with whom she has been in the metropolis:

"Who are these people? How old are they? What do they do for a living? Are they students?" "Why do you want to know?" "Because I'd like to know what you're doing. You're alone in New York on Saturdays. Not everyone's parents would allow a sixteen-year-old girl to go that far." "I go in... I, you know, there are people and dogs and streets ..." "You come home with all this Communist material. You come home with all these books and pamphlets and magazines." "I'm trying to learn. You taught me to learn, didn't you? Not just to study, but to learn. C-c-c-communist ..." "It is Communist. It says on the page that it's Communist." "C-c-c-communists have ideas that aren't always about C-commu-nism." "For instance." "About poverty. About war. About injustice".

(ibid., p. 104)

When the revolutionary Patricia Cohen (the only link Seymour has with his daughter, by now at large) first meets him, she tells him her own narrative about social differences and exploitation. Patricia's narrative is incompatible with the Swede's values and personal experiences; thus he replies with the story of Vicki, the black forelady in his glove factory in Newark, an example of loyalty to her role and of intergenerational upward social mobility, hence a clear instance, according to Seymour, that the system works after all:

Obediently he listens. She tells him that imperialism is a weapon used by wealthy whites to pay black workers less for their work, and that's when he seizes the opportunity to tell her about the black forelady, Vicky, thirty years with Newark Maid, a tiny woman of impressive wit, stamina, and honesty, with twin sons, Newark Rutgers graduates, Donny and Blaine, both of them now in medical school. He tells her how Vicky alone stayed with him in the building, round the clock, during the '67 riots. On the radio, the mayor's office was advising everyone to get out of the city immediately, but he had stayed, because he thought that by being there he could perhaps protect the building from the vandals and also for the reason that people stay when a hurricane hits, because they cannot leave behind the things they cherish. For something like that reason, Vicky stayed.

(ibid., p. 161)

Regardless of rapid and violent social changes, which are transforming Newark and the USA, the Swede may make reference to the loyalty to the values he and Vicki still share, no matter how different their ranking is in the structure of stratification. This is Seymour's desperate effort to present his own view of modernity, with its beauty and rationale, to a sceptical Patricia Cohen, who vehemently proposes her own alternative portrayal. The narrative probably sounds unrealistic to Seymour himself, an untimely, ultimate, attempt to revive his American pastoral (ibid., p. 121 ff.). Vicki and Seymour are thus presented as examples of integrated personalities (one would dare say in Parsonsian terms), people who are likely to adapt to one's collocation in the social ranking and accept the consequences, as well as the opportunities, deriving from complying with the expectancies of their social position. The Swede (and in her specific way Vicki) act according to the values they have interiorized during their socialization. Both are causal instances of the idea, so typical of Parsons' theory, according to which system integration is possible only provided that the actor is prone to convert system needs into motivation for individual social action. In this superficial representation, the Swede may remind a social scientist of what Harold Garfinkel called the "cultural dope" (Garfinkel, 1964), hopelessly addicted to social values and norms, cognitively monitoring the consistency of his action with the requirements of the cultural system. Yet Seymour is more than that: the reader will learn that something deeper than norms and values drives his action and that his emotional life does not overlap with his hedonistic attachment to the values of the American societal community.

4 Action and the mask of reasonableness

When Merry grows up into a complex and rebellious adolescent, Seymour's world begins losing its integrity. He has now to negotiate, since his representation of the world is at odds with his daughter's and with present-day social changes. Here the space opens up for deep acting, that is a kind of acting where "display is a natural result of working on feeling; the actor [...] expresses spontaneously, as the Russian director Constantin Stanislavski urged, a real feeling that has been self-induced" (Hochschild, 1983a, p. 35). More than expressing a self-induced feeling, Seymour is compelled to conceal from himself and others his disappointment and rage, constantly reproducing the social image of himself as calm, patient and rational. He has to adjust his expectations about his daughter, who appears not to have developed in the perfected portrayal of himself he had wrongly anticipated. His intelligent daughter begins to stutter, has eating disorders and becomes eventually the left-wing advocate of anti-capitalism and anti-Americanism, that is the opponent of all Seymour worships as sacred. The conflict is much about emotional rules and emotional display. The adolescent Merry is unrecognizable to her parents because she no longer complies with the idea they have of the proper behaviour of a middle-class, educated girl. Dawn may be emotionally correct when crying in despair at the change of her daughter, whereas the Swede has to reproduce the social model by which a man has to be rational and to abide by the social image he has of himself. He has thus to look and at the same time to be calm. In his deep acting, he has in fact to convince not only his wife, but also himself that all will eventually settle down:

> Night after night now Dawn went to bed in tears. "What is she? What is this?" she asked the Swede. "If someone simply defies your authority, what can you do? Seymour, I'm totally puzzled. How did this happen?" "It

happens," he told her. "She's a kid with a strong will. With an idea. With a cause." "Where did this come from? It's inexplicable. Am I a bad mother? Is that it?" "You are a good mother. You are a wonderful mother. That is not it." "I don't know why she's turned against me like this. I don't have any sense of what I did to her or even what she perceives I did to her. I don't know what's happened. Who is she? Where did she come from? I cannot control her. I cannot recognize her. I thought she was smart. She's not smart at all. She's become stupid, Seymour; she gets more and more stupid each time we talk." "No, it's just a very crude kind of aggression. It's not very well worked out. But she is still smart. She's very smart. This is what teen-agers are like. There are these very turbulent sorts of changes. It has nothing to do with you or me.

(Roth, 1997, p. 101)

In his calm, reassuring attitude, Seymour demonstrate the complex process by which emotions are socially constructed and made individually and socially plausible. In his confrontation with the unexpected, in his contrast with imper-fection, Seymour is not calm, rational, relaxed. He only tries to be so. In Arlie Hochschild's words:

We often say that we try to feel. But how can we do this? Feelings, I suggest, are not stored "inside" us, and they are not independent of acts of manage-ment. Both the act of "getting in touch with" feeling and the act of "trying to" feel may become part of the process that makes the thing we get in touch with, or the thing we manage, into a feeling or emotion. In managing feeling, we contribute to the creation of it.

(Hochschild, 1983a, pp. 17–18)

In contrast with her father, Merry is vindicating her freedom, but she is also stigmatizing Seymour's constructed calm. In her enraged attack against family constraints, Seymour becomes Mr. Cool, the one who is still rationally anticipat-ing possible futures for his daughter and his family. He is, in Merry's words: "[a]lways planning. Always trying to figure out the most reasonable course" (ibid., pp. 111–112). The contrast is not only about behaviours and ideas. The contrast is chiefly about emotions and emotional management. Here follows conversation #44 about New York:

"I'm not driving you to the train. You're not leaving the house." "What are you going to do? B-barricade me in? How you going to stop me? You going to tie me to my high chair? Is that how you treat your daughter? I can't b-b-believe my own father would threaten me with physical force." "I'm not threatening you with physical force." "Then how are you going to keep me in the house? I'm not just one, of Mom's dumb c-c-c-c-cows! I'm not going to live here forever and ever and ever. Mr. C-cool, Calm, and Collected. What is it that you're so afraid of? What is it you're so afraid of people for? Haven't you ever heard that New York is one of the world's great cultural centers? People come from the whole world to experience New York."

(ibid., pp. 108–109)

The reader experiences the contrast in the form of an everyday paradox, one with which most parents of teen children are acquainted: the calm demeanour of Seymour causes Merry's rage:

> Conversations #24, 25, and 26 about New York. "I can't have these conversations, Daddy. I won't! I refuse to! Who talks to their parents like this!" "If you are underage and you go away for the day and don't come home at night, then you damn well talk to your parents like this." "B-b-but you drive me c-c-c-crazy, this kind of sensible parent, trying to be understanding! I don't want to be understood – I want to be f-f-f-free!" "Would you like it better if I were a senseless parent trying not to understand you?" "I would! I think I would! Why don't you fucking t-t-try it for a change and let me fucking see!".

(ibid., p. 106)

As long as Merry is just a problematic adolescent, Seymour is condemned to perceive himself and consequently act as calm, patient, rational. His whole world is at stake and he finds no other way out but reproducing his reassuring attitude:

> And so, hopeless as it seemed, he talked, he listened, he was reasonable; endless as the struggle seemed, he remained patient, and whenever he saw her going too far he drew the line. No matter how much it might openly enrage her to answer him, no matter how sarcastic and caustic and elusive and dishonest her answers might be, he continued to question her about her political activities, about her after-school whereabouts, about her new friends; with a gentle persistence that infuriated her, he asked about her Saturday trips into New York.

(ibid., p. 103)

In the conflict between Seymour and Merry two worlds clash: the Swede's pastoral America, with its values of self-realization and inclusion, and Meredith's, the emotional embodiment of the removed contradictions and inequalities of the American life. Seymour is "just a liberal sweetheart of a father. The philosopher-king of ordinary life. Brought her up with all the modern ideas of being rational with your children. Everything permissible, everything forgivable, and she hated it" (Roth, 1997, p. 69). Hate, rage, contempt are on the contrary the specific emotions connoting the stuttering, fat, protesting Merry. Here is a long passage from the novel:

> "You f-f-fucking madman! You heartless mi-mi-mi-miserable m-monster!" she snarled at Lyndon Johnson whenever his face appeared on the seven

o'clock news. Into the televised face of Humphrey, the vice president, she cried, "You prick, sh-sh-shut your lying m-m-mouth, you c-c-coward, you f-f-f-f-filthy fucking collaborator!" When her father, as a member of the ad hoc group calling itself New Jersey Businessmen Against the War, went down to Washington with the steering committee to visit their senator, Merry refused his invitation to come along. "But," said the Swede who had never belonged to a political group before and would not have joined this one […] had he not hoped his conspicuous involvement might deflect a little of her anger away from him, "this is your chance to say what's on your mind to Senator Case. You can confront him directly. Isn't that what you want?" "Merry," said her petite mother to the large glowering girl, "you might be able to influence Senator Case—" "C-c-c-c-c-c-case!" erupted Merry and, to the astonishment of her parents, proceeded to spit on the tiled kitchen floor.

(ibid., p. 99)

Whereas Meredith's action is determined chiefly by negative aggressive emotions, and her mother's by despair and depression, the Swede is still trying to mend and repair. Reasonableness is all Seymour may propose as a solution to his pessimistic wife:

"All we can do, Dawn, is to continue to be reasonable and continue to be firm and not lose hope or patience, and the day will come when she will outgrow all this objecting to everything." "She doesn't want to outgrow it." "Now. Today. But there is tomorrow. There's a bond between us all and it's tremendous. As long as we don't let her go, as long as we keep talking, tomorrow will come. Of course she's maddening. She's unrecognizable to me, too. But if you don't allow her to exhaust your patience and if you keep talking to her and you don't give up on her, she will eventually become herself again."

(ibid., p. 103)

When the bomb breaks off, things change abruptly for Seymour too. Life seems to have lost its meaning, and reasonableness is now useless: "The Swede – Roth writes – as he had always known himself – well-meaning, well-behaved, well-ordered Seymour Levov – evaporated, leaving only self-examination in his place" (ibid., p. 92). Merry's stuttering, which had been his and his wife's chief preoccupation, becomes now the metaphor of the lost order:

It was all stuttering. In bed at night, he pictured the whole of his life as a stuttering mouth and a grimacing face – the whole of his life without cause or sense and completely bungled. He no longer had any conception of order. There was no order. None. He envisioned his life as a stutterer's thought, wildly out of his control.

(ibid.)

Tragedy and sufferings enter an otherwise self-satisfied life, in which obedience to the social rules and values had been wrongly conceived as being capable of reducing the risk of drama:

> How could he – Roth writes – with all his carefully calibrated goodness, have known that the stakes of living obediently were so high? Obedience is embraced to lower the stakes. A beautiful wife. A beautiful house [...] He was really living it out, his version of paradise. This is how successful people live. They're good citizens. They feel lucky. They feel grateful. God is smiling down on them. There are problems, they adjust. And then everything changes and it becomes impossible. Nothing is smiling down on anybody. And who can adjust then? Here is someone not set up for life's working out poorly, let alone for the impossible. But who is set up for the impossible that is going to happen? Who is set up for tragedy and the incomprehensibility of suffering? Nobody. The tragedy of the man not set up for tragedy – that is every man's tragedy.
>
> (ibid., p. 86)

Yet, the sentiment of the tragic is not separated in the Swede from the need to understand. A simple man, or what other people perceived as a simple man, hedonistically content in his position in society, converts into a self-reflexive, cogitative actor:

> Some people thought he was simple because all his life he was so kind. But Seymour was never that simple. Simple is never that simple. Still, the self-questioning did take some time to reach him. And if there's anything worse than self-questioning coming too early in life, it's self-questioning coming too late. His life was blown up by that bomb. The real victim of that bombing was him.
>
> (ibid., p. 68)

Seymour's life is from now on defined by the nostalgia for his lost child (and the lost pureness of his personal pastoral) as well as by a cognitive necessity to understand the reasons why imperfection abruptly entered his flawless biography. In the attempt to explain to himself his failure as a father, he recurrently connects the tragedy to a candid kiss between him and his daughter when Merry was eleven:

> The kiss bore no resemblance to anything serious, was not an imitation of anything, had never been repeated, had itself lasted five seconds... ten at most... but after the disaster, when he went obsessively searching for the origins of their suffering, it was that anomalous moment – when she was eleven and he was thirty-six and the two of them, all stirred up by the strong sea and the hot sun, were heading happily home alone from the beach – that he remembered.
>
> (ibid., p. 92)

Thus, a rational quest for motives, an emotional need for explanation, shame for a hypothetically broken emotional rule are all intermingled in Seymour's quest for meaning. In the Swede's normalized life, where there was no room for emotional deviance, the single episode of a rapid kiss becomes the fault that may explain the tragedy:

> [n]ever in his entire life, not as a son, a husband, a father, even as an employer, had he given way to anything so alien to the emotional rules by which he was governed, and later he wondered if this strange parental misstep was not the lapse from responsibility for the rest of his life.
>
> (ibid., pp. 91–92)

The emotional quest for his daughter and the cognitive quest for a meaning converge in Seymour's biography, showing how any gap between sentiment and cognition is only artificial. As social scientists have recently argued, "[s]ense-making is saturated with emotion and cognition in complex feedback loops and in equal measures" (Jensen and Pedersen, 2016, p. 101). Cognition and emotions are intermingled in Seymour's personal quest for sense: they are both ways of engagement with a world which is rapidly losing its consistency.

In the first stage of his socially ascending life, Seymour had no need to simulate sentiments, either to himself or to the others: his emotional and social world overlapped in fact with the consolidated American values and the American way of life. In the period of struggle with his daughter he had to learn the difficult art of deep acting: by reassuring himself and his relatives that all would eventually go right, he condemned himself to a self-induced reassuring calm. The bombing reduces his trust in the rationality of his world and himself and what is now left is the simulative make-believe of his surface acting. As opposed to deep acting, in surface acting feelings are not internally induced, they are just pretended. One does not need to deceive oneself before deceiving others. In fact, "[i]n surface acting we deceive others about what we really feel, but we do not deceive ourselves" (Hochshild, 1983a, p. 33). Seymour's tragedy is due to the fact that at once his titanic effort at self-deception does no longer work and he can now only dissimulate, in a life-long Goffmanian game of make-believe. A further passage from the novel is particularly meaningful. Since Merry had disappeared:

> all he'd been wanting was to weep or to hide; but because there was Dawn to nurse and a business to tend to and his parents to prop up, because everybody else was paralyzed by disbelief and shattered to the core, neither inclination had as yet eroded the protective front he provided the family and presented to the world.
>
> (ibid., p. 120)

But underneath the mask of simulation, lies Seymour's complexity, his being driven by the sense of a loss which impels him to search for his daughter and the nostalgia for a prefigured, by now unrealizable future.

5 Seymour Levov and the pain of surface acting

Like all great novels, *American Pastoral* is an open work (Eco, 1965), hence available for a plurality of interpretations. Yet, a plausible key is to read the novel as the clash of sentiments between the Swede and his daughter, Meredith. While the first loves America and what it represents in term of social mobility, well-being and prestige, in her attitude of *cupio dissolvi* Merry seems to hate all that her father holds as sacred. The Swede is an example of perfect assimilation: he "oversees a successful business, marries a Catholic former Miss New Jersey, fathers an attractive and gifted child, and owns a stunning country home built at the time of the American Revolution" (Parrish, 2000, pp. 86–87). Seymour has assumed the WASP model of life as his own, within a liberal perspective which should neither deny nor emphasize ethnic, cultural, religious differences. Yet dissolution (as opposed to integration) gradually emerges in his life, due to his adolescent daughter and her refusal of what, in the restricted vision of her father, has been removed from contemporary American society (inequality, injustice, exploitation, etc.). The stuttering Merry represents the insertion of imperfection and contradiction in the perfect world of Seymour Levov. He tries to mend Merry's everyday splits with a liberal attitude to dialogue. But when Merry set off a bomb at the local post office, kills an incidental bystander and goes into hiding, Seymour's American dream of integration crumbles:

> she went out one day and blew up the post office, destroying right along with it Dr. Fred Conlon and the village's general store, a small wooden building with a community bulletin board out front and a single old Sunoco pump and the metal pole on which Russ Hamlin – who, with his wife, owned the store and ran the post office – had raised the American flag every morning since Warren Gamaliel Harding was president of the United States.
>
> (Roth, 1997, p. 113)

From this moment on, the solid self-identity which the Swede has tried to construct, by complying with the norms and values of the American societal community, falls apart: Seymour's action may appear rational, adequate to the social expectations connected to his roles. He still complies with emotional norms, being able to exteriorly control his demeanour. But his emotional conformity is no longer the spontaneous, effortless adjustment to societal values and norms. Being quiet and reasonable in a world which has lost its meaningfulness is not easy for Seymour: surface acting and dissimulation are now necessary.

Seymour learns at his expense that the solid identity he had constructed through a life-long exercise is nothing more than social pretension: he learns, as it were, to cope not only with the loss of his daughter but also with the demise of his stable, solid, modern identity (Parrish, 2000, p. 98). According to Heinz-Günter Vester (1999), we live in a post-emotional culture. This does not entail that emotions are eliminated from the social scene. On the contrary, emotions persist, but, whereas in former times they were strongly related to a well-defined emotional culture, post-modern emotions are situated in what Vester calls a post-emotional culture, devoid of an adequate set of symbols and norms able to give social sense to individual or collective emotionality. In post-emotional culture the individual is at a loss, unable to handle emotions both in their social and in their interior dimensions (Vester, 1999, p. 20). As long as the system of values and expectancies works, Seymour is able to cope with his emotionality. But as the system crumbles, he loses his bearings. As Roth writes: "[t]he old system that made order doesn't work anymore. All that was left was now his fear and astonishment, but now concealed by nothing" (Roth, 1997, p. 422).

If the difference between order and disorder vanishes, it is ever more difficult to find one's bearings, especially when it comes to the management of one's emotions. In a disordered world, emotions are, as it were, indifferent: they are not authentic or inauthentic, correct or incorrect (Vester, 1999, p. 25). Seymour's problem is now how to manage his own complex emotionality, neither reducible to the hedonistic compliance to shared social values, nor concealable behind well-established feeling rules. He has to learn how to cope with the unpredictable, the unthinkable, the deviant: "What should be did not exist. Deviancy prevailed. You can't stop it. Improbably, what was not supposed to happen had happened and what was supposed to happen had not happened" (Roth, 1997, pp. 441–442). Thus, Seymour's story converts into a narrative about emotions in a post-emotional culture, that is about having feelings without possessing a code of plausible meanings or a system of shared norms which may give sense to one's own feelings.

The sentiment of loss makes Seymour Levov aware of himself, of the platitude of his life and the uselessness of his constant efforts to conform. We are thus induced, as readers, to get to know another aspect of Seymour's apparently simple personality:

> A man whose discontents were barely known to himself, awakening in middle age to the horror of self-reflection. All that normalcy interrupted by murder. All the small problems any family expects to encounter exaggerated by something so impossible ever to reconcile.
>
> (ibid., p. 84)

Seymour's anguish is not caused only by his daughter's misdeeds. It is also connected to the loss of the expectations of an integrated life within the American societal community:

> The disruption of the anticipated American future that was simply to have unrolled out of the solid American past, out of each generation's getting smarter – smarter for knowing the inadequacies and limitations of the generations before – out of each new generation's breaking away from the parochialism a little further, out of the desire to go the limit in America with your rights, forming yourself as an ideal person who gets rid of the traditional Jewish habits and attitudes, who frees himself of the pre-America insecurities

and the old, constraining obsessions so as to live unapologetically as an equal among equals,

(ibid.)

The loss of Merry is physical, social and at the same time symbolical. It is the loss of trust in the idea of progress, that is the idea that the future represents a perfected image of the present. The idea that the process of integration would keep on, in an incremental mechanism such that the next generation would be the improved version of the previous. The loss of Meredith is unrecoverable because it reveals the contradictory character of Seymour's personal American dream.

> And then the loss of the daughter, the fourth American generation, a daughter on the run who was to have been the perfected image of himself as he had been the perfected image of his father, and his father the perfected image of his father's father ... the angry, rebarbative spitting-out daughter with no interest whatever in being the next successful Levov, flushing him out of hiding as if he were a fugitive – initiating the Swede into the displacement of another America entirely, the daughter and the decade blasting to smither-eens his particular form of Utopian thinking, the plague America infiltrating the Swede's castle and there infecting everyone.
>
> (ibid., pp. 85–86)

Parsons stressed that complying with the set of culturally shared norms and values could produce a sort of hedonistic pleasure, a sense of belonging and of appropri-ateness of what one has accomplished. The bomb and Meredith's escape put an end to the sense of hedonistic adequacy in Seymour's life. Emotions are no longer the agreeable output of self-gratification. They are now strongly connected to a loss of certainties and identity. And this radical change may be imputed to a single person, "[t]he daughter who transports him out of the longed-for American pas-toral and into everything that is its antithesis and its enemy, into the fury, the vio-lence, and the desperation of the counterpastoral – into the indigenous American berserk" (ibid.).

After his life has crumbled, a sort of repetition compulsion leads Seymour to reproduce the ideal which had been hopelessly broken: a new selfish wife, three kids, an apparently faultless life. The reader does not learn much about Seymour's second life. Nonetheless, he understands that it is partly a simulation, functioning only provided that the sense of inadequacy and the sentiment of loss are removed and suppressed from everyday activities and intercourses. It is a life of make-believe, of surface acting, of masking the feeling underneath the apparent normal-ity. Here follows Roth's acute remark:

> Never again will the Swede be content in the trusting old Swedian way that, for the sake of his second wife and their three boys – for the sake of their naive wholeness – he ruthlessly goes on pretending to be. Stoically he suppresses

his horror. He learns to live behind a mask. A lifetime experiment in endurance. A performance over a ruin. Swede Levov lives a double life.

(ibid., p. 80)

Yet the apparent suppression of feelings does not imply that they have been actually eliminated. When Nathan Zuckerman asks Seymour's younger brother Jerry if his brother had ever told him how horrible it was, Jerry replies telling the story of the only circumstance in which the Swede poured out his anguish. All the family is eating together in Florida: Seymour's new family, Jerry's family and the grandparents: "We all went to this stone-crab place. Twelve of us for dinner. Lots of noise, the kids all showing off and laughing. Seymour loved it. The whole handsome family there, life just the way it's supposed to be" (ibid., p. 70). But at the end of dinner, Seymour disappears. Jerry finds him in his car, in tears.

I'd never seen him like that. My brother the rock. He said, 'I miss my daughter.' I said, 'Where is she?' I knew he always knew where she was. He'd been going to see her in hiding for years. I believe he saw her frequently. He said, 'She's dead, Jerry' I didn't believe him at first. It was to throw me off the track, I thought. I thought he must have just seen her somewhere. I thought, He's still going to wherever she is and treating this killer like his own child – this killer who is now in her forties while everybody she killed is still killed. But then he threw his arms around me and he just let go, and I thought, Is it true, the family's fucking monster's really dead?

(ibid., p. 71)

Eventually emotions break out: they become physical, a perceivable part of Seymour's behaviour. And we apprehend, from the peculiar, cynical perspective of Seymour's brother that the loss of Merry, the quest for Merry, the puzzle of finding her somewhere in Newark, the pity for Merry and the nostalgia for the life Seymour has not been able to live have always been conspicuous (although hidden) components of the Swede's emotional biography.

6 The dependable father, and the daughter who is chaos itself

In the construction of its methodological *homunculus*, the theory of action gives relevance to cognition rather than emotions. Literature, on its turn, shows how difficult it is to seclude the emotional from the rational aspects of individual action. The emergence of the sociology of emotions has given the social sciences a greater awareness of the deep interconnection among action, cognition and emotions. Emotions are understood as a constitutive component of the way the social actor locates himself in the world, focuses his attention on selected aspects of reality, including his fellow people and determines the content and direction of social interaction (Boiger and Mesquita, 2012, p. 222). Although it would be methodologically plausible (think of Weber's ideal types) to neatly separate the emotional component of individual behaviour from its cognitive or strategic features, such separation works only if it is consciously understood as a fictional construct. Yet, the exclusion of emotions from our model of the social actor by necessity excludes emotions as an object of inquiry and reveals itself inadequate from a substantive and analytical point of view. Emotions and cognition are cognate, in the sense that we experience the world through emotions and then we understand it by making recourse to our rationality. Arlie Hochshild writes of emotions as cues, through which we unveil the world and, by stigmatizing the Western divide between emotions and rationality, she ironically adds:

> The word objective, according to the Random House Dictionary, means "free from personal feelings." Yet ironically, we need feeling in order to reflect on the external or "objective" world. Taking feelings into account as clues and then correcting for them may be our best shot at objectivity.
>
> (Hochshild, 1983a, p. 31)

The theoretical reduction of action to some form of cognitive interpretation of the environment, though ill-posed, may depend on the traditional "division of labour" among sociology, psychology and biology. Emotions have been conceived as an expression of one's genetic make-up or psychological drives, both considered as inappropriate for sociological analysis. On the contrary, upon a more accurate scrutiny, emotions are part of our daily experience and are a relevant, ineludible, component of social interaction. They are not to be isolated in some psychological or biological process, since they are characterized by what phenomenologists call about-ness, that is the fact that emotions are:

> intentionally oriented towards events or objects in the world, which are appraised as attractive or unattractive, good or bad, and so forth. In this view, they are not to be seen as inner 'mental states' alone but rather as part of active striving and world-orientation.
>
> (Jensen and Pedersen, 2016, p. 85)

Emotions are therefore experienced as a central feature of our perception of the social world, being inextricably intermingled with volition and cognition. Once the idea emerges of a strong interconnection between action, cognition and emotions, one may conceive the cognitive and the emotional sphere "as part of our whole-bodied behaviour" (ibid.). Emotions are thus an integral component of action in so far as they are embodied, hence are inseparable both from the acting body and from the cogitative self. Furthermore, emotions are a relevant support for cognition, in the sense that it is through emotions that we experience facts and events as facts and events of a certain kind (Nussbaum, 2001). And indeed "a core quality of emotions lies in the way in which they saturate experiences with value. In and through emotions, we experience something as 'something' – fearful, exciting, boring, scary, attractive, or repulsive" (Jensen and Pedersen, 2016, p. 84).

In the process of reading, we learn that even Seymour's behaviour is emotionally linked to the world of social interaction. When the tragic manifests in his life, emotions become the unexpected which drives the Swede's action, at first in his contrast with his adolescent daughter, then in the nostalgic quest for Merry. At one point in the novel, Seymour receives an information about where Merry is. She is living in Newark, no longer the industrious city of the Swede's youth but a devastated place after the riots of the late 1960s. Merry has eventually become a Jain, a solitary member of an Indian sect whose adepts live an ascetic life. She lives on nothing. She eats only some vegetables out of respect for life. She wears a mask made up of a piece of stocking, so as to avoid killing any possible living being by breathing. She does not even wash, so as not to contaminate water. She is skinny, dirty, filthy. She is the unexpected, entering once again into Seymour's life. Yet, when the elegant, still handsome father and his unrecognizable daughter meet and recognize each other, these two utterly different human beings are irresistibly driven towards one another. Emotions are embodied and inescapable, and are the main elements drawing father and daughter towards one another. Here is Roth's masterful description of the meeting:

> Merry had seen him. How could she miss him? How could she have missed him even on a street where there was life and not death, where there was a throng of the striving and the harried and the driven and the decisive and not this malignant void? There was her handsome, utterly recognizable six-foot-three father, the handsomest father a girl could have. She raced across the street, this frightful creature, and like the carefree child he used to enjoy envisioning back when he was himself a carefree child – the girl running from her swing outside the stone house – she threw herself upon his chest, her arms encircling his neck. From beneath the veil she wore across the lower half of her face – obscuring her mouth and her chin, a sheer veil that was the ragged foot off an old nylon stocking – she said to the man she had come to detest, "Daddy! Daddy!" faultlessly, just like any other child, and looking like a person whose tragedy was that she'd never been anyone's child. They are crying intensely, the dependable father whose center is the source of all order, who could not overlook or sanction the smallest sign of chaos – for whom keeping chaos far at bay had been intuition's chosen path to certainty, the rigorous daily given of life – and the daughter who is chaos itself.
>
> (ibid., pp. 230–231)

In the scene as represented by Roth, differences are replaced by the need of bodily contact, of feeling one another's presence. Cognition, the need to understand, to state one's reasons or to recriminate are irrelevant now. What is relevant is the concrete emotional intentionality of their being-here-now.

7 Seymour Levov as the tragic hero of solid modernity

American Pastoral is, *inter alia*, a book on the liquefaction of solid modernity. Seymour Levov is the hero of the values Zygmunt Bauman (2000) ascribed to modern society in the second post-war period. National identity, biographical stability, welfare, inclusion, economic growth, all described in the novel as American values, are the main features of integrative processes which were still capable of connecting the individual social actor to his environment. As the novel proceeds, social stability crumbles, conflicts emerge as unavoidable aspects of a complex society and personal identities seems no longer able to hold the increasing contradictions of social roles. The Swede had lived in a world of open possibilities, where self-content was the chief emotional tone. Yet he is forced to apprehend that life may cut off his long-cherished expectations, and thus self-content is transformed into negative emotions, such as disillusion, fear, despair. Seymour's personal choice is to start anew, pretending that nothing has happened, thus disguising his personal tragedy under a reconstructed pretension of respectable normality:

> The Swede had got up off the ground and he'd done it – a second marriage, a second shot at a unified life controlled by good sense and the classic restraints, once again convention shaping everything, large and small, and serving as barrier against the improbabilities – a second shot at being the traditional devoted husband and father, pledging allegiance all over again to the standard rules and regulations that are the heart of family order. He had the talent for it, had what it took to avoid anything disjointed, anything special, anything improper, anything difficult to assess or understand.
>
> (Roth, 1997, p. 81)

Yet the Swede's talent for the ordinary is not enough. The pretended compliance with social values is only at the surface of Seymour's life. Underneath, lies the inescapable need to recover his lost daughter, and his lost life:

> And yet not even the Swede, blessed with all the attributes of a monumental ordinariness, [...] could go all the way and shed completely the frantic possessiveness, the paternal assertiveness, the obsessive love for the lost daughter, shed every trace of that girl and that past and shake off forever the hysteria of "my child." If only he could have just let her fade away. But not even the Swede was that great.
>
> (ibid.)

Yet, complying with the old rules and values is now only pretension. In this sense, in the last phase of his life, Seymour Levov is the incarnation of Goffman's social actor (Goffman, 1959). His reconstructed normality is the stage where he plays the role of the happy husband, the proud father, the average middle-class citizen. By adjusting his action to social standards, he controls his acts, not his emotions. His behaviour is just disenchanted surface acting (Hochshild, 1983a, p. 33). But concealing one's emotions has its cost. Seymour Levov is the hero of solid modernity and at the same time the demonstration that social action may not be understood properly once it has been deprived of its emotional component. The Swede is not the fictional *homunculus* of social theory. He is a literary character, whose complexity is in the tension between his pretended inaffectivity and the real intricacy of his emotional world. As a literary character, he may expose the contradiction of any reduction of life to reason (or to the reasonable) and that is what we, as social scientists, may learn from him. By understanding the inconsistency of social values, he learns the hard lesson of the lack of meaning, the meaninglessness of the whole, the artificiality of pretended happiness and the reality of his tragic nostalgia:

> He had learned the worst lesson that life can teach – that it makes no sense. And when that happens the happiness is never spontaneous again. It is artificial and, even then, bought at the price of an obstinate estrangement from oneself and one's history.
>
> (ibid.)

6   The emotional crowd

1 The crowd, literature and social theory

The topic of this chapter is collective behaviour, which will be specified by analyzing a single (perhaps the most elementary) social phenomenon which may
be qualified as such, that is the crowd. The crowd as a sociological topic will
be theoretically dealt with by making reference to two great 19th century novels, belonging to two different national and cultural traditions. The first is Émile
Zola's *Germinal* (1885), a novel written according to the rules set by its author
in his *The Experimental Novel* (1880), in which the French novelist conceives of
literary narrative as a form of objective, scientific knowledge of reality. The protest of the miners, ending up in a raging rally, is analyzed as an illustration of Le
Bon's theory of the psychology of crowd (1895). The second is one of the most
important novels in the history of Italian literature, namely Alessandro Manzoni's
I Promessi Sposi (also known in English as *The Betrothed*), first published in 1827
and in its definitive version in 1842. Manzoni devotes two central chapters of his
historical novel to the bread riot which took place in Milan in 1628. Manzoni's
complex presentation of the crowd will be used in order to test two 20th century theories of collective behaviour, namely Niel Smelser's added value theory
(1962) and Turner and Killian's emergent norm theory (1957). Both the novels
I have selected predate the theories they are summoned to explain. Nonetheless,
the question is, from my specific point of view, irrelevant, since my attempt is
not to demonstrate some possible mutual influences between social theory and
literature but to employ literary sources as a powerful tool for the understanding
of human and social action, within complex narratives and descriptions which are
available for a variety of analysis, including sociology. My attempt is to be understood as a sort of intellectual *divertissement*, showing the potentiality of literature
as a tool to illustrate theoretical conceptions, even in the case of classical works
which were written much earlier than the sociological material I try to illustrate.
I assume here as reference model Schutz' (1964) masterful use of *Don Quixote* as
to explain his theory of multiple realities.

Before turning to the work of Émile Zola and Alessandro Manzoni, I will try
to qualify collective behaviour, by briefly making reference to the available literature, so as to sketch problems and potentiality of the sociological analysis of

this relevant aspect of social life. In my sketch of collective behaviour, the topic of emotions and their relevance will be always the underlying question: collective behaviour has generally been conceived of by early social scientists as an emotionally driven behaviour. In the development of social thought, a trend may be detected towards a gradual bracketing of emotionality in the analysis of collective behaviour. Although more recent works (Jasper, 1998; Jasper, 2011; von Scheve and Ismer, 2013; Goodwin, Jasper and Poletta, 2001; Flan and King, 2005) show a renewed interest in emotions and feelings, the general tendency is one emphasizing the rational component of collective action (Miller, 2011; Borch, 2012; McPhail, 1991/2017). By describing what happens in the crowd, literary sources are, as it were, able to represent the complex phenomenon of behaving in collectives, both in relation to personal motives, collective pressure, conflict and cooperation, and this is reason enough to resort to narratives as a way to compensate the somewhat schematic representation of sociological speculation.

2 Negative affects, social contagion and the crowd

The first problem with collective behaviour is of a definitory kind. Collective behaviour is a general term by which social scientists define a large variety of different social phenomena, ranging from the imitative propensity typical of fashion to the much more structured and ideologically aware participation in social movement. What all these social phenomena have in common is that a plurality of individuals shares tendencies, action and feeling, often (but not necessarily) in a situation of co-presence. The first problem with the definition of collective behaviour has to do with its extreme generality: how can we put under the same theoretical category such different phenomena as the dancing mania affecting Europe from the 14th to the 17th century, delirious fans at a rock concert and a social movement vindicating specific rights? The second problem has to do with the tautological character of most of the available definitions: in order to specify the features of collective behaviour, current definitions often make reference to the causes which generate it. In such a way, social scientists anticipate in their definition the causes of the phenomenon which, on the contrary, should be empirically investigated (McPhail, 1991/2017, pp. 155–156). Another theoretically intriguing aspect is the conception of the single actors who contribute to the constitution of a collective unity. Sociologists are used to thinking of social phenomena from the collective rather than from the individual point of view. Indeed, in the case of collectives, the role of the individual tends to be delimited, as the single actor is conceived as cast adrift by social forces behind his control. This is particularly so in the case of crowds, which have often been described as a social space where individuality dissolves in favour of shared collective emotions, as if crowd phenomena were expression of a unitary collective mind. Indeed, the first scientific attempts to understand collective behaviour made reference to the crowd and its capacity to transform otherwise mild people into dangerous subverters of the social order. The first theoretical characterizations of the crowd were as one possible output of the deep social changes which were affecting Western societies during the 19th century. Modern social sciences (sociology in particular) developed in that period, as an intellectual reaction to a turbulent social environment, characterized by radical changes in the social structure, which often expressed themselves in popular discontent and mobilization. Moreover, violent crowd outbursts were scientifically puzzling, as they put into question the idea, which had developed at least since the Enlightenment, of the individual as a rational being, able to give order and to control not only his own demeanour but also the unstable social and natural environment (Longo, 2005, p. 19 ff.). In a gloomy representation of a world by now devoid of order, which was gaining relevance in the social representation of modernity, the raging crowd played a relevant role:

> From its very inception, the notion of crowds has referred to the dark side of modern society: to something which is intrinsic to the edifice of this social order, and which is associated with all sorts of negative features – and therefore looked upon with terror. Of course, there are notable exceptions to this image, but it is remarkable how seldom crowds are conceived as a solution to the challenges of modern society rather than as the embodiment of its immanent dangers.
>
> (Borch, 2012, p. 15)

Collective behaviour was thus understood by making reference to the alarming phenomenon of protesting crowds, which seemed able, with their overwhelming strength, to upset the rational order of hierarchical society, dissolving it in the generalized irrational uniformity of crowd behaviour. The crowd is seen as a single organism, endowed with its own destructive psychology, independent of the partaking individual actors. Moreover, the crowd has a transforming power, as the individual is compelled by some hypnotic force, to assume as his own the prevailing mood of the collective unity (be it anger, distress or joy). Clark McPhail effectively calls transformation theory all those hypotheses which "hold that crowds transform individuals, diminishing or eliminating their ability to control their behavior rationally" (McPhail, 1991/2017, p. 1). In all these conceptions, the crowd is, as it were, able to radically transform individuals who now act in ways which they themselves, once freed from the influence of the mob, would consider inappropriate or utterly wrong.

This approach to the crowd took its more eloquent form in Gustave Le Bon's (1895) highly influential essays, *La psychologie des foules*, a book whose effects on the analysis of collective behaviour were felt up to the second half of the 19th century. This strong, politically influenced, description of the crowd, now become commonplace and part of our non-specialized representation of mob-behaviour, stresses the unifying power of collective behaviour, which eventually entails a break-up of the individual rational minds within a generalized sentiment, shared by all who partake.

Gustave Le Bon, if not the first, was the most successful advocate of such a perspective, which was imbued with the diffuse preoccupation for the destabilizing power of politically self-aware city masses.[1] Contemporary society may be labelled, according to Le Bon, as the era of crowds.

> Organised crowds – he writes – have always played an important part in the life of peoples, but this part has never been of such moment as at present. The substitution of the unconscious action of crowds for the conscious activity of individuals is one of the principal characteristics of the present age.
>
> (Le Bon, 1895, p. V)

The envisaged substitution of the individual awareness with the collective subconscious is perceived, by the conservative Le Bon, as a menace to long-established hierarchies and values. The negative power of the crowd may end up in the destruction of society and its evolutionary trend, which has guaranteed so far the advancement of culture and civilization. And indeed, the power of crowd is not only destabilizing, it is also able to trigger a devolution process, which would eventually make "it hark back to that primitive communism which was the normal condition of all human groups before the dawn of civilisation" (ibid., p. XVII).

The negative account of the crowd as a regressive phenomenon is strengthened by the description of its inner mechanisms. As Le Bon explains, the very quality of the crowd is the emergence of new psychological characteristics, which may not be imputed to the single participants. A community of sentiments and intents may be witnessed, which are specific of the crowd as such and which justify the interest of the social scientist in the new social figuration. Here is how Le Bon explains this process:

> The sentiments and ideas of all the persons in the gathering take one and the same direction, and their conscious personality vanishes. A collective mind is formed, doubtless transitory, but presenting very clearly defined characteristics. The gathering [...] forms a single being, and is subjected to the *law of the mental unity of crowds*.
>
> (ibid., p. 2, italics in original)

This new social entity does not result from the summing up of the single intelligences; it is, on the contrary, intrinsically naïve, since the process by which the individual actors come to be part of a crowd overrides their rationality: "In crowds – as Le Bon sarcastically put it – it is stupidity and not mother-wit that is accumulated" (ibid., p. 9). Thus, the crowd, imagined as an almost autonomous living being, is able to downgrade the intellectual capacities of its members, due to a process of emotional and motivational contagion. The irrationality of the crowd is the output of its capacity of blunting the participants' cognitive abilities, reinforcing at the same time their excitability. Thus, the principle of self-interest, one of the bases of the economic action founded on the individualistic pursuit of one's own utility, is now sacrificed to the collective, undistinguishable interest of the crowd.

In this brief synopsis of Le Bon's arguments, an utterly negative account of the crowd is evident, based on the description of violent collective moods, provoking abrupt, irrational transformations rather than a planned and orderly process of social change: "It was – as David L. Miller writes – the intense emotions of widespread and mindless expectations, hero worship, hatred, and fear that eliminated the possibility of orderly social change and made precipitous and bloody revolutions inevitable" (Miller, 2011, p. 10).

What is evident in Gustav Le Bon is both a negative conception of the crowd and an explanation of crowd behaviour as based on negative emotionality. The individual becomes readily influenced amidst the crowd, the co-presence of other individual exerting a sort of hypnotic power, able to erase his self-constraints and self-control. The single actor is thus induced to give vent to the irrationality and instincts which had been successfully blunted by civilization. The increased suggestibility that the crowd produces results eventually in a sort of collective mind, by which collective behaviour may be considered as the output of an undetermined collective consciousness, not be imputed to any one of the partaking individuals. Thus, the crowd manifests itself as a multiform and yet unified organism, whose absent rationality results in the manifestation of the most primitive, negative instincts and emotions which the individual, in his normal social intercourses, is able to repress or control (McPhail, 1991/2017, pp. 4–5). Clark McPhail (ibid.) has effectively referred to the line of thought set up by Le Bon as the myth of the madding crowd. This myth has specific features: 1. the individual disappears within the crowd; 2. he loses the control of his rationality; 3. his emotionality is expression of the emotionality of the crowd; 4. collective behaviour is conceived as characterized by converging individual action, which has lead Turner and Killian (1957) to critically speak of the illusion of unanimity.

Regardless of its naïve presentation of the crowd as a unanimous acting (and feeling) organism, Le Bon's conception exerted a durable influence. When, at the beginning of the 20th century, collective behaviour became a relevant academic topic, the institutionalizing American sociology drew so much from Le Bon that the American description of the psychological mechanism of the crowds could be understood as the liberal translation of Le Bon's theory. Indeed, American sociologists tended to propose a more optimistic, less gloomy presentation of crowd and collective behaviour: social unrest and the crowd may be dangerous, yet they are to be understood as relevant steps in the process of social change. In this specific regard, the difference with Le Bon is evident: whereas the latter connected the crowd to de-evolution processes, American social scientists conceived the crowd as a potentially positive social factor, able as it was to foster social transformations.

In their *Introduction to the Science of Sociology* (1921), Park and Burgess qualify collective behaviour quite generically as a behaviour influenced by the presence of others: "each individual acts under the influence of a mood or a state of mind in which each shares, and in accordance with conventions which all quite unconsciously accept, and which the presence of each enforces upon the others" (Park, Burgess, 1921, p. 865). Collective behaviour is essential to social life, and indeed Park and Burgess detect a number of different forms of collective behaviour, from social unrest and the crowd to social institutions. Social unrest and the crowd, understood as de-institutionalized forms of collective behaviour, may give birth to new institutions, thus playing an important role in social change:

> Rather than seeing the crowd as an irrational threat to society, [Park] conceived of it as an entity in social evolution through which individuals may generate new social relations. Hence, in Park's account, the crowd did not evoke an image of societal destruction and disorganization, but rather of social creation and reorganization. On this affirmative view, society and democracy were believed to profit from the new social forms generated by crowds.
>
> (Borch, 2012, p. 144)

The appraisal of the crowd as a regenerating factor of social change is highly compatible with the American translation of the European speculation about the crowd. Indeed, what Christian Borch says about Park may be extended to even later American sociology, including Herbert Blumer and Lewis Coser. By connecting collective behaviour and social change, Park and Burgess were able to mitigate Le Bon's conservatism, resulting in a gloomy conception by which mass society could produce the eventual dismantlement of civilization as we know it. Nonetheless, their analysis of the internal mechanisms of the psychology of the crowd was much in line with the French scholar's. Drawing from Tarde, Park and Burgess distinguished in the first place the crowd from the public, the latter being a dimension of collective behaviour characterized by the rational discussion of public issues. Thus, the crowd may be effectively represented starting from its lack of rationality:

> The crowd does not discuss and hence it does not reflect. It simply "mills." Out of this milling process a collective impulse is formed which dominates all members of the crowd. Crowds, when they act, do so impulsively. The crowd, says Le Bon, "is the slave of its impulses."
>
> (Park and Burgess, 1921, p. 869)

Yet, regardless of the reference to Le Bon, Park and Burgess contest him the apparent unanimity of the crowd, as conforming crowd behaviour does not imply a total dispersion of the individual in the collective entity. As they write: "the crowd carries out the suggestions of the leader, and even though there be no division of labor each individual acts more or less in his own way to achieve a common end" (ibid., p. 877). Eventually, a social unanimity is actually achieved, by a process which will be analyzed with further detail by Herbert Blumer, that is the establishment of rapports among the crowd members, hence "a mutual responsiveness, such that every member of the group reacts immediately, spontaneously, and sympathetically to the sentiments and attitudes of every other member" (Park, 1921, p. 895). This mutual responsiveness has, as one of its main outputs, a diminished control on one's actions, so that long repressed attitudes may find expression in a crowd situation. Here Park anticipates one of the main elements of transformation theories: the exceptionality of crowd behaviour, which entails that what social actors do and feel in a crowd is different from what social actors would do and feel in their daily occupations. The crowd is an autonomous social space, where normal relations based on social rules are substituted by a contagious responsiveness to the states of mind and feelings of other partakers.

Herbert Blumer (1951) starts his analysis from the exceptionality of collective behaviour, since he describes collective behaviour as a specific, de-institutionalized kind of demeanour. Drawing from Park and Burgess (1921, p. 886), elementary collective behaviour is according to Blumer recursive, in that "the response of one individual reproduces the stimulation that has come from another individual and in being reflected back to this individual reinforces the stimulation" (Blumer, 1951, p. 170). Elementary collective behaviour entails therefore a mutual stimulation of feelings, which is quite evident in the case of collective excitement.

By stressing the character of exceptionality, Blumer seems at odds with his own theoretical perspective, that is symbolic interactionism. Whereas symbolic interactionism is a cognitive approach, stressing the relevance of mutual interpretation in social interactions, the crowd is conceived by Blumer as a separated social space, endowed with its own rules, where social actors are driven by shared impulses and collective feelings. Indeed, this kind of behaviour is different from what is usually experienced by individual actors in normal interactions: whereas these are characterized by a process of interpretation, whereby social actors interpret the actions of their fellow people and act in consequence, collective behaviour is a direct response to the emotional stimuli from other people's demeanour. This accounts for the uniformity of people's behaviour in a crowd; indeed, crowd behaviour tends towards the homogenization of the individuals, whereas normal behaviour tends towards differentiation (ibid., p. 171). In specific circumstances, Blumer states, collective behaviour may be transformed in a form of collective unrest. Individual restlessness is converted into a fluid action which is socially relevant insofar as it may represent the precondition of social change (ibid., pp. 172–173).

This specific kind of behaviour manifests itself chiefly in what Blumer calls the acting crowd, where the individual tends to behave in relation to other people's demeanour and manifestation of feelings and emotions. Blumer states that in the acting crowd collective excitement may rise, a form of mutually growing emotionality which breaks "the personal make-up of individuals" (ibid., p. 175). People tend to become "more likely to be carried by impulses and feelings; hence rendered more unstable and irresponsible" (ibid.). In order for this process to be achieved, a number of elementary mechanisms are to be performed. The first is the milling, in which the individual move around, meet and become more responsive with one another. The second step is what Blumer calls rapport, that is a situation in which crowd members become "increasingly preoccupied with one another and decreasingly responsive to ordinary objects of stimulation" (ibid., p. 174).

It is this responsiveness to crowd-internal behaviours and moods rather than crowd-external objects which qualifies, according to Blumer, the milling process as essential to collective behaviour. In fact, from the greater responsiveness to other members of the collective unity derives the possibility for social contagion, being understood as "an intense form of milling and collective excitement" (ibid., p. 176). Like Park before, even Herbert Blumer's argument may be understood as a positive and liberal representation of the crowd and social unrest (McPhail, 1991/2017, pp. 8–9). Yet the crowd representation remains highly compatible with Le Bon's: the crowd is a sort of collective individual, endowed with its constitutive rules by which the single actor almost dissolves, in favour of mutually reinforcing collective emotions and feelings.

3 Émile Zola, Gustave Le Bon and the crowd

In his *Sociology through Literature*, Lewis Coser (1963) proposes the first systematic attempt to use literature as an instrument to illustrate abstract sociological concepts. The book is a reading, employing literary passages, chiefly drawn from narratives, in order to clarify the conceptual tools developed within sociological thought. Section fourteen is devoted by Lewis Coser to collective behaviour, to the crowd in particular. In the brief introductory remarks to the section, Coser clarifies his conception of collective behaviour. Being a conflictualist theorist (although of the mildest type), Coser associates, more sharply than Park and Blumer ever did, collective behaviour and social change. He starts from the usual differences between collective behaviour and normal social action, the first being more loosely structured. He then stresses the relevance of collective behaviour as a symptom of a decaying social order. Collective behaviour is "relatively unorganized and lack[s] the stability and predictability of cohesive social groups" (ibid., p. 328). It is a kind of behaviour "arising spontaneously, and not based on pre-established norms or traditions". It deserves anyway great sociological attention "because such behaviour may enlighten us as how an old order dies and a new social order may emerge" (ibid.). Collective behaviour is thus, according to Coser, a sign of a senescent society and, at the same time, the first, potential symptom of an emerging process of re-institutionalization. Yet, regardless of the attention reserved for conflict and change, Coser's conception of collective behaviour is much in line with the transformation theories which I have analyzed so far. The crowd is qualified as "a temporal and ephemeral group requiring the physical presence of its participants; it rubs out the distinctive characteristics of individuals and instead brings to the fore crude and generalized emotions" (ibid., p. 329).

Indeed, the description of the crowd as an organic unit, often qualified as a ferocious beast, was elaborated in literary accounts before becoming a topic of the social sciences. It is difficult to say whether and in what sense the "subtle, concrete observations" of novelists, which are, according to Coser "superior in many respects to the theoretical informed findings of sociologists" (ibid.) influenced coeval sociological and psychological speculation. Indeed, in the second half of the 19th century, sociology and literature were competing for the better representation of social reality, conflict going together with mutual influences and cross-fertilization (Lepenies, 1985). Thus, it should be no wonder if one finds, prior to Le Bon's influential book on the topic, literary representations of the mob which are compatible with transformation theory. One of these works is in the selection proposed in Coser's reading, notably a passage from Émile Zola's *Germinal* (1885), describing a crowd of striking miners. It goes without saying that Coser's choice was appropriate: Émile Zola is, in fact, a fitting example of the mutual influences between the novel and the social sciences in the last decades of the 19th century. By setting the principles of Naturalism in his *The Experimental Novel* (1880), Zola advocates a new kind of realism, which should be based on scientific principles and be understood as a scientific representation of the social and psychological world. Observation, understood as the accurate description of a phenomenon, is typical of realistic literature. In the experimental novel, Zola states, observation must be coupled with experiment, that is a manipulative approach by which human actions and psychology are described as determined by scientific laws.

> In fact, the whole operation consists in taking facts in nature, then in studying the mechanism of these facts, acting upon them, by the modification of circumstances and surroundings, without deviating from the laws of nature. Finally, you possess knowledge of the man, scientific knowledge of him, in both his individual and social relations.
>
> (Zola, 1885, p. 9)

In his scientific approach to narrative, Zola equates the naturalistic novelist with the scientist. Indeed, the experimental novelist, when describing individual characters and their actions, should be consistent with social and psychological forces, which are in their turn produced by deterministic laws. The experimental attitude, according to which plots and characters should evolve following universal laws, gives naturalistic narratives a scientific quality, since they are supposed to produce an articulated, objective knowledge of the individual actor in his social context. When describing the crowd, Zola was adhering to the principles of Naturalism, his intent being a clear-cut, scientific representation of the behaviour of people in a mob. *Germinal* (1885) is the novel where Zola's scientific approach to the novel is at its best (Walker, 1984, Chapter 1, *passim*). The novel is the naturalistic representation of the living conditions of miners in the North of France. Set at the end of the Second Empire (about 1860), it depicts social unrest and social protest due to the extremely harsh conditions to which miners and their families are subjected. The central character, Étienne Lantier, is the stranger with a strong political awareness, coming to the North in search of a job. Shocked by the hardness of the miners' living conditions, he tries to spread revolutionary ideals and organizes a strike. The crowd scene is part of the unsuccessful protest Étienne organizes against the mine management. It may be conceived as a plastic representation of a series of ideas (the association of crowd with violence, contagious emotions, the relevance of instincts and the suppression of rationality) which would later be developed in disciplinary speculations (Borch, 2012, p. 28).

The mob is represented as a natural phenomenon, and as natural phenomena, it is not pliant to reason; as natural facts, it can be devastating and uncontrollable. Zola compares the approaching crowd to the blasts of wind preceding a storm: "The noise grew louder, but nothing could yet be seen; along the vacant road the wind of a tempest seemed to be blowing, like those sudden gusts which precede great storms" (Zola, 1885, p. 232). Two rallies, the one made up of a thousand women, the other, double in size, consisting of men, converge. The representation Zola gives of the mob is of a compact entity, swept by anger and fury, a common sentiment which enhances the bestiality of people, a representation highly compatible with transformation theories according to which the individual rationality is supplanted by generalized emotions. Here is the representation of women in the mob:

> The women had appeared, nearly a thousand of them, with outspread hair dishevelled by running, the naked skin appearing through their rags, the nakedness of females weary with giving birth to starvelings. A few held their little ones in their arms, raising them and shaking them like banners of mourning and vengeance. Others, who were younger with the swollen breasts of amazons, brandished sticks; while frightful old women were yelling so loudly that the cords of their fleshless necks seemed to be breaking.
>
> (ibid.)

In Zola's narrative, the generalized emotionality of the crowd affects women in particular, since women are, according to the coeval mentality, closer to nature, such that the crowd as a natural phenomenon is likely to exert a deeper influence on feminine personalities. In the late 19th century representation, the crowd is depicted as a feminine entity, which entails a double critique: against women and the mob, both being supposedly definable for their lack of rationality and their propensity to uniformity (Borch, 2012, p. 43). These features of the mob affect men too, once they are in a crowd situation: the rally of men marches in close yet disorganized ranks, characterized by a visual uniformity which makes single individualities undistinguishable. Even the Marseillaise, which is sung by the mob, becomes a blurred roar:

> And then the men came up, two thousand madmen—trammers, pikemen, menders—a compact mass which rolled along like a single block in confused serried rank so that it was impossible to distinguish their faded trousers or ragged woollen jackets, all effaced in the same earthy uniformity. Their eyes were burning, and one only distinguished the holes of black mouths singing the Marseillaise; the stanzas were lost in a confused roar, accompanied by the clang of sabots over the hard earth.
>
> (Zola, 1885, p. 232)

An axe is passed from hand to hand, the symbol of revolt, its profile reminding of the guillotine, hence the Reign of Terror of the French Revolution: "Above their heads, amid the bristling iron bars, an axe passed by, carried erect; and this single axe, which seemed to be the standard of the band, showed in the clear air the sharp profile of a guillotine-blade" (ibid.).

All the elements of Le Bon's theory of the crowd are here present. The crowd is portrayed as a single organism, endowed with its specific features and, as a unique social entity, it is able to transform individual psychology, imposing on single actors its prevailing mood. Within the furious mob, characters are transformed. Even the otherwise mild Catherine is cast adrift by the crowd's collective emotion of anger and starts throwing stones, as other women do. Rationality and sensibility are no longer driving her acts: Catherine's actions are now led by a sentiment of anger and revenge, and while casting stones she closes her eyes, blindness being the symbolic image of the irrational conditions of those who take part in the mob.

> And suddenly, in the midst of these furies, Catherine was observed with her fists in the air also brandishing half-bricks and throwing them with all the force of her little arms. She could not have said why, she was suffocating, she was dying of the desire to kill everybody. Would it not soon be done with, this cursed life of misfortune? She had had enough of it, beaten and driven away by her man, wandering about like a lost dog in the mud of the roads, without being able to ask a crust from her father, who was starving like herself. Things never seemed to get better; they were getting worse ever since she could remember. And she broke the bricks and threw them before her with the one idea of sweeping everything away, her eyes so blinded that she could not even see whose jaws she might be crushing.
>
> (ibid., p. 233)

As Herbert Blumer would some half a century later write, in the acting crowd the "individual loses ordinary critical understanding and self-control as he enters into rapport with other crowd members and becomes infused by the collective excitement which dominates them" (Blumer, 1951, p. 180). This tuning up process has, as its extreme consequence, the suppression of the reflexive component of interaction, which according to symbolic interactionism is on the contrary the basis of interaction in normal social situations. In the crowd, so it would seem, the cognitive reflexivity of social actors is supplanted by a negative form of emotionality, in which action is determined by an irreflexive suppression of one's sensibility and the generalized tuning into others' behaviour.

In Zola's representation, the transformation process affects not only the individual actors, it concerns the mob as a whole, converting the single partakers into a collective beast. Taking part in the crowd may be well motivated (anger, hunger, sufferings), yet, regardless of the solidity of motives, the extreme output is the transformation of individuals into "wild beasts", "bloody butchers" ready to exert violence.

And in fact anger, hunger, these two months of suffering and this enraged helter-skelter through the pits had lengthened the placid faces of the Montsou colliers into the muzzles of wild beasts. At this moment the sun was setting; its last rays of sombre purple cast a gleam of blood over the plain. The road seemed to be full of blood; men and women continued to rush by, bloody as butchers in the midst of slaughter.

(Zola, 1885, p. 232)

With an intelligent narrative device, Zola contrasts the description of the crowd with the narration of what happens in the houses of the local middle class. Descriptions of anger and violence are set against narratives of disconcertion and fear. The narrative device emphasizes the abnormal nature of the crowd, its capacity to put long-established hierarchies and normative order into question. The crowd is potentially able to show the injustice of the everyday arrangement of social inequalities. Yet, it is not capable of presenting plausible alternatives. The mob is characterized by brutality and violence, the absence of a clear-cut division of labour and roles (a characteristic that transformation theories would later remark) which reminds one of Durkheim's account of the horde (1893, p. 126). Within a horde, coordination is impossible since there is no differentiation: the actions of its members consist of the constant repetition of the same model. According to Durkheim, the horde is a protoplasmatic society, the realm of the undifferentiating; this means that there is neither role distribution nor any incipient form of specialization. Specialization is indeed impossible: it would imply a rational distinction of functions, whereas the mob is characterized by the indistinctiveness of collective emotions and demeanour. Rationality may emerge in the crowd but only as the autonomous attempt of some individuals to control collective emotions and drive them towards a specific aim. Yet, according to Zola, this attempt is doomed to be unsuccessful:

Étienne had remained at the head of his mates. But while he was hoarsely urging them on to Montsou, he heard another voice within him, the voice of reason, asking, in astonishment, the meaning of all this. He had not intended any of these things; how had it happened that, having set out for Jean-Bart with the object of acting calmly and preventing disaster, he had finished this day of increasing violence by besieging the manager's villa?

(Zola, p. 237)

In a messianic forecast of further social developments, Zola describes the mob of striking miners as an anticipation of a gloomy future, one in which the old order will be demolished, with no hints at possible alternatives. This aspect may deserve a long quotation:

It was the red vision of the revolution, which would one day inevitably carry them all away, on some bloody evening at the end of the century. Yes, some evening the people, unbridled at last, would thus gallop along the roads, making the blood of the middle class flow, parading severed heads and sprinkling gold from disembowelled coffers. The women would yell, the men would have those wolf-like jaws open to bite. Yes, the same rags, the same thunder of great sabots, the same terrible troop, with dirty skins and tainted breath, sweeping away the old world beneath an overflowing flood of barbarians. Fires would flame; they would not leave standing one stone of the towns; they would return to the savage life of the woods, after the great rut, the great feast-day, when the poor in one night would emaciate the wives and empty the cellars of the rich. There would be nothing left, not a sou of the great fortunes, not a title-deed of properties acquired; until the day dawned when a new earth would perhaps spring up once more. Yes, it was these things which were passing along the road; it was the force of nature herself, and they were receiving the terrible wind of it in their faces.

(ibid., p. 233)

The crowd is here represented as pure violence, a destructive and irrational force which may not be rationally controlled. The passage accounts for the deep pessimism which Zola, although sympathizing with socialist ideals, manifested concerning the nature of humanity and history. As Philip Walker clearly states:

In his blacker moods, Zola not only rejected on positivistic grounds the more glowing idealistic conceptions of mankind's future that many of his contemporaries embraced; he veered toward a philosophy of history sharply at odds with them. There were moments when he found himself in agreement with the view that nature never changes and that history, whether human or natural, will always be a grim, bloody, endlessly repeated kaleidoscopic process.

(Walker, 1984, p. 14)

Thus, the crowd, which one could suppose to be the output of a reawakened sense of justice, fostered and controlled by a politically aware leader, turns out to be just the outburst of uncontrollable collective hyper-excitement. This is the conclusion to which Étienne himself comes, by admitting that the crowd is uncontrollable, as it is equatable to an irresistible force of nature:

Besides, he had never led them, it was they who led him, who obliged him to do things which he would never have done if it were not for the shock of that crowd pushing behind him. At each new violence he had been stupefied by the course of events, for he had neither foreseen nor desired any of them [...] But he felt himself at the end of his courage, he was no longer at heart with his mates; he feared this enormous mass of the people, blind and irresistible, moving like a force of nature, sweeping away everything, outside rules and theories.

(Zola, 1885, p. 293)

The exceptionality as a specific feature of mobs (one of the main characteristics of the crowd for transformation theories) is here anticipated by the genius of Zola. And in fact, in the crowd – as Herbert Blumer would later write – the social actor "responds immediately and directly to the remarks and actions of others instead of interpreting these gestures as he would do in ordinary conduct" (Blumer, 1951, p. 180). This qualifies collective behaviour in the acting crowd as due to the suppression of ordinary critical interpretation of the surrounding action, which is now replaced by collective aroused impulses and excited feelings. Crowd behaviour is not only determined by the blind and irresistible collective acting of a horde of people, it is also outside rules, a delimited form of social conduct where – according to Zola's gloomy pessimism – the norms of rationality and social conventions are suspended. Yet the suspension is ineffective in *Germinal* (and one could plausibly suspect that this holds for Zola as a general social law) as the final output of the strike and crowd action is the eventual return to the *status quo* (Borch, 2012, p. 25).

4 Manzoni, Smelser and the theory of the emerging norm

Transformation theories give relevance to collective emotions as a specific feature of collective phenomena. This entails that they characterize collective behaviour as substantially irrational, a form of action in which social actors are driven by emotions and in which rationality has a scant role. As I have tried to sketch above, this theoretical approach expresses itself at its best when social scientists try to depict the mob. Mobs are indeed easily characterizable by the prevailing emotions (be it joy, sadness or anger) that their partakers manifest in unison. Thus, the idea of a unitary organism, able to supplant individual rationality with collective emotionality and sensibility, was apparently consistent with empirical experiences of crowd behaviour. Up to the 1960s, social scientists, regardless of their theoretical or political position, conceived of the mob as a fluid structure, devoid of clear-cut norms and expectations, in which individual behaviour was moulded by the circular reinforcement of the emotions manifested by participants. In their reduction of the complexity of social phenomena which sociological constructs produce, the sociological image of mob action may be understood as a mirror image to the theoretical representation of the individual action; the former was devoid of any rationality, whereas the latter was conceived as chiefly rational or cognitive. The idea of collective behaviour as based on contagious emotionality was so strong that even the interactionist Herbert Blumer or the conflictualist Lewis Coser adhered to this simplified conception of collective behaviour. Coser considered mob phenomena as the symptoms of a crumbling social order, yet the crowd was not in itself ordered or controllable, being the momentary expression of a normative social void. Blumer was even more categorical: the social void which the crowd produced was not only normative, but even cognitive, since in the mob symbolic interpretation was replaced by the emotional contagion.

In the second half of the 20th century, research on collective behaviour was characterized by an attempt to bring cognition back in. The central idea, which developed within a plurality of different approaches, was that collective behaviour was not in itself abnormal. It was therefore erroneous to oppose every-day behaviour and collective behaviour, chiefly because the idea of the unanimity of crowd feelings and of crowd actions was theoretically misleading and empiri-cally invalid (McPhail, 1991/2017, p. 61 ff). The consequence of this new attitude was a conception of collective behaviour and collective action as based on the rational actions of those who partake, coupled with the exclusion of emotions and emotionality. The sociological analysis of collective behaviour and action was affected by the same strain of cognitivism which characterized social theory along the 20th century, whose main effect went in the opposite direction as com-pared with earlier conceptions of the crowd, leading to the eventual bracketing of emotions as sociologically irrelevant. Attempts have been made, even in the field of collective behaviour, to override this tendency (Lofland, 1981). Yet, the final output of the process was the eventual exclusion of the crowd as a relevant topic of collective behaviour. The crowd, being more easily understandable in terms of collective emotionality, tended to fade outside the interests of mainstream socio-logical theorizing and researching. The semantic of crowd was replaced by the semantic of collective action, centred chiefly on social movements, a branch of collective behaviour more adequately understandable as the result of rationally motivated choices. Christian Borch (2012, pp. 16–17) is probably right when he proposes that this shift, which would eventually produce "the crowd topic's gradual expulsion from the central sociological agenda", was determined by the fact that the crowd as a social phenomenon, with its capacity to impose uniform collective behaviour and collective sentiments, was constitutively at odds with the idea, reinforced in the social sciences, of a rational liberal subject.

In what follows I will try to test two highly cognitive approaches to collec-tive behaviour (the emergent norm theory and the added value theory) by using a riot episode drawn from the masterpiece of Italian romantic narrative, namely *The Betrothed* (*I Promessi Sposi* in Italian) by Alessandro Manzoni. The novel was published in its first version in 1827, thus almost sixty years before Zola's *Germinal*. Yet, chiefly thanks to the author's ironical gaze upon human vicis-situdes, it shows a more complex representation of the crowd as compared to Zola's. The crowd is not portrayed as a unitary unorganized structure. It is, on the contrary, made up of single actors, suggestible as they may be, but still endowed with individual emotions and rationality, both emerging in their action within the crowd as a collective phenomenon. Manzoni's account seems consistent with more recent conceptions, where crowds "are more accurately characterized as consisting of alternating and varied sequences of individual and collective behav-ior—not continuous and unanimous behavior" (McPhaid, 1991/2017, pp. 43–44). Yet in Manzoni's description feelings and emotions still play a relevant role; they are not suppressed as irrelevant or subsidiary.

Alessandro Manzoni's approach to the crowd is connected to his idea of soci-ety: his early adherence to the Enlightenment was replaced, in his maturity, by a strong Catholic faith, by which he rejected the revolutionary idea of equality as dangerous. In his ideological approach to politics, Manzoni aimed at a regulated society, in which differences were justifiable in so far as they were mitigated by a form of government driven by the principles of equity and justice. This meant that social equality was superfluous in that people are equal in front of God, a religious principle which should replace the revolutionary ideas which had proven dangerous and ineffective (Sottong, 2012, pp. 32–33). The literary representation of the crowd in action, which the reader may find in Chapters 12 and 13 of Manzoni's masterpiece, is affected by the author's ideas, yet his treatment of the crowd is also informed by an accurate historical knowledge, by referring to which Manzoni is able to trace the economic and political causes of the riot. Given the great historical accuracy of Manzoni's narrative, and his ability to portray the emotional and rational action within the crowd, I attempt, in what follows, an explanation of the bread riot in the terms of two theories: Smelser's added value theory and Turner and Killian's theory of the emergent norm. Both theories tend to bracket the role of emotions since, although a relevant component of collective behaviour, they are seen as insufficient as the explanatory cause of mob action. The general reaction against emotionality as a cause of collective behaviour may be made explicit by referring to Smelser, who considered the emotional reaction to collective behaviour as an impediment to its scientific understanding. As he wrote "because many forms of collective behavior excite strong emotional reactions, they resist objective analysis" (Smelser, 1962, p. 4).

Let me briefly hint at some methodological questions. Regardless of the startling convergence between Smelser's theory and Manzoni's acute analysis of the causes of the bread riot, regardless of the convergence of Manzoni's treatment of the crowd and some of the features of the emergent norm theory, I would be theoretically naïve, if I suggested that both theories are anticipated in the beautiful pages of the masterpiece of the Italian romantic novel. Smelser's account is an attempt to explain collective behaviour from the vantage point of Parsons' theory of action (ibid., Chapter 2, *passim*). Turner and Killian's analysis may be understood as issuing from the theoretical need to reconcile reflexivity and collective behaviour, within an interactionist framework, which had been too quickly dismissed in Blumer's account of crowd action. Manzoni uses a highly artificial combination of fiction and historical facts within a complex narrative whose main ideological aim is to show the relevance of divine providence in the vicissitudes of human beings and in the destiny of a whole nation. What we do when using literary narrative for sociological purposes is reducing the complexity of the work of genius, adapting it to our specific argumentative tasks. Yet *I Promessi Sposi*, as any great work of narrative, although suitable to a large variety of readings, including the sociological, is reducible to none of them. The possible use of the novel to explain some traits of both Smelser's and Turner and Killian's theories is a demonstration of the profundity of great narratives which, although often representing reality for the sole sake of narration, tend to be more multifaceted and rich than sociological theories, whose representation is motivated chiefly by argumentative and cognitive purposes.

Neil Smelser's theory is incremental, which means that collective behaviour may manifest only provided that a number of sequential conditions are available. A general structural condition is indispensable (structural conduciveness in Smelser's wording) as well as a more specific structural tension, perceived by social actors as an appropriate motive to take part in collective behaviour. "Real or perceived economic deprivation" is conceived by Smelser (ibid., p. 17) as an appropriate structural strain for the hostile outburst. When Renzo, the protagonist of the novel, arrives in Milan, the city is stricken by a severe famine. The causes, Manzoni writes, were chiefly natural, yet they had been worsened by the lack of judgement of the vice governor of the city, Antonio Ferrer, who, in order to secure himself the favour of people, had imposed the backers to sell bread at a non-market price. Since this situation could not last, city bakers being now almost bankrupt, the bread was put again at the due price. The tension derived from the famine and the rise of the price of bread, perceived by the Milanesi as an injustice, may be understood in Smelser's terms as a structural strain, a precondition for the violent outburst. The strain would be ineffective, if it did not fall "within the scope established by the condition of conduciveness" (Smelser, 1962, p. 16), which entails a set of general structural conditions without which collective behaviour is doomed not to trigger. In the case of 17th century Milan, structural conduciveness may be explained as a consequence of the highly differentiated access to economic resources, the great inequality between the better and the worse-off and a foreigner government which vexed the Milanese with "insupportable taxes, levied with unequalled cupidity and folly" (Manzoni, 1842, p. 204). In his historically and economically aware treatment of the bread riot, Manzoni gives us a brief account of the structural tension anticipating the riot:

> No sooner had this deficient harvest been gathered in, than the provisions for the army, and the waste which always accompanies them, made such a fearful void in it, that scarcity quickly made itself felt, and with scarcity its melancholy, but profitable, as well as inevitable, effect, a rise of prices.
>
> (ibid.)

The third condition of collective behaviour is the spread of a generalized belief, by which faults are imputed to social actors, often scapegoats, so as to personify the often abstract structural strains, now made clear and meaningful for those who will potentially partake in the collective action. In Smelser's words:

> Before collective action can be taken to reconstitute the situation brought on by structural strain, this situation must be made meaningful to the potential actors. This meaning is supplied in a generalized belief, which identifies the source of strain, attributes certain characteristics to this source, and specifies certain responses to the strain as possible or appropriate.
>
> (Smelser, 1962, p. 16)

In the accurate account of the riot, Manzoni traces as one of the motives of the hostile outburst the ill-posed conviction that bakers and speculators are hoarding wheat in order to promote an unmotivated rise of bread price:

> But when the price of food reaches a certain point, there always arises [...] an opinion among the many that it is not the effect of scarcity [...] Corn

monopolists, either real or imaginary, large landholders, the bakers who pur-
chased corn, all, in short, who had either little or much, or were thought to
have any, were charged with being the causes of the scarcity and dearness of
provisions; they were the objects of universal complaint, and of the hatred of
the multitude of every rank.

(Manzoni, 1842, pp. 204–205)

The fourth condition of collective behaviour is that of precipitating factors.
Precipitating factors are able to confirm and specify the negative sentiments
connected to generalized belief. They indeed "give the generalized beliefs concrete, immediate substance. In this way they provide a concrete setting toward
which collective action can be directed" (Smelser, 1962, p. 17). In the case of
the bread riot, the precipitating factor may be detected in the decision of a city
council to allow bakers to sell bread once again at the market price, so that
bakers could be perceived as the enemies towards whom to address the protest.
As Manzoni writes "The bakers once more breathed, but the people raved"
(Manzoni, 1842, p. 207). Given the four above described conditions, a mobilization may start.

   In his felicitous treatment of the crowd action, Manzoni is able to give an
highly sophisticated representation of the mob: the mob is not, as in Le Bon's
treatment, an unanimous beast, since it is made up of individual actors, some of
whom are endowed with a critical capacity, hence rationally able to criticize the
mob's misdoings or to use to their advantage a diffuse sentiment of hatred and
hostility. Thus, the crowd is represented as a complex collective phenomenon, in
which both rationality and emotionality play an important role. The representation of the crowd in its early stage is compatible with the process which Herbert
Blumer defined as milling:

> The evening preceding the day in which Renzo arrived at Milan, the streets
> and squares swarmed with men, who, transported with indignation, and
> swayed by a prevailing opinion, assembled – whether acquaintances or
> strangers – in knots and parties without any previous concert, and almost
> without being aware of it, like rain-drops on a hillside. Every conversation
> increased the general belief, and roused the passions of both hearer and
> speaker.
>
> (ibid., pp. 207–208)

Yet, even in the milling crowd, in which emotions play a relevant role and to
which people are driven by some external natural forces (see in the above quotation the comparison with *rain-drops on a hillside*) there are some who rationally
employ the excitement for their own purposes:

> Amongst the many excited ones, there were some few of cooler tempera-
> ment, who stood quietly watching with great satisfaction the troubling of
> the water, who busied themselves in troubling it more and more, with such
> reasonings and stories as rogues know how to invent, and agitated minds are

so ready to believe, and who determined not to let it calm down without first catching a little fish.

(ibid., p. 208)

The process of communication among crowd members is also important. At an early stage, they tend to reinforce the generalized belief which will eventually strengthen the collective impulse to act:

> Crowds assembled before day-break: children, women, men, old people, workmen, beggars, all grouped together at random; here was a confused whispering of many voices; there, one declaimed to a crowd of applauding bystanders; this one asked his nearest fellow the same question that had just been put to himself; that other repeated the exclamation that he heard resounding in his ears; everywhere were disputes, threats, wonderings; and very few words made up the materials of so many conversations.

(ibid.)

Collective action starts when the crowd attacks the bakery boys who are carrying baskets of bread for their daily delivery: "The first appearance of one of these unlucky boys in a crowd of people, was like the fall of a lighted squib in a gunpowder magazine" (ibid.). Once the first act is performed, the crowd is ready for further violent action, one of which being the assault on a bakery. Yet the crowd is upset by contrasting forces. It is not an impetuous and irrational compact unit *à la* Le Bon;[2] rather it needs constant communicative reinforcements to keep its action alive:

> The flame had again sunk; no one was seen approaching with fresh combustibles, and the crowd was beginning to feel impatient when a rumour was spread that at the Cordusio (a small square or cross-way not far distant) they had laid siege to a bake-house. In similar circumstances, the announcement of an event very often produces it. Together with this rumour, a general wish to repair thither gained ground among the multitude: I am going; are you going? Let us go, let us go were heard in every direction; the crowd broke up, were set in motion, and moved on.

(ibid., p. 216)

Resentment, an ill-posed sense of justice and anger undoubtedly drive the crowd. Yet, this does not happen in a complete void of rationality: the crowd is not lead by collective emotions which drive social actors beyond their normal attitudes (as is the case in Zola's account). Rather, communication among individual actors and some form of reflexivity is needed in order for the crowd to keep being a collective entity. This reminds one of the theory of the emergent norm, elaborated by Turner and Killian (1957). The theory is a symbolic interactionist attempt to give a plausible answer to the complexity of collective behaviour. The theoretical approach rejects the idea of unanimity which is typical of transformation theories, by assuming:

> the presence of heterogeneous actors with different backgrounds, perceptual abilities, and motives about what is going on, what should be done to respond to the crisis, and who should do it. ENT assumes that collective behavior is not irrational but social, normative behavior.
>
> (Aguirre, Wenger and Vigo, 1998, p. 302)

The complex representation of the crowd which Manzoni proposes to the reader, with its moments of excitement, collective perplexity, acceleration, in which individual motives clash, one of which eventually prevailing, prefigures a conception of collective behaviour as an arena, where differences and identities of emotions and purposes cooperate and conflict, the final output being the result of complicated processes (a conception highly compatible with the idea of an emergent norm).

Another relevant aspect of the emergent norm theory is that "[e]ven in crowded settings where excitement is high people retain critical ability and a sense of personal identity, and they behave in terms of personal motives" (Miller, 2011, p. 32). The idea of personal motives is made explicit when Turner and Killian single out five social types within the crowd. In the crowd, no longer considered a homogeneous set where individual characteristics disappear, it is possible to detect different attitudes and modes of participation. The first type is the highly committed; thus, one who is likely to incite and lead the action; the second type is motivated by a generalized concern. He is likely to actively partake, following the lead of others; the third type is the insecure, who take part in the collective action out of psychological motives (e.g. to strengthen his self-esteem); the fourth type is the curious, who is attracted by unusual situations, whereas the fifth type is the ego-detached whose motivation is to exploit the situation (ibid.). In Manzoni's account, I have been able to detect at least four of the five types. We have already met in Manzoni's narrative those who belong to the fifth type ("some few of cooler temperament, who stood quietly watching with great satisfaction the troubling of the water, who busied themselves in troubling it more and more" [Manzoni, 1842, p. 208]). The first type is critically portrayed by Manzoni in the figure of an old man who incites the mob when partakers assault the house of the superintendent of provisions, considered responsible for the rise of the price of bread. Here follows Manzoni's description of the man. Among the people laying siege to the house of the superintendent

> appeared one, who was himself a spectacle, an old and half-starved man, who, rolling about two sunken and fiery eyes composing his wrinkled face to a smile of diabolic complacency, and with his hands raised above his infamous, hoary head, was brandishing in the air a hammer, a rope, and four large

nails, with which he said he meant to nail the vicar to the posts of his own door, alive as he was.

(ibid. pp. 221–222)

In the economy of the narrative, the old man is much more than the personification of a sociological type: he is the embodiment of evil, as well as the personification of unmotivated and irrational hatred. The second type is represented by those who " […] are a mixed body of men" (ibid., p. 224) who let themselves be influenced by the highly committed. The protagonist, Renzo, belongs to the third category. He represents the voice of reason, the curious who is able to keep his rationality even amidst the most furious manifestation of violence and hostility. A brief passage, characterized by Manzoni's usual irony, should confirm the narrative role of the mountain dweller brought to the big city by the vicissitudes of life:

To say the truth, the destruction of sieves and kneading- troughs, the pillaging of bake-houses, and the routing of bakers, are not the most expeditious means of providing a supply of bread; but this is one of those metaphysical subtleties which never enter the mind of the multitude. Renzo, without being of too metaphysical a turn, yet not being in such a state of excitement as the others, could not avoid making this reflection in his mind.

(ibid., p. 216)

The riot is eventually quelled, in a collective scene in which two opposite tendencies (the one of those who would like to have the superintended killed and the one of those who would like to have him given up to the authority) contend for the favour of the crowd. The intervention of the vice-governor Antonio Ferrer, idolized by the crowd as the one who had imposed price control on bread, solves the tension. The crowd let him take the superintendent in charge, with the promise that he will operate as to have him put in jail. Accompanied by a row of soldiers at each side of his carriage, Ferrer is eventually able to take the superintendent far from the raging crowd. The crowd is eventually left without a purpose. The power of the state (although in the farcical form of the intervention of Ferrer) is eventually able to re-establish order, which is consistent with the last phase of Smelser's treatment of collective behaviour, that is the operation of social control (Smelser, 1962, p. 17).

What is striking in Alessandro Manzoni's representation of the crowd is its subtlety. There is no predefined uniformity but a complex social process by which the sentiment of hostility is driven either in the direction of the tumult or in the direction of the appeasement. Social unrest may result one way or the other, according to those in the crowd who are better able to excite emotions or to calm hostility down. Such a penetrating sociological gaze, expressed in the first modern example of Italian narrative, may deserve a final long quotation:

In popular tumults there is always a certain number of men, who, either from overheated passions, or from fanatical persuasion, or from wicked designs, or from an execrable love of destruction, do all they can to push matters to the worst they propose or second the most inhuman advice, and fan the flame whenever it seems to be sinking [...] But, by way of counterpoise, there is always a certain number of very different men, who, perhaps, with equal ardour and equal perseverance, are aiming at a contrary effect: some influenced by friendship or partiality for the threatened objects; others, without further impulse than that of a pious and spontaneous horror of bloodshed and atrocious deeds [...] Those who make up the mass, and almost the materials of the tumult besides, are a mixed body of men, who, more or less, by infinite gradations, hold to one or the other extreme: partly incensed, partly knavish, a little inclined to a sort of justice, according to their idea of the word, a little desirous of witnessing some grand act of villainy; prone to ferocity or compassion, to adoration or execration, according as opportunities present themselves of indulging to the full one or other of these sentiments craving every moment to know, to believe, some gross absurdity or improbability, and longing to shout, applaud, or revile in somebody's train.

(Manzoni, 1842, p. 224)

5 Brief concluding remarks

The crowd has always been a puzzle for the social sciences. It makes the strong interconnection between the individual and collectivities evident. Moreover, it forces social thinkers to question the idea that modernity can be understood as a time of sole rationality, a period in which passions have been, if not suppressed, at least tamed, civilized and controlled. When social sciences developed, raging mobs were not only attacking old hierarchies and privileges, they were at the same time showing how idealistic the idea of progress (hence of a rationally achieved social change) could be. The raging crowds put the long-established Western tradition of the rational individual actors into question, together with the idea that social change could be rationally achieved through accurate and well-thought human planning. The individual and his rationality dissolved within the crowd, in a process by which collective emotions heavily conditioned and eventually replaced the rational self-control of individual actors. Crowd behaviour was hence conceived as chiefly emotional, the evident demonstration that modernity could not only be represented as increasingly rational, but also as increasingly emotional. The emotional component of individual and collective behaviours could not be suppressed by modern progress since, on the contrary, modernity itself seemed able to produce new forms of emotionally driven behaviours.

At the outset of the scientific representation of the crowd, one finds an oversimplified conception by which the mob is negatively qualifiable as irrational, violent, impulsive. "According to 19th-century semantics – writes Christian Borch – crowds are endowed with characteristics of suggestibility, femininity, immaturity, in short, irrationality" (Borch, 2006, p. 84). The endeavour of

20th century social theory has been to bring rationality and individuality back into the analysis of collective phenomenon. This process, which has been accurately analyzed by Clark McPhail (1991/2017), has produced a gradual change in the objects of analysis of those scholars who deal with collective behaviour. On the one hand, the idea of emotional contagion has been questioned, at least since Turner and Killian (1957) and Smelser (1962) developed their theories. This has led to a conception of emotionality understood not as the cause but, at most, as the consequence of crowd action (McPhail, 1991/2017, p. 109). Emotionality tended to be considered, as it were, as the psychological by-product of collective behaviour, which, in so far as it was connected to inner processes, did not deserve sociological investigation. The model of the emotional, irreflexive actor was replaced by a rational individual, who could act rationally even in the midst of a collective chaos. It is evident that both contrasting models are mock-representation, both hyper-simplifying what actually happens in a crowd.

The crowd lost its appeal as an object of investigation, being substituted by other topics (chiefly social movement) which could be better analyzed by making reference to cognitively oriented approaches (Borch, 2012, pp. 259–260). This accounts for a normalization of collective behaviour, no longer perceived as a negative dimension of social action but, on the contrary, as an utterly normal form of interaction, based on gathering in public spaces (ibid.). In the present day revival of emotions and sociology, collective behaviour and social movement have been once again analyzed in connection to the emotion they are able to arouse and the role emotions play in the reinforcement of collective ties (Jasper, 1998; Jasper, 2011; von Scheve and Ismer, 2013; Goodwin, Jasper and Poletta, 2001; Flan and King, 2005). Yet, as Borch (2012) convincingly argues, the disappearance of the crowd as one of the main topics of sociological investigation accounts for a persisting rationalism and individualism affecting social sciences today. The questions are relevant, since they have to do not only with collective behaviour but also with the present-day semantics of the individual and its relation to society and the social bond. Regardless of the emotional turn, social theory still conceives actor and action as essentially rational.

Literary works may override this gross simplification, allowing the reader a sort of quasi-ethnographic experience and showing how collective action is the complex output of emotionality, strategic thinking, simulation, cooperation and conflict, all inextricably incorporated in the acting bodies of those who partake. This chapter does not even attempt at tackling such manifold theoretical problems. It suggests, more modestly, the potentiality of literature as a fictive yet appropriate field for the sociological observation of the complex relation between emotionality, quasi-rational choices and collective behaviour. Literary accounts may be adopted so as to illustrate a sociological theory (as they are here in the case of Zola's *Germinal*) but may also be capable of overcoming the reduced complexity of sociological theorizing, its taking part for rational subjectivity or emotional unanimity, showing (as Manzoni masterfully did) the intricacy of crowd behaviour, its being difficultly reducible to a single dimension, hence its being the appropriate object of a renewed sociological interest.

Notes

1 The Italian school of criminology anticipated much of the ideas which would later be developed by Gustave Le Bon (McPhail, 1991/2007, p. 2).
2 Interpretations of Manzoni's crowd based on Le Bon are available (Sottong, 2012).

7 Envy, social order and social change

1 Envy as a sociological concept

Envy is the topic of this chapter. More specifically, I will try and analyze the role of this sentiment as a tool to explain social phenomena, both on the micro and on the macro level. The literary works which have been selected are analyzed in the attempt to show the implications of envy as a sentiment able to foster social order, social change and social mobility. My hypothesis is that the social representations of envy change over time and that semantic innovations have specific structural and functional relevance. Simple social structures usually restrain envy, as envy is understood as a negative feeling, endowed with a destabilizing power, hence capable of undermining social order. On the contrary, modern society tends to mitigate the negative conception of envy, which, even if it is not converted into a positive feeling, is tolerated as a factor promoting social mobility. Nonetheless, the mitigation of the negative conception of envy is never totally achieved, and it functions only in connection to specifically modern phenomena (here I will analyze social mobility and consumerism). In micro and meso contexts, on the contrary, envy is still understood as a destabilizing sentiment, able to disturb social processes and established hierarchies and values, for example within modern organizations (Vidaillet, 2008). The present chapter will hence analyze envy from a limited point of view, as both an obstacle and an instrument of social mobility.

But how can we qualify envy from a sociological point of view? Envy is, according to Schoeck (1966) transcultural. As compared to other emotions or sentiments, whose definitions are often culturally specific, every known culture seems to have felt the necessity to define envy, for example as:

> the state of mind of a person who cannot bear someone else's being something, having a skill, possessing something or enjoying a reputation which he himself lacks, and who will therefore rejoice should the other lose his asset, although that loss will not mean his own gain.
>
> (ibid., p. 12)

Not only have all societies defined envy. They have also detected "conceptual and ritual mechanisms designed as protection against those of their fellow men who are prone to this condition" (ibid.). This may depend on the perceived disruptiveness of envy which, by questioning established order and defined structures, is chastised in traditional and pre-modern cultures. Since envy is perceived as a possible danger, it is, Schoeck writes, the premise for the activation of instruments of social control:

> If we were not constantly obliged to take account of other men's envy of the extra pleasure that accrues to us as we begin to deviate from a social norm, "social control" could not function. In all the cultures of mankind, in all proverbs and fairy tales, the emotion of envy is condemned. The envious person is universally exhorted to be ashamed of himself. And yet his existence, or the belief in his ubiquity, has at the same time always provided enough latent apprehension of other people's views to allow a system of social controls and balances to evolve.
>
> (ibid., p. 3)

As to its social function, envy is therefore ambivalent. It is a sentiment potentially able to trigger social change, since it may stimulate social emulation or social conflict, and, at the same time, it may be understood as a pre-condition for social order. This ambivalence is rooted in the semantics of the word. In English, envy has a double origin: it derives both from the old French *envie*, which entails admiration, and the Latin *invidere*, meaning malice for the accomplishments or qualities of other people. And in fact:

> [a] feeling of envy may be the price we pay for the recognition of another's qualities or abilities that we do not possess but to which we aspire. It is a twinge of pain in the midst of a surge of admiration.
>
> (Britton, 2008, p. 126)

It is the swinging of the meaning of the term between hate and admiration which characterizes envy as a sentiment and accounts for its potential when it comes to its social function.

One of the first sociologists who attempted to define the sentiment of envy was Georg Simmel. With his usual terminological accuracy, he distinguishes envy from jealousy. Envy, writes Simmel, is the desire for an object which is not in our possession and upon which we may not have a claim (Simmel, 1904, p. 521). In this sense, it is to be distinguished from jealousy, which, on the contrary, refers to an object which one possesses or may claim.

> Both sentiments – Simmel writes – are undoubtedly of the widest significance for the molding of human relationships. With both there comes into question an object of value which a third party either actually or symbolically hinders us in attaining or controlling. When it is a case of attaining, we may more properly speak of envy; if it is a matter of retaining, jealousy is the passion involved.
>
> (ibid.)

By claiming his/her own right on a person, the jealous partner engages in a relation which implies both unity (the dyad is perceivable as a dyad) and disjunction (jealousy is the consequence of a fracture). The relation entails, at any rate, a conflict issuing from some sort of former integration. This produces an unusual combination of passionate love coexisting with passionate hatred, which makes Simmel speak of jealousy as "that sociological phenomenon in which the erection of antagonism above unity reaches subjectively its most radical form" (ibid., p. 525). Whereas jealously is based on the sentiment of a broken relation (or broken trust), envy is a claim for what is in principle not claimable, hence for some aspects of social life (a quality, a property, an object or a person) belonging to someone else. This characteristic of envy accounts for its productive role in social change. Envy in fact entails at least the possibility to envisage alternatives to the actual social order, to the distribution of privileges, wealth, socially scanty rewards. And as such, envy is socially more dangerous than jealousy, as the envious Iago (the disruptive advocate of alternative futures) is for the jealous Othello (longing to re-established order after the supposed infidelity of his lover).

In his intelligent pamphlet on the topic, Epstein (2003) states that envy is the output of the question *why not me*? When confronted with troubles or serious problems, the question we pose to ourselves is *why me*? By confronting our conditions with that of our fellow people we may happen to notice the difference in fortune between us and the others. People may be richer, more powerful or luckier than we are. Thus, envy is an utterly social sentiment, since it originates from comparison and from the possibility to differentiate between us and the others. The object of envy is, as it were, always part of social interaction (Ferguson, 2002, p. 889). Not surprisingly, justice as an ideal balance among people's attributes is often understood as an intellectualized output of envy (Frye, 2016) with political consequences when it converts into a vindication of a more equal society (Schoeck, 1966; Barbalet, 1992). This connection between envy and the vindication of equality is, at any rate, a late development of the culturally determined conception of envy.

Simple and traditional societies tend to consider envy always as a negative sentiment in so far as it may undermine social order and social stability. Anthropological researches, in particular, have shown how traditional cultures try to guarantee social stability. In segmentary societies equality among members is the norm, since social differences are generally connected to specific natural attributes (e.g. sex or age) on which the differentiation and distribution of social roles is grounded. In such societies, any deviation from equality is perceived as abnormal, thus "the primitive man [...] explains any deviation upwards, or downwards, from the supposedly normally, emotionally acceptable society of equals as having been caused by the deliberate and malicious activity of fellow tribesmen" (Schoeck, 1966, p. 49). Thus, on the one hand, envy is generally censured as the malevolent product of black magic, on the other, one tends to stigmatize those who emerge over the average, since their achievements are often imputed to the summoning of dark forces (ibid., p. 40). The equalizing function of envy in simple society is therefore twofold: the envier is stigmatized as the dangerous upsetter of the social order; moreover, those who could potentially gain social rewards (more wealth, more power or more prestige) or accede to a superior social status through social mobility, tend to avoid any action aiming at their social improvements, so as to ward themselves off the negative effects of the evil eye (i.e. other people's envy).

The above-sketched hypothesis of the relations between envy, social change and social order will be tested in reference to literary texts. My attempt is not the construction of an all-encompassing theory, but rather the illustrative use of literary materials so to describe small scenarios in which envy is actually at work. What I intend to do is, by following Robert Nisbet's lesson (Nisbet, 1976), to construct analytical dioramas, small scale representations of the social, able to let us penetrate the complex relations between the individuals and social structures, personal feelings and social constraints, in specific social and historical contexts. Starting from the illustrative use of the selected materials, an attempt will be made at detaching the relation among the individual sentiment of envy, the semantics developed in order to represent it and the transformation of the social structure over time.

2 Envy. A sentiment and a deadly sin

Envy has been understood by the theologians of the great monotheistic religions as a source of social destructiveness (Britton, 2008, p. 126). Here is the definition of envy in a 1914 catechism meant for student priests:

> Envy is a feeling of sadness, uneasiness, or discontent excited at the sight of another's superiority or success: whether in the spiritual or in the temporal order; and this because we fancy our own merit to be lessened thereby. Envy is not only contrary to charity, but leads to rash judgement, calumny, detraction, hatred and to rejoicing at another's ill-fortune.
>
> (Hart, quoted ibid.)

In the tradition of the Catholic Church, envy is both a sentiment and a sin, actually one of the seven deadly sins. Among the seven deadly sins, only two are to be understood as emotions or sentiments (envy and wrath) whereas the others are connected with attitudes, dispositions or actual habitual behaviours (gluttony, sloth, lust, pride and greed). Locating a sentiment (hence what one feels, not what one does) among the most dangerous sins is clear evidence of the perceived dangerousness of envy, that is of its anti-social and destructive character.

The envious are located by Dante Alighieri (ca. 1313/1956) in the 13th Canto of the *Purgatorio*. Due to the logic of retaliation (i.e. the principle regulating the distribution of punishment according to the features of sins) the sinners who had cast their malice eyes on others when alive (*invidere*, the Latin root of envy, actually means to stare fiercely at someone) are now blind, their eyelids sewed with iron wires. They are dressed in poor clothes, resembling beggars, since charity is the virtue opposite to envy and, as beggars waiting for handouts, they are to listen to examples of charity, uttered loudly by invisible spirits. Moreover, since during their lifetime, the spirits were part of no community, because envy separates the envier from his fellow people, they have now to stick close together, cooperation being the only way to avoid falling down the Purgatory hill. The description Dante provides of envy stresses its disruptiveness. Whereas charity is stirred by our interests for other people's well-being, envy is motivated by our desire for other people's ruin. As a sentiment, it overlaps with what the German call *Schadenfreude*, that is the joy deriving from other people's misfortune. And indeed, the protagonist of the 13th Canto of *Purgatorio* is Sapia, a woman from Siena devoid of any sense of belonging to her community, such that she had exulted at the defeat of her own city in the Battle of Colle Val D'Elsa against Florence (1269). For the politically engaged Dante who, even as an exile had always experienced his belonging to the city of Florence as a specific feature of his identity, the rejection of one's city bonds is a deplorable sin, resulting in the self-exclusion of Sapia from the original community.

Dante wrote his *Purgatorio* around 1313. Almost coeval (1303–1305) to Dante's *Purgatorio* are Giotto's frescos at the Scrovegni Chapel in Padua. The frescos are a complex representation of salvation, based upon three cycles of scenes: Joachim and Anna, the Life of Jesus and the Life of the Virgin. At the bottom of the chapel, Giotto paints monochrome allegories of vices and virtues and, among them, Envy opposite to Charity as its antithetical quality. The allegory of Envy has been masterfully described by John Ruskin in his *The Stones of Venice*:

> Giotto has [...] represented her [...] as having her fingers terminating in claws, and raising her right hand with an expression partly of impotent regret, partly of involuntary grasping; a serpent, issuing from her mouth, is about to bite her between her eyes: she has long membranous ears, horns on her head and flames consuming her body.
>
> (Ruskin quoted in Grauso, 2010, p. 231)

The monstrosity of the allegorical portrait Giotto gives of envy hints at the idea that being envious recoils on the envier. In psychoanalytical terms, indeed, envy may be understood as a sentiment which affects both the actor and his fellow people. And, in fact, "a person afflicted with an envious nature is not only a potential aggressor, but also a victim of his own disposition" (Britton, 2008, p. 126). From a sociological point of view, Giotto's portrayal emphasizes the self-destructiveness of the envier, represented as one who, by setting himself (as Sapia did) outside the community of his fellow people, produces social distress and, at the same time, self-exclusion. It is this anti-social character of envy which accounts for the disgraceful place this sentiment holds among vices. In Giotto's representation, Envy (the only polychromatic image among the symbolic representations of vices and virtues) is burning into the flames which she herself has produced, which once again stresses the dangerousness of envy, both for the envier and the social context.

Still in the *Puritan Age*, envy may be configured not only as a sin, but as the origin of sins as such. *Paradise Lost* (1667) (hence another allegorical and metaphorical poem) is, in this regard, particularly eloquent. Envy is here understandable in psychoanalytic terms as a projective identification with an "imputably privileged, enviable person [...] [who] is felt to possess attributes that the envious person thinks should rightly be his: thus he feels himself impaired" (Britton, 2008, p. 127). Such a psychological process is at the base of Satan's mutiny. In Milton's words:

> Satan, so call him now, his former name
> Is heard no more in heav'n; he of the first,
> If not the first Archangels great in power,
> In favour and pre-eminence, yet fraught
> With envy against the Son of God, that day
> Honoured by his great Father, and proclaimed
> Messiah king anointed, could not bear
> Through pride that sight, and thought himself Impaired.
>
> (Milton, *Paradise Lost*, Book V, v. 658–665)

Envy leads Satan to plot against Adam and Eve in Eden, their happiness being perceived as unbearable:

> Sight hateful, sight tormenting! Thus these two
> Imparadis'd in one another's arms
> The happier Eden, shall enjoy their fill
> Of bliss on bliss, while I to Hell am thrust.
>
> (Milton, *Paradise Lost*, Book IV, v. 505–508)

Still in the 17th century, within the modernizing yet strongly religious context of Puritan England, envy is perceived as a highly negative sentiment, able to describe the condition of man, a fallen creature whose destiny has been determined, from the outset, by the ill-posed belief of deserving what one does not possess. The implicit message is that envy has to be tamed, mastered, controlled in order to avoid further catastrophic consequences for the individual and the community to which he belongs.

3 Iago, or the envier in a society in transition

Iago, the antagonist of Shakespeare's *Othello* (1604), is probably the literary envier *par excellence*, the archvillain whose cruelty is utterly incomprehensible in so far as it seems devoid of any actual motive, except the destruction of those he hates and of himself. His envy appears indeed so much ill posed that Samuel Taylor Coleridge, in his reading of Othello (Coleridge, 1907, pp. 167–177), talks about it in terms of a "motiveless malignity". Coleridge describes the Shakespearian character as endowed with a rationality aimed to grasp the weaknesses of those he wants to oppress, and use their weak points so as to destroy all that they consider essential. In pursuing his evil tasks, Iago is fully modern. Indeed, Coleridge compares him to a cool experimenter, who is also a *connoisseur* of human feelings and actions, able as he is to identify the objects of other people's affection and to work as a destructive force against those objects. Iago is endowed with all those features (self-awareness and rational choices for example) which characterize the modern individual (Wells Slights, 1997, pp. 380–381). Although his action is rationally modern, it is in fact understood as a means to oppose the advancing modernity, represented by his antagonist, Othello. His unmotivated wickedness entails an instrumental capacity to evaluate his social surroundings and the motives and feelings driving other people's actions (Ferguson, 2002, pp. 892–893). Nonetheless, Iago's envy results in a sort of *zwecklos Rationalität*, a *cupio dissolvi*, which, although devoid of rational motives (as opposed to Weber's *Zweckrationalität*), is pursued by rational means. One could state that Iago's envy, although already modern (it is not perceived as a sin but as the output of a disturbed morality) is still endowed with the specific features of envy as conceived in an earlier period. The envier is satisfied with the annihilation of the community to which he belongs, which entails his self-exclusion and eventually his self-destruction. Thus, his "motiveless malignity" configures Iago as a character in between the rationality of rising modernity and the destructing, self-excluding attitude typical of envy in a previous age. Othello is Iago's counterpart, in so far as he may be understood as the personification of a new modern human prototype, who acts rationally for his military honour and the superior good of the state.

The partial modernity of Iago's behaviour accounts for the necessity to understand his misdeeds as conditioned by a social structure which is no longer fully hierarchical (as the medieval society was) and is not yet fully modern. And indeed, a sociological understanding of Iago's "motiveless malignity" would probably take advantage of a reading of the tragedy which should carefully take into account the structural changes of English society in the 17th century. A society structured upon pre-established, unchangeable differences is characterized, as it were, by a frozen complexity. Differences rigidly establish what is allowed to each individual actor, according to his social origins and belongings. Social belongings, in their turn, pre-define a set of actions allowed to specific social categories, hence they predetermine individual destinies. Thus differences, once they are conceived as unchangeable (in the jargon of sociology, when they are ascribed) produce a highly predictable social context. On the other hand, the less predictable social differences and the more varied social actions are, the more complex the social structure. In the 17th century, English society (which is reflected in the Venice of the tragedy) was radically changing in the direction of a more dynamic structure, whose features began to be properly modern. English economy "came to rely more strongly on merchandizing, trade and venturing" (Logan, 2004, p. 354), thus destabilizing the old social order based chiefly on aristocratic privileges. In this changing context, the state was to assume a new, fundamental role, emerging as a modern organization able to guarantee stability and unity to the nation. The new functions of the state are better represented by Nicolò Machiavelli (1469–1527), who proposed a de-moralized conception of politics, by which the Prince has to act not for the interests and privileges of single individuals, but for the progress of the nation, understood as a political and moral entity: "The Prince must reject socially supported moral imperatives in order to ensure the strength and stability of the state – figured by Machiavelli as the source of generalized benefit – ignoring subjects' needs, interests or desires" (ibid.). The authority of the Prince has to be consolidated as compared to the Middle Age, when power is generally segmented among the king and his feudal lords, the main task of the Prince now being to harmonize the plurality of colliding interests and values and define general objectives.

Sandra Logan (2004) proposes an interesting reading of the Shakespearean tragedy, by which Othello and Iago represent contrasting ideologies: Othello is the promoter of a new conception of humanity and the state, whereas Iago is the advocate of the old order and the predestined victim of social and political transformations. In Logan's interpretation, Othello is the tragedy where "the personal and the political violently collide, and the early modern family/state homology collapses" (ibid., p. 351). Venice represents the new, emerging world, a world where acquired characteristics are more relevant than birth and social origin and where the *raison d'état* is becoming the shared ideology of the developing modern state. In this new social and political context, Othello emerges as a *homo novus*, a *morisco* (i.e. a converted Muslim) who, although not totally forgetful of his origins, grounds his social identity on personal achievements. Moreover, his capacity for personal choice is deeply rooted in his adherence to the new ideology of the forming modern state. Here follows an effective description of Othello, proposed by Camille Wells Slights:

> Valuing personal freedom more than family lineage and inherited loyalties, Othello assumes that his position in society derives from conscious choice and service to the state. Unlike such protagonists as Hamlet, Lear, or Macbeth, who are tightly embedded in networks of kinship and feudal allegiance, Othello's sense of personal and social identity is based on individual achievement and merit. He owes his position in Venetian society to personal ability and the chances of war. Though he proudly claims descent from "men of royal siege" (1. 22), he sees no disjunction between his origins and his current position; his sense of social identity derives from "My services which I have done the signiory" (1. 18).
>
> (Wells Slights, 1997, p. 379)

The development of a unitary state able, as it were, to unify the individual intentions and values for the common good, appears to be a gross idealization. And indeed, the vicissitudes of the characters and the tragic ending of the play is interpreted by Sandra Logan as evidence that the modern state has in itself the seeds of its own failure. Unity is not achieved without injustice, increasing disparities and discontent. Thus, whereas Othello represents the new citizen, self-conscious of his qualities and in agreement with the new social configuration and values, Iago represents the unsuccessful resistance against the new order. In such a perspective, the motives which induced Iago to his unrestrained hatred (the suspicion that his wife has betrayed him with Othello and his being preferred to Cassio as lieutenant) may be understood under a new light: no longer trivial motivations partially justifying a boundless hatred, but a sort of active resistance against the new order. The first motive (the betrayal) has to do with traditional family ties which are being upset by advancing modernity. An example of the conflict opposing the old and the new conception of the family is evident in the contrasted marriage between Desdemona and Othello. When Barbantio, Desdemona's father, lodges a claim before the Senate of Venice, in order to vindicate the honour of his daughter and his right to revoke her marriage to the Moor, the Senate disregard Brabantio's requests. Considering the military value of Othello, and comparing it to Brabantio's patriarchal claims, the Senate decides in favour of the superior interests of the state, which is now leading a crucial war against the Turks. Even family ties, once subsumed under the control of the *pater familias*, are now reinterpreted according to the new values of individual mobility and the unitary interests of the state. With her active choice, Desdemona is the character who represents this relevant change at its best:

> [her] desires – writes Sandra Logan – coincide with the state's support of social mobility: her acceptance of Othello, despite his visible difference and lack of social standing in Venice, reinforces the shift away from blood-based hierarchy and "natural" social order. In its place, and in the service of emergent modern political interests, a new system of merit-based social advancement begins to assert itself.
>
> (ibid.: 362)

When Iago emphasizes his situation as a betrayed husband, he is actually vindicating his right to the honesty of his wife, within a patriarchal conception of the family, now diminished by the power of Othello as the embodiment of the *raison d'état*.

The same incapacity to adapt to social and political changes is visible in the second motive triggering Iago's conduct, that is his usurped advancement. Iago seems unable to adapt to the new order by which Othello is left free to choose his lieutenant, thus disregarding the influence and prestige of aristocracy, represented here by the request made by three noble Venetians in favour of Iago ("three great ones of the city,/In personal suit to make me his [Othello's] lieutenant,/Off-capped to him but were unsuccessful" [I.1, 8–10]). As often is the case with huge literary characters, Iago's action is not to be imputed to a single sentiment. Indeed, envy mixes up with jealousy, at least in the sense in which Simmel (1904) understood this sentiment as a malaise generated by the loss of something which the actor considers his own. Thus, Iago's envy, tainted with jealousy, is not fully understandable if we stick to Coleridge's idea of a malignity devoid of any motivation. It is, on the contrary, chiefly determined by Iago's incapacity to adapt to the new world, one where old costumes, mores and ideals are by now valueless, replaced as they are with personal merits, social mobility and the reason of state (Logan, 2004, p. 364). On its turn, Othello is the representative of the new order, able to assume the new values of the modern state and its objectives as his own, and his compliance with the state's expectations (hence his capacity to adapt to the new social context) is the principal reason for his success. Against the interpretation according to which Othello is only loosely part of the Venetian establishment due to his ethnicity, Camille Wells Slight (1997) has stressed the fact that the Moor is, on the contrary, a conspicuous component of the new social order:

> In opposition, then, to the now-dominant view that Othello's vulnerability lies in his position as an alien, a Moor not fully secure within Venetian society, I see Othello as not merely a Moor in Venice but the Moor of Venice, whose deepest values and sense of self are fully consonant with those of Venice's other inhabitants.
>
> (Wells Slights, 1997, p. 384)

The excluded is, on the contrary, Iago, whose passionate envy is addressed to the destruction of those who support the new order. His modernity, that is his capacity to rationally control his emotions and direct them rationally towards the intended result, is motivated by an anti-modern attitude, expressed in his unrestricted desire to oppose the overcoming novelties.

> "Control" – Logan writes – then, is in actuality a rechannelling of passion into vengeance. Reason is brought into play against those who are perceived as threatening to the patriarchal control of the home and family, or to the socioeconomic security of the male subject [...] For Iago, on the other hand, reason serves as the basis for establishing both his right to vengeance and the method he will pursue. He is, in this sense, embedded in the old order. His plot is specifically one of traditional – almost biblical – vengeance, as he seeks to return in kind the wrongs he imagines to have been perpetrated against him.
>
> (Logan, 2004, p. 366)

The apparent "motiveless malignity" of Iago may be thus explained as the motivated resistance to social changes. It could hardly emerge in a stable social context, in which roles are set once and for all and the individual is, as it were, defined by his location in the social order (hence no Moor could be appointed general). Iago's envy is an instrument to oppose transformations; the world is changing as well as the rules which define social coexistence and social roles. In this changing world, Iago is ill at ease; thus he transforms his insufficient capacity to adapt to the new social environment into rational scheming and destructive actions. Standing at the juncture of two ages, he is the output of a still unaccomplished social change. Envy is no longer able to produce social stability, as in pre-modern societies. It is not yet an instrument of social change and social mobility, as in full modernity. The sentiment is still endowed with a destructiveness of its own, a capacity to elicit unease and support social estrangement. Hence the motiveless-ness of Iago's envy, which eventually results in his capacity to produce a rational behaviour, whose final output is not a benefit for the envier but, as in previous times, the annihilation of the community and of the envier himself.

4 Enviers claiming their lost status. *The Way We Live Now*

The 19th century in English literature is qualified as the *Age of the Novel*. One may talk of a sort of strong ideological bound between the middle-class reading public and the early and mid-Victorian novelists, by which the reader could easily identify in the novel characters, values, forms of behaviours and social structures as he had already experienced them in his everyday life. The average Victorian reader – as David Daiches writes:

> wanted to be entertained with a minimum of literary convention, a minimum of "aesthetic distance". He wanted to be close to what he was reading about, to have as little suspension of disbelief as possible, to pretend, indeed, that literature was journalism, that fiction was history.
>
> (Daiches, 1969, p. 1049)

But although realistic novels could, at a first sight, be equated with objective accounts of reality, they were on the contrary the output of the mastery of the novelists, able to produce apparent faithful representations but only in so far as they complied with the rules and tropes of an artificial literary genre. Rather than describing an objective reality, the novelist proposed his own version of contem-porary England and "often created complexes of symbolic meaning that reached far deeper than the superficial pattern of social action suggested to the casual reader" (ibid.)

The words of Daiches are to be assumed as a warning against a naïve use of realism as a faithful representation of reality but also as an appreciation of the ideological and cognitive qualities of literary narratives. In the case of realistic novels, the temptation to conceive the narrative as a mirror of reality is particu-larly strong. As a matter of fact, a narrative is never a mechanical representation of reality. It is, on the contrary, a selection of disparate aspects, characters and events which eventually converge so as to give a plausible and unitary represen-tation. This *fictional* character of narratives (regardless of the fact that they are made up – e.g. a novel – or related to actuality – e.g. a journalist report) is stig-matized by Paul Ricoeur who describes this form of communication as a process of grasping together otherwise disconnected events and actions, thus conveying a new, unitary meaning (Ricoeur, 1984, p. 66). One needs therefore to be cautious when assuming narrative material (especially fiction) as mirroring the real.

A narrative report consists always of socially conditioned forms of the narra-tions, yet, although it may manifest values and knowledge specific to the social context in which it emerges, it may never overlap with reality (whatever one may mean with this polysemous term). Among the Victorians, Anthony Trollope has been considered as an accurate witness of his age. The Italian literary critic Mario Praz, while imputing to Dickens' and Thackery's novels a certain distorting power, attributes Trollope an artful fidelity to the original. According to Praz, indeed, Trollope has the essential quality "of acting as the supremely faithful mirror of Victorian Age between the years 1860 and 1880" (Praz, quoted in Banks, 1968, p. 177). Yet, if at all, Trollope's novels mirror only a small portion of the Victorian society. Anthony Trollope describes reality from his peculiar standpoint, that of a conservative member of the upper middle class, focusing his attention chiefly on gentry, living in a delimited geographical area (London, small towns in the south of England and the nearby countryside) (Banks, 1968, p. 181). Thus, the representation is by necessity partial, with little hints to important social phenomena, such as industrialization, and almost no regard to important parts of the country, such as the unstable industrial North.

Nonetheless, Trollope's novels are rich in sociological suggestions, such that he has been considered, perhaps too emphatically, as both a novelist, a historian and a sociologist *malgré lui* (Hewitt, 1963). Some of the topics in his fiction are particularly relevant for the sociological eye. The first is the bewilderment and ill ease of English upper middle classes at the social, cultural and economic changes which were taking place in the second half of the 19th century. Trollope's novels may be thus understood as a plausible representation of the reaction of the social élite to current changes. This is one of the reasons why the great amount of fictional material Trollope left us is an effective representation of "the way certain of Trollope's contemporaries saw the world of their days", notably the upper-middle-class Victorians (Banks, 1968, p. 181). But the occasional sociological quality of Trollope's novel is at its best when he attempts, as it were, to "realistically develop the interplay of personality in social situations" (ibid., p. 186). Trollope is, one could say, a micro-sociologist and an unaware interactionist *ante literam,* able to subtly analyze the mutual obligations of characters in their everyday reciprocally oriented action. Thus, the sociological reader may take advantage of characters who either adhere to the socially shared conventions or deviate from them, in an interesting interplay able to reveal the ideological substratum of social values (ibid., p. 188).

In Trollope's representation of social relations, envy has an important role. In a rapidly changing world, one where social differences are chiefly determined by achievement, envy may assume the character of a vindication of old privileges and statuses, which are by now anachronistic. In order to test this hypothesis, I propose here a tentative analysis of one of the best among Trollope's novels, that is *The Way We Live Now. The Way We Live Now* was written in 1875 and is chiefly centred around the figure of Augustus Melmotte, an unscrupulous financier whose past is unknown and who is able, regardless of his rudeness and unfitness to the manners of London high society, to gain the favour of part of London's upper class and obtain a seat in the Parliament, being eventually overrun by his financial misdeeds, which leads him to the final suicide. *The Way We Live Now* is first of all a strong satire against the transformation of English society: no longer chiefly based on the values of aristocracy and birth. Money and achievements are now able to establish the social status of individuals, which results in an inter-mingling of people of different origins and in an ever more anomic social behav-iour. The old values and way of living are represented by Roger Carbury, stoutly resisting any contact with Augustus Melmotte, the *homo novus* conceived both as an impostor and a threat to the established social order. Yet, regardless of the critique against the rapid changes affecting English society, personified in the character of Roger Carbury, Trollope is at his best when depicting the entangle-ment of the individual in the new complex network of social relations and rules, within which the social actor finds himself often alone. This social isolation char-acterizes Trollope's sympathetic representation of the misfits, including Augustus Melmotte, in his final decision to take his own life (Gilmour, 2004, p. 124).

According to William A. Cohen (2009), envy is a systematic sentiment in *The Way We Live Now*. It affects most of the characters, and its vivid representation may be configured as an underlining critique against capitalism not much as an economic system, but for its social and moral destructiveness. Envy is a relevant element in the plot machinery. It motivates decisions and triggers social actions and that in almost all the social spheres the novel deals with: the business world and the affair of the Mexican Railway Company, the world of journalism, pub-lishers and authors, the social world of clubs where members of the upper classes meet chiefly to gamble (ibid., p. 300). The sentiment is, as it were, diffuse and unavoidable since it reflects the ill ease of the individuals in an ever more unsta-ble social structure, characterized by the new values of achievements which have replaced the position once held by honour and rank.

As a matter of fact, the ideal of social upgrading was by now a consolidated character of society, yet it was perceived both as an opportunity and a risk in the mid-Victorian period (about 1850–1870). Progress, which was a key word of the century, had to be controlled and socially directed, which in the coeval sociologi-cal thought was wonderfully expressed by Auguste Comte's combination of sta-bility and social change or, in his jargon, of social statics and dynamics (Comte, 1875). Robin Gilmour (2004, p. 103) has stressed the relevance of the combina-tion of progress and social stability in the political discourse of the period, by making reference to a speech which the Prime Minister Lord Palmerston gave in 1865 at the *South London Industrial Exhibition* to an audience of artisans and workmen. In the speech, Palmerston stressed that, although the higher positions in society are difficult to reach, yet a certain degree of mobility is now available, provided that the privileges and power of the monarchy and the aristocracy are not put into question (ibid., p. 105). Social stability is still perceived as a value and social mobility may be guaranteed provided that the fundamental order of society is accepted by the generality of the population. In this rapidly changing context, which still devotes social relevance to ascribed hierarchies, envy has a specific function: it overlaps with the vindications of old privileges, once they have been swept away by *the way we live now*. Thus, while the general function of envy works somewhat underground in the novel, motivating actions and conflicts among the characters, its specific narrative role is connected to the resentment for lost prestige and wealth of those who still represent themselves as belonging to the best part of the English society. As a matter of fact, the narrative role of envy as a vindication of the lost social position emerges also elsewhere in Trollope's huge literary production. Here is a brief quotation from Terry (1977) referring to the character of Reverend Mr. Crawley in *The Last Chronicle of Barset* (1867), in which envy mixes up with shame for one's decadence and with a persisting awareness of one's own value:

> One notes a curious sense of the stigma felt in loss of station, and it is this shame and envy, as such as secret pride in his own worth giving luxury to his woe, that almost drives Crawley insane. Trollope makes the point that reputation in the eyes of the community is necessary to man, and moreover that social standing and money are vital to self-respect.
>
> (Terry, 1977, p. 228)

In Trollope's novels, envy has a similar function as compared to Othello: it is the envy of those who, belonging to the high ranks of society, find themselves taken aback by the new system and enviously look at those who have power and wealth without socially deserving them. As in the character of Iago, envy combines with jealousy, understood as the injustice for a social position which has been lost and is yet imagined as due. Yet the demise of the old order is by now irreversible, so much that the envier does not even attempt to oppose the representatives of the new one (as Iago did) but strategically tries to come to terms with them. The old sociological distinction between class and status is here at work, class being conceived as connected to wealth, whereas status as expression of one's social prestige (Weber, 1958). The conflagration between wealth and social esteem entails a kind of conservative envy, whose output is a useless vindication of the privileges of the past and at the same time the active desire to belong to the new privileged class, which results in a process of self-degradation and further loss of prestige.

William A. Cohen (2009) has detected this specific declination of envy in two characters of *The Way We Live Now*. Mr. Adolphus Longstaff and his younger daughter Georgiana. The Longstaff family belongs to the lesser nobility of English squirearchy. Their intermediate social position makes them particularly vulnerable in a period of rapid social change. And indeed, their relevance in the plot is connected with their unsuccessful attempt to keep pace with the times, yet maintaining a snobbish attitude and a largely unmotivated status pride (Terry, 1977, p. 242). They are, as it were, the negative counterpart of the preserved values of landed gentry represented by Roger Carbury. Old Longstaff is portrayed as a contemptuous man, caught up in the prejudices of his status and unable to manage his difficult financial situation. Here is Trollope's description:

> He entertained an idea that all who understood the matter would perceive at a single glance that he was a gentleman of the first water, and a man of fashion. He was intensely proud of his position in life, thinking himself to be immensely superior to all those who earned their bread. There were no doubt

gentlemen of different degrees, but the English gentleman of gentlemen was he who had land, and family title-deeds, and an old family place, and family portraits, and family embarrassments, and a family absence of any useful employment. He was beginning even to look down upon peers, since so many men of much less consequence than himself had been made lords.

(Trollope, 1875/1941, p. 116)

His self-content combines with a set of ill-posed certainties on what is proper for a country gentleman:

There was very little that his position called upon him to do, but there was much that it forbad him to do. It was not allowed to him to be close in money matters. He could leave his tradesmen's bills unpaid till the men were clamorous, but he could not question the items in their accounts. He could be tyrannical to his servants, but he could not make inquiry as to the consumption of his wines in the servants' hall. He had no pity for his tenants in regard to game, but he hesitated much as to raising their rent. He had his theory of life and endeavoured to live up to it; but the attempt had hardly brought satisfaction to himself or to his family.

(ibid., p. 117)

His incapacity to arrange his financial difficulty by changing his habits results in Mr. Longstaff's idea that "the word in general was very hard on him" (ibid.). In this combination of self-esteem and ineptitude, envy emerges as the disregard for those who enjoy better social positions, in terms of status and wealth, or both. In psychological terms, it implies "turning the good things that someone else has, into a bad one as a way of disavowing the wish to possess it" (Cohen, 2009, p. 300).

The decline of the family is even more effectively portrayed in the character of Georgiana Longstaff. Her envy is systematic, tainted with "ravenous pride, covetousness and rage" (ibid.). Georgiana feels that she deserves a place among the members of the best society, which should actualize through an appropriate marriage. Yet, as time goes by, and the financial situation of her family gets worse, she downgrades her aspirations and eventually accepts the marriage proposal of the rich Jew Breghert, generating scandal among her relatives and social circle. Georgiana is convinced that marriage has nothing to do with love; it is a way to establish her role in society, and although she, as her father, over-esteems her social status, the marriage with a Jew is conceived as an opportunity to lead a comfortable and wealthy life. The engagement is eventually broken due to Georgiana's impossible economic demands and she, in a process which Cohen has effectively described as a "condensed anti-bildungsroman", eventually elopes with the local curate, a person whose status and wealth are incompatible with Georgiana's initial pretensions.

Mr. Longstaff and his daughter represent envy as a form of social and personal degradation: both characters only apparently stick to the old values and look to the new ones with contempt and resentment. Yet, by assuming that their social status should make them deserve a better social position, they are prone to mitigate their social scorn towards the parvenus. Envy for the wealth and social position of the new rich leads both father and daughter to intermingle with them, in the hope to share part of their success. Mr Longstaff aims at a position on the board of the Mexican Railway Company, whereas his daughter is ready to barter her social status for an advantageous marriage with a Jewish member of the new caste. Yet, envy is not sufficient motivation for successful action, and their attempt is bound to be unsuccessful, resulting in the final descent of both in the social scale.

5 Uriah Heep or the envy punished

David Copperfield is the *summa* of Charles Dickens' narrative and one of the masterpieces of the Victorian novel. Written when his career as a novelist was well established, in the novel one can find all of Dickens, since "his essential strengths and weaknesses as a novelist, are in this novel, published serially (1849–1850), nearly midway in his career" (Dunn, 1965, p. 789). The first-person narrative simulates an autobiographical report, yet:

> [d]espite its first person narrative viewpoint and its many allusions to Dickens' life, David Copperfield is an amalgamation of actual and imaginary experience and is not autobiography. The narrator carefully manipulates his story by cleverly foreshadowing his own future and by directing attention to interesting people he meets.
>
> (ibid.)

Here the manipulative character of the realist novel is clearly at work: the intrusiveness of the narrator, the partial presentation of aspects of social life, the novelist's biases conditioning the representation of characters and social figures. All these elements led Mario Praz to speak of the distorting power of Dickens' fiction (see *supra*) and motivated the turn to a more rigorous kind of fiction, fostered in the late 19th century by Henry James, which eventually led to the partial rejection of the Victorian novel by the Anglo-Saxon literary criticism and the Modernist movement (Stevenson, 2004, p. 47). In Dickens' novels, the novelist is the intruder, commenting on what he narrates from his personal points of view, thus disclosing the moral world which he shares with his reading public.

The story is well-known and hence a synopsis is not necessary here. Suffice it to say that David Copperfield may be understood as a *Bildungsroman* with autobiographical references, describing the ordeals the protagonist goes through and his eventual success in life. Relevant for the topic of envy is the figure of Uriah Heep, his relation with David Copperfield and the consequences of Uriah's negative sentiment for the solution of the plot. At a first, simplistic sight Uriah is the arch-villain of the novel, combining the desire for social acknowledgement and the *cupio dissolvi* which we have seen as a typical trait of Iago as a tragic character

(Titolo, 2003, pp. 183–184). According to Matthew Titolo, Uriah synthesizes two Shakespearian characters: Malvolio of *Twelfth Night* and *Othello*'s Iago:

> As Malvolio, Uriah is the uppity steward of the household, comically proud of his symbolic authority. As Iago, Uriah's seething resentment threatens to compromise his attempt to achieve recognition; at times, his anger threatens to boil over and destroy his coveted status distinctions altogether.
>
> (ibid.)

In his role as the secretary of Mr. Weakfield, he is able to combine apparent servility with an envious quest for social ascent. Here envy is not motivated by the vindication of a lost status (like in the Longstaffs) but is the sentiment triggering Heep's scheming, aimed at social achievement. Uriah Heep personifies evil concealed as humility and servility. As most minor characters in the Dickens menagerie, Uriah Heep is caricatured, so as to mock the traits of his personality and disposition to their extremes. Uriah is the servant who attempts to become master and who almost achieves his goal by plotting against those who still deserve the place in society he covets to acquire. His social position forces him to conceal his envy and malice until he is eventually unmasked (Dunn, 1965, p. 792). Yet Uriah is both a caricature and a tragic character, since his failure is inscribed, as it were, in the social class where he belongs and in the restricted opportunities that the social structure allows the members of his class.

Contemporary criticism has shown that the relation between David Copperfield and Uriah Heep is not simply based on deception and disgust. Against Uriah, David is at loss, and in fact the reader owes the final exposure of Uriah to Mr. Micawber, not to the protagonist. A further clue of the intricate relation between David and Uriah is the fact that they are named after two biblical characters, King David and Uriah the Hittite, whose wife Bathsheba the king covets. In order to get rid of the husband, the biblical David sends Uriah to fight for him and he is eventually killed. The comparison with the Bible, where the relation between the wicked and the victim is inverted (in the Bible the victim is in fact the Hittite) (Bar-Yosef, 2006), gives the opportunity for a subtler interpretation: the real victim is Uriah Heep, that is he is the victim of a social structure that may allow David Copperfield to emerge but cannot tolerate the humble clerk's rise. Matthew Titolo (2003) has stressed the critical, self-reflexive features of *David Copperfield*, especially in connection with the liberal idea, so typical of the coeval political and social thought, according to which the social actor is able to construct his own biography. Uriah Heep's parable shows plastically the ideological component of liberalism: a pretended openness of opportunity which conceals persisting social differences. Powerful cultural and social forces are still at work, preventing Uriah's acquired qualities from guaranteeing his advancement. In order to justify his final unmasking, his action is to be represented as well-planned schemes, whose lack of morality deserves punishment, not success. Dickens is not yet ready to adhere to the liberal conception of acquired qualities as a sufficient reason for social ascendant mobility. And in fact, no upgrading is possible for those social actors who, as Uriah Heep does, disregard moral values and neglect socially defined differences (ibid., p. 186). This explains why Uriah is represented as morally unfit before his final exposure, which ratifies his social inadequateness. Early modernity has structural constraints, against which the individual is at a loss, since they may impede or hinder his social ascent. Uriah Heep thus presents himself as a perfect scapegoat, "the vulgar, social climbing clerk" who allows the novelist to distract his reader's attention from systemic constraints and inequalities, thus solving the potentially political tension of the plot in the trivial pleasure of the reader for unmasked evil.

Joseph Litvak (2012) writes of a homoerotic attraction which links the protagonist to both James Steerforth and Uriah Heep. In the first case, it is the attraction to beauty, wealth and status. In the second, it is a more devious draw to the unctuous behaviour of a deceivingly humble social climber. Both the aristocrat and the servant are doomed to fail in the novel, since the future belongs to the middle class, represented in the novel by David Copperfield's eventual achievements (Bar-Yosef, 2006, p. 959). Social ascent is reserved to the members of the middle class, where Uriah does not belong. This is reason enough for the secretary to stress his servitude, concealing his malice and envy under a pretended disposition to serve. In Uriah, flattery and machination combine (the first being used to cover the second); yet Uriah has no other choice if he wants to emerge. He belongs to a social status from which any ascent is still conceived as undue, which is why Dickens converts the parvenu into a pariah (Litvak, 2012, p. 139). Uriah is socially unfit for the role to which he aspires: he lacks "mastery over […] complex 'symbolics' of success" (Titolo, 2003, p. 187). This is why he is, regardless of his ambition, doomed to occupy the:

> uncharted social territory somewhere between the autonomous, middle-class professional and the deferential, hat-tipping worker. Uriah Heep anticipates the emergence of a new class of organization men who may never achieve autonomy in exchange for the working-class culture they have left behind.
>
> (ibid.)

Although envy motivates Uriah's scheming, Dickens uses the word seldom in the novel and never in relation to the secretary. Uriah's behaviour, once exposed, may show malice, hatred, insolence, not envy. Exposure is the moment in which Uriah's false humility may give way to manifest resentment, which is the consequence of his frustrated desire to ascend. Times are not ripe for a servant to become a master, which is a disturbing truth for the liberal thinker and a reassuring one for the conservative reader. Uriah understands this logic in the moment of his defeat and, turning to Copperfield, cries: "You were always a puppy with a proud stomach from your first coming here; and you envy me my rise, do you?" (Dickens, 1850/1953, p. 712). For Uriah, envy is a conservative sentiment, belonging to those who, like David Copperfield, assume structural constraints as a matter of fact, thus impeding the social climb of those who seem at odds with the values of the rising middle class.

6   Experiencing status change. Verga's *Mastro don Gesualdo* and Larsen's *Passing*

What happens when status changes have actually occurred? What may, in this case, be the social role of envy? In order to illustrate this point, I make reference to two novels belonging to utterly different geographical, historical and literary contexts. The first is *Mastro Don Gesualdo*, the masterpiece of Giovanni Verga, one of the Italian authors who adapted French Naturalism to the late 18th century Italian narrative (McWilliam, 1961, p. 12). The second is Nella Larsen's *Passing*, a novel belonging to the so-called *Harlem Renaissance*, in which the topic of envy may be connected to race relations and the new models of living fostered by the emerging consumerism. The two novels are not to be compared here, belonging as they do to distant literary worlds. They nonetheless illustrate, from their very peculiar perspectives, what may happen when status change, by whatever means, is actually achieved.

Giovanni Verga is known to the English reading public through the translations by David H. Lawrence, who was fascinated by both the original language of Verga's novel (the reproduction in Italian of pace and tropes of the Sicilian dialect) and by the isle's primitive world which is depicted in Verga's novels and short stories (ibid.). If one thinks of Lawrence' attraction to primitivism, sentiments and behaviours not yet spoiled by social conventions (Daiches, 1969, p. 1165), one may easily perceive the difference between Verga's world and the civilized, modern societies of Northern Europe in which Lawrence lived. The structure of Sicilian society at the end of the 19th century is very different from the one portrayed by the Victorians. It is a society chiefly based on rural economy, in which the decaying aristocracy still enjoys a declining prestige and social reputation. In such a society, social upgrading may be possible but with disastrous consequences for those who, by socially ascending, destabilize the apparently unchangeable order of society. Italian literary criticism (Luperini, 1982) has stressed how, in Verga's mature works, a deep understanding of social changes is closely connected with a conservative political position, by which any attempt to ascend the social scale has deep, negative consequences. Verga had planned to write the so-called "Ciclo dei Vinti" (or cycle of the defeated), which was to consist of five novels of which only two were eventually issued: *I Malavoglia* (1881) and *Mastro Don Gesualdo* (1890). The five novels were to portray the consequences of modernity for members of different social statuses. In the first novel, a family of fishermen tries to start a business as merchants of lupin beans, but a shipwreck puts an end to the attempt, casting the family into poverty, moral bewilderment and social anomie. The unsuccessful attempt "to escape from their crushing poverty" results in the family being "exterminated either in body or in spirit by the hostile forces of the world outside" (McWilliam, 1961, p. 17).

The second novel is the account of a successful ascent, yet at the cost of social exclusion. Gesualdo Motta, a former millwright, is able to make his way and to marry a member of a decayed aristocratic family. Envy is a triggering element of social ascent and is symbolically represented by the desire the protagonist has to acquire wealth (*la roba* – the stuff, in Verga's wording) (Caldarone, 1987, p. 65). The desire to possess marks the shift from basic survival needs, typical of the former novel, to the desire for wealth and power, which will allow Mastro Don Gesualdo to rise in the social hierarchy. Envy directed to Gesualdo is, as it were, evidence of his achievements. When the Marquis Lìmoli tries to convince his niece Bianca to marry Gesualdo Motta, he shows that he has interiorized the new philosophy of capitalism. Rumours about the marriage are caused by envy, not by some ill-posed defence of the old values of aristocracy "Listen ... the world nowadays belongs to those who have money ... they are all clamouring out of envy. If the baron had a daughter of marriageable age, he would most certainly give her to Mastro Don Gesualdo" (Verga, 1890, p. 49). Envy is a leitmotiv in the novel, combined with a sense of ill ease which appears to be the output of the class boundaries that Gesualdo has broken. The price to be paid is huge: Gesualdo will never be able to build up sincere social relations, condemned to remain estranged even among close relatives. In this sense, Mastro Don Gesualdo is a Durkheimian hero *ante-litteram*, a literary personification of the concept of anomie.

And indeed, his ascent will alienate him both from his original social class and from the upper class, where he would like to belong. Gesualdo's ascent produces a diffuse envy towards his success, yet envy alone is no longer a socially effective barrier against social achievements. The economic structure of Sicily at the end of the 19th century, including the conditions of part of the Sicilian aristocracy, makes Gesualdo's rise plausible and envy ineffective as an antidote to social change. Nonetheless, Gesualdo Motta remains an enriched outcast. The very title of the novel ironically hints at the impossibility to shift from one status to another, as one's qualities ascribed by birth may not be erased. Mastro is approximatively the Italian equivalent for master craftsman, which indeed Gesualdo was, while Don corresponds to the English Sir, which Gesualdo is striving to become. By naming him a combination of the two qualifications, a strong ironic effect is produced. Mastro Don Gesualdo's defeat is, therefore, produced by the diffuse social disdain which surrounds him, a complement of social envy for what he has been able to acquire. Despise is a mechanism for social exclusion, which accounts for the fact that Gesualdo, it being by now impossible for him to return to his old social position, will never be able to integrate in the new social status he has gained in working so hard. He will hence die alone, almost a stranger in the palace of his only daughter, now Marquise of Leyra.

Passing (1929) is located in a different social context as compared to the rural Vergan Sicily of the end of the 19th century. The setting is the American metropolis, with its multifaceted structure and its complex social relations. Yet, like *Mastro Don Gesualdo*, *Passing* is in its own peculiar way a story of a status change in which not only class boundaries but also the race border is deceptively crossed. It is, moreover, the story of a relationship between two women, Clara and Irene, based on a weird balance of attraction, repulsion and envy. The background is the American modern city (namely New York and Chicago) where relations are anonymous, no longer based on the mutual knowledge of each other's personal and family history and where a mulatto woman can manage to pass as white.

The city is both the place where classes and races mingle and where women may enjoy a new liberty, since they are now allowed to attend the public sphere. The big city has been one of the favourite settings for contemporary American fiction. At the beginning of the 20th century, the American metropolis was a sort of experimental field, where new forms of sociality emerged, transforming the consolidated social structure, allowing new social types to emerge and new forms of behaviours to be accepted or tolerated. It is no surprise that both sociologists and novelists assumed the new social space as a privileged object of their specific interest (Cappetti, 1993). Yet barriers among classes, sexes and races were still effective features of social relations, regardless of the apparent liberalism of the American modern urban society. The metropolis produced new differences and confirmed old ones; nonetheless, its complex social mix of people and the weakening of informal control made crossing the borders of class, gender and race more likely (Park, 1928).

Race passing was a diffuse phenomenon in the USA in a period between the end of the 19th century and the beginning of the 20th. Race crossing, which in the contemporary system of inequalities implied a status upgrading as well, was possible in the systematic chaos of the metropolis, by which cultural and ethnic belonging were replaced by new ones, in a deception game which always entailed the danger of being unmasked. The dramatic implication of the change of one's race status affected both black and white narrative, so that the passing plot was diffuse at the beginning of the 20th century (Sullivan 1998, p. 373). The topic of deception and the unmasking of one's concealed race identity is central in Nella Larsen's *Passing*, together with the clash of values between Irene, a middle-class black woman, apparently content with her social status, and Clare, who personifies the new ideals of self-realization and self-fulfilment.

In the novel, the city is not a mere background. It guarantees the social conditions of passing and, at the same time, represents an innovative social context, where the new culture of consumerism takes its contemporary form. Gregory Askew (2005) has analyzed the novel from this peculiar perspective, underlining the relevance of envy, ambivalence and the new culture of consumption. *Passing* is in fact, inter alia, an effective portrayal of the contradictions of the emerging consumer society, which was then eroding the ideological basis of the American conservatism (ibid., p. 309). The old Protestant ethic, based as it was on parsimony and self-control, is no longer functional to the new economy, which relies upon the artificial construction of new needs, hence on the constant increase in consumption. Yet, the old barriers persist, in particular as far as race is concerned. Thus, the act of passing is Clare's only possibility to adhere to the new culture, an act which is produced by an envious protest against those who possess (both wealth and status). As Clare says:

> [W]hen I used to go over to the south side, I used almost to hate all of you. You had all the things I wanted and never had had. It made me all the more determined to get them, and others.
>
> (Larsen, 1929/2004, p. 17)

Irene, on the contrary, accepts her position as a black middle-class wife, although that implies her belonging to a diminished social status. In the new consumer society black people almost disappear, as they are symbolically excluded from the social representation of the affluent society. One of the options left to them is mimicking the white middle class, their values and their consumption models, without ever being fully part of the new dynamic social environment. And this is the option Irene chooses: Irene accepts the logic of social differences, provided that her social position (the wife of a black doctor) may guarantee a semblance of social distinction, not to be compared yet to its equivalent in the community of white people.

We have already seen how envy is a constitutive part of consumption society (see *supra*, Chapter 3). According to the historian Susan Matt (2009) consumption was in fact fostered by envy and emulation, such that envy came to lose part of its negative connotations. Clare adheres totally to the new model of consumption, as a way to reinforce her new simulated identity. As an object of envy, Clare shows Irene that consumption may result in a restless (although never completely satisfying) activity. This put Irene's consumption models into crisis, since she uses goods as a way to confirm her black middle-class identity. The relationship between the two characters is complex, since both finds in the other's life something they lack: a stable identity in the case of Clare, a more satisfying and free existence in the case of Irene. The final death of Clare gives a further sense to the novel's title, since the word "passing" carries death as a colloquial meaning (Sullivan, 1998). The tragic finale re-establishes the broken order, confirming Clare's identity as a black woman and showing the dangers of a life without roots and devoid of any self-constraint.

As compared to the previous works we have analyzed, both *Mastro Don Gesualdo* and *Passing* make the possibility of upgrading one's own status a key element of their plot. Envy is, in both cases, understood as a sentiment triggering social mobility. It is hence productive for social change. The negativity of the sentiment is mitigated by the idea that social position is somewhat independent of social origins, as it now relies, at least in part, on achieved rather than on acquired qualities. Yet the social structure is still largely defined according to the traditional distinctions based on birth, sex and race. The structure of society is no longer capable of stopping social upgrading, yet it is not ripe enough to hinder any forms of social exclusion in retaliation for social achievement. In their own specific ways, both novels end with the tragic dissolution of those who have emerged regardless of the lack of prestige of their original class or original race.

7 Brief final remarks

Nella Larsen's novel hints at a constitutive problem of American society, that is the race question which was conceived by Gunnar Myrdal as the fundamental American dilemma (1944). During the 20th century, sociology has attempted to cope with the growing structural complexity of modern society and has elaborated new conceptualities, trying to describe the location of the individual within the social structure. Inclusion has become both a sociological concept and a task to be pursued. In the so-called solid modernity, differences do persist but may be mitigated thanks to the equalizing function of the modern nation-state, understood as a powerful means to produce equity through social differentiation, hence integration through the maintenance of social differences (see *supra*, Chapter 5). Sociology owes Talcott Parsons a conception of modernity as characterized by inclusiveness and social mobility. In the new social structure, acquired skills are more important than ascribed qualities, since a highly differentiated system needs ever more complex competences so as to guarantee system and social integration. Society is thus represented as an open structure, as it allows the individuals the realization of their professional and biographical tasks, regardless of ascribed qualities (including social or ethnic origins) (Parsons, 1951, p. 187). Inequalities are not suppressed but are now justified as means to distinguish individual merits. Moreover, social inclusion is guaranteed to all citizens provided that they comply with the values of their societal community (Parsons, 1965). Citizenship and the values which it fosters become the ideological tie guaranteeing integration to an increasing number of social actors, regardless of their different status or social roles. A society based on these principles should mitigate the social destructiveness of envy. Envy is indeed a sentiment based on the idea that we have been unjustly deprived of something we deserved. A society based on merit and shared values should tame envy, by distributing social rewards according to the actual competences and guaranteeing achievement for all through emulation.

Parsons' model, simplified by necessity here, was of course not the sole representation of modern Western society. Alternatives were elaborated, chiefly in the direction of theoretical portrayals of society stressing the relevance of inequalities and conflict. Yet, Parsons' approach was, in the period between the 1950s and the early 1970s, highly influential, assuming almost the character of a sociological paradigm. Therefore, Parsons' theory may be assumed as a plausible representation of solid modernity, one in which the *liaisons dangereuses* between envy and social change could be institutionalized in the form of merit and social inclusion, so limiting their potentially negative consequences for social order. This theoretical description worked as a plausible representation of industrial modernity in so far as it portrayed an inclusive society, based on the idea that the equality of citizens should guarantee the full enjoyment of civil, political and social rights (Parsons, 1965).

It is by now difficult to deny that a radical change has recently occurred in the integration of the individual in the social system. In the period of liquid or late modernity, we are experimenting with a dramatic passage from the idealized inclusiveness as proposed by Parsons to the multiplication of actual exclusion. The process by which the state fosters inclusion was dramatically limited by the crisis (both ideological and fiscal) of the welfare state dating back to the late 1970s (Hill, 1995, p. 294 ff.). This resulted in a new social structure whose specific character is exclusion as a political, economic and social practice. It is a social structure in which the individual is left alone, cast adrift by market forces, which make his life precarious from a social, economic and ontological point of view (Young, 1999, p. 6 ff.). It is, moreover, a world of increasing differences, ever less mitigated by welfare policies. And it is a world where the ideal of a unitary set of values, which characterized Parsons' concept of "societal community" has been replaced by a plurality of unstable values, lacking any unifying principle. The individual shares ephemeral values with transient social groups or tribes (Maffesoli, 1988) which may guarantee only provisional, nomadic identities.

The analysis of our contemporary modernity is beyond the scope of these brief remarks. What is probably plausible when it comes to the topic of this chapter is that, whereas solid modernity had produced a socially tamed form of envy, which had become an important psychological tool to foster consumption and emulation, envy may, in late modernity, assume a renewed disruptive character: an increasingly negative sentiment, unable to transform social inequalities into motives for the vindication of social and economic justice. Apparently, envy is a diffuse yet individualized sentiment, whose effects on the social structure are limited by the lack of alternatives. It may no longer function as an instrument of social control, neither can it be assumed as a propellant for cultural and societal changes. Reduced to its individualized and psychological component, it shows its potential destructiveness without hinting at alternative futures.

8   Of love, its semantic and its social function

1 Love as a syndrome and as a social fact

A Lover's Discourse: Fragments (1977) is the title Roland Barthes gives to his book on the speech of love. The book is an interesting attempt to reconstruct the characteristics and topics of verbalized love. Love is analyzed by Roland Barthes as an introspective observation of the effects of being in love on lovers. Barthes describes love as a syndrome, rather than a sentiment, thus anticipating contemporary definitions of love within the neural sciences and philosophy (Pismenny and Prinz, 2017; de Sousa, 2015, pp. 3–4). Love is a recursive adaptation of the lover to a set of trivial situations which are emphasized in his discourse in so far as they have the beloved as their object. They are not sequential, in the sense that they may occur in whatever order. These situations, as Barthes writes, condense into figures, that is speech acts which identify a specific moment of a lover's discourse (i.e. absence, adoration, affirmation, etc.), arranged by Barthes in alphabetic order, so as to stress that no hierarchy other than random may be imputed to love. Each figure may be recognized by the reader as a specific kind of love speech act.

Regardless of their randomness (Barthes compares them to arias in an opera) (Barthes, 1977, p. 5), anyone who is or has been in love may employ them to reconstruct his personal story: the emotional history of the lover, in which emotions appear only to be substituted by new ones, according to the inner development of the love syndrome. Solitude, jealousy, exaltation, desperation, hope all may converge in a lover's discourse, in a tangle of feelings and speeches, often contradictory with one another, each qualifying the momentary emotional situation of the lover. Roland Barthes was a semiologist with a structuralist background; thus he was chiefly interested in the structure of the speech rather than in the loving subject and his feelings. By making reference to a variety of literary sources, Barthes's work shows the inner structure of the love discourse and, in this restricted sense, its universality. The act of speech driven by an "amorous feeling" (Barthes, 1977, p. 4) converges into a discourse in which the reader may recognize his own love experience, regardless of time and culture. It is a speech "woven of languorous desire, of the image-repertoire, of declarations" (ibid.) each understandable as figures. Yet, even if the discourse of a lover may recurrently make use of a set of defined figures, Barthes is aware that it changes over time.

And indeed, his book is a tribute to the marginality of love speech in contemporary society. As he puts it:

> The necessity for this book is to be found in the following consideration: that the lover's discourse is today of an extreme solitude. This discourse is spoken, perhaps, by thousands of subjects (who knows?), but warranted by no one; it is completely forsaken by the surrounding languages: ignored, disparaged, or derided by them, severed not only from authority but also from the mechanisms of authority (sciences, techniques, arts). Once a discourse is thus driven by its own momentum into the backwater of the "unreal," exiled from all gregarity, it has no recourse but to become the site, however exiguous, of an affirmation
>
> (ibid., p. 2)

Barthes's elegant approach to love as a discourse shows indirectly that love as an experience is universal. Yet Barthes gives us hints, from the very beginning of his argument, that the location of the loving speech within society may change, fading in contemporary modernity into a marginal, shadowlike position. In this chapter, I assume the universality of the experience of love as a matter of fact and, from a sociological perspective, I will use literary descriptions of love (including lover's discourses) in order to show how love may be differently integrated within different social contexts or structures. My departure point is somewhat different from Barthes's: love as an emotional syndrome is relational, in the sense that it implies, at least in principle, the presence (or the absence) of the other.

Among the founding fathers, the relational dimension of love has been stressed by Georg Simmel (1911, 1919), who considers love as an essential element of sociality. In its micro-sociological component, love is the triggering element of flirting, a social activity to which Simmel devotes an interesting essay (the original having been published in 1911). The essays on flirting start with a differentiation from the classical conception of love. Love is not, as Plato put it, "an intermediate state between having and not having" (Simmel, 1911, p. 133). If this were the case, Simmel writes, love would exhaust "with the fulfilment of its yearning" (ibid.). Love, on the contrary, does not expire when the object of our desire is achieved. It entails in fact more than the mere fulfilment of a desire, as it may reproduce itself anew in a sort of oscillatory re-actualization of the desire for the loved object. "The being of love – Simmel writes – the pure phenomenon of which is desire, cannot be terminated by the appeasement of this desire" (ibid.). This feature of love (its constant re-actualization) is the premise of the social practice of flirtation, a social game based on the alternation of denial and approval, assent and dissent (ibid, p. 134). Thus, the complex sentiment of love activates social relations and practices which are analyzed by Simmel with his usual acuteness.

Let me overlook an appropriate analysis of the work on flirtation to briefly focus on the much more complex and patchy *Fragment on Love*. Published posthumously in 1919, the fragment is a complex attempt to analyze love from both a sociological and philosophical perspective. Simmel begins his essay by analyzing the primordial relation between the I and the Thou; the temporal priority of this relation implies that the way we direct our behaviour towards personal or impersonal others is determined by the opposition between altruism and egoism (Simmel, 1919, p. 153). This distinction between altruistic and egoistic actions does not apply to love, since in both cases our interest in the Thou is too narrow and unspecified; we may in fact act altruistically or egoistically towards people who are indifferent to us (ibid., p. 154). On the contrary, love as a motivation for action is intimately connected to the object at which our action is aimed. In Simmel's words: "[l]ove for another person as what might be called the general motive for a particular action is more indivisibly connected with its content" (ibid, p. 155). Love produces its object, in the sense that it develops irrespective of its qualities; the lover imputes qualities to the object of his sentiment by the very development of his sentiment towards it (ibid, p. 161). As Simmel writes, "the object of love, in its categorical significance does not exist prior to the love itself but only by means of it" (ibid., p. 162). Moreover, love, as it were, nullifies the distances between the I and the Thou without nullifying the individuality of both subjective positions (ibid.).

The relational component of love qualifies it as a sociological question (Bianco, 2011, p. 55). As a relation, it may not be reduced to its biological function. Sexuality is intrinsically connected to love, yet love is able to transcend the simple biological drive, resulting in complex processes which subvert the vital task of the perpetuation of the species. Love, as it were, transforms itself into its own teleology. In simpler term, even if sexuality is a relevant component of love, love may not overlap with sexuality as it assumes an autonomous meaning and suffices to itself (Simmel, 1919, p. 167).

In order to explain the gap between the biological function of sexuality and love as a social and psychological phenomenon, Simmel makes hints to the process of individualization of love. This phenomenon is illustrated by making recourse to literary sources, namely Goethe's *Faust* and *Elective Affinities*. In the first work, the love of Faust for Gretchen is the de-individualized love of a man for a woman: Faust loves the eternally feminine which Gretchen represents, not her as a specific individual, and this holds also for Gretchen, who loves what Faust represents more than his uniqueness. Simmel writes "As regards the nature of the love between Faust and Gretchen, the possibility of replaceability is by no means inconceivable" (ibid., p. 175). The love between Eduard and Ottilie is on the contrary starkly individualized, based as it is on the uniqueness of both the partners of the love relationship. Uniqueness makes the implicit reference to sexuality and the perpetuation of the species less dramatic; sexuality and reproduction are not expunged, of course, but are seen as complementary, the main task of love being to strongly connect two persons (ibid., p. 178). Another relevant aspect distinguishes modern love from its previous configurations: love in modern society is relational, as it is meant to be reciprocated. Whereas love in ancient cultures is chiefly understood as possession, modern love resides in the sharing of two different visions of the world. It is, as it were, a creative act by which two people cooperate in a dual production of sense (Bianco, 2011, p. 55).

Niklas Luhmann's *Love as Passion* (1982), one of the best sociological books ever written on the topic of love, starts from the same interest in the relational relevance of love. The book is a complex attempt to analyze the semantic evolution of the concept of love in order to understand its function as a communicative medium for intimacy (ibid., p. 11 ff.). Luhmann connects the contemporary semantic of love to the development of modern society, where a new conception of the individual has emerged: the individual is no longer defined, as in archaic and traditional societies, by his birth or origin, but by his performances. This entails a neat separation of the single social actor from the supportive reference to the social groups to which he belonged by birth. Paradoxical as it may sound, the individualized social actor needs intimate relationships: as he is formally included in all social systems, and as all social contexts are available in principle to him, intimate relationships become now relevant as a compensation for his chanceful solitude. Intimacy is thus codified, writes Luhmann, in order to guarantee to intimate relations both a specific area of communication and an appropriate social system in which to manifest.

Understood in these terms, as Luhmann writes:

> love as a medium is not itself a feeling, but rather a code of communication, according to the rules of which one can express, form and simulate feelings, deny them, impute them to others, and be prepared to face up all the consequences which enacting such communication may bring to him.
>
> (ibid., p. 20)

Love is one of the generalized symbolic communication media, that is instruments to be understood as partial solutions to the Parsonsian problem of double contingency. A double contingency is at the core of the problem of social order, as it thematizes the question of the interaction of psychic systems. The other's intentions are opaque to me, as are mine to him; yet we succeed in coordinating within social interaction. In an ever more individualized society, where the old mores and hierarchies are no longer able to predefine human action, symbolically generalized media evolve in order to make the improbability of coordination plausible (Luhmann 1997, p. 316 ff.). In Luhmann's terms "[g]eneralized symbolic media are primarily semantic devices which enable essentially improbable communications nevertheless to be successful" (Luhmann, 1982, p. 18). Such media (money, power, truth, values, art and love) are means by which social systems guarantee the continuance of communication, hence the reproduction of society. How can we indeed explain the fact that someone accepts money (e.g. a piece of paper) in exchange for goods? Or that nobody will lay claim on our property? How can we explain the fact that we accept as scientific truth something we cannot even faintly understand? By fostering the acceptance of highly improbable contents, generalized symbolic media make the actions of psychic systems predictable even in our complex society, where most communication takes place outside the simplified context of social interaction.

As a medium, love guarantees a specific form of communication: the possibility to express one's own world as a world to be shared with the loved one. In modern society the individual is often evaluated for his role, which entails that the reference to the subject is de-substantialized: one is relevant for the functions one assumes rather than for one's complex psychological or personal features (ibid., p. 25). In modern society, love re-establishes the possibility of the reciprocal communication of one's inner world. Thus, the medium love makes a radical form of personalized communication possible – a result which should not be taken for granted, if one thinks that communication is always based on the intransparency of the inner psychological processes of those who partake. A system thus emerges (a sort of transitory bridge between the constitutive reciprocal intransparency of two psychologies) which makes the possibility for each partaker to share the inner world of his/her mate plausible.

Keeping the idea in mind, according to which love is both a sentiment (or a syndrome) and a social fact, the chapter intends to explore the relational dimension of love, its evolution both as a code and as a tool able to legitimize individual choices and specific forms of interaction. The relational dimension of love implies its inconsistency as an instrument of social stability. This aspect will be explored, chiefly in reference to romantic love, often understood as the emotional foundation of the modern nuclear family.

2 Love as an ideal: courtly love and Dante's *Vita Nova*

R. Howard Bloch (1987; 1991) has explored the topic of misogyny in the Middle Ages, connecting it to the theme of the so-called *Molestiae Nuptiarum*, that is the conception of marriage as a misfortune, which men should do all their best to avoid. Bloch quotes Jean de Meun's *Roman de la Rose* (end of the 13th century), in which the pernicious features of marriage are imputed to women. In the coeval literature, the critique against women is escapeless: if a woman is beautiful, all will desire her and she will be likely to be unfaithful. If she is ugly, she will try to please and will also betray. If she is reasonable, like Penelope, she will be subject to seduction; all the more if she is irrational (Bloch, 1987, pp. 3–4). Misogyny is deeply rooted in Western religious culture, as in the Bible woman is a derived element of the creation, owing in part to man (not only God) her coming to the world. She is, moreover, ornamental. Her seductive capacity derives from this quality, which enables her to beguile man only to harass him once she has become his wife. As Bloch writes, a visual paradox is here at work:

> before marriage the senses are seduced and distorted by desire, yet after marriage they are distorted by abuse, or by the tears of lamentation that distort vision. There is, then, no moment at which woman does not trouble vision, distort and destroy the senses.

(ibid., p. 17)

The irrationality of women is hence capable of distorting man's sensibleness, acting as a perturbing force.

The stark misogyny, which affects the representation of women in the High Middle Age, is part of a complex, at places contradictory, conception of love which emerged in Southern France and would influence the coeval literature in Europe. Courtly love was directed to the lady of the castle, thus idealizing women which were conceived as *dominae*, hierarchically superordinate to the lovers. In this restricted sense, courtly love reproduces in the relation between the poet and his lady the structure of Medieval vassalage (a relation which one may still trace in the double meaning of the English word mistress). Thus, a double conception of woman emerges, in which women are either denigrates as the devil's gate or idealized (ibid, p. 65 ff.). Howard Bloch (1991) demonstrates how complex the conception of love in Medieval Provençal literature was, combining courtly love with a rejection of love and an exaltation of chastity. Both attitudes may be traced in the same author, or in the same book, as it is the case with Adreas Cappellanus' *The Art of Courtly Love* (about 1190).

What may strike the modern reader is a neat disjunction of love and marriage. Love may be longed for or rejected, conceived as a necessity or a disease; it is hardly connected with nuptial relations. Historians have explained the expulsion of love from marital relations as a consequence of the practice of arranged marriages, especially among the aristocrats. Arranged marriages are bound to be unhappy, hence another topic of Medieval literature, the theme of the *mal mariée*, a woman who is compelled to suffer from a marriage whose partner she has not been allowed to choose (ibid, p. 171).

Bloch makes it evident that the diffuse practice of arranged marriages was being opposed by the juridical and ecclesiastical conception of the marital union, conceived as a sacrament based on mutual consensus, which had been evolving at least since the late 11th century (ibid., p. 184 ff.). The religious conception of marriage, understood as valid provided that the two partners were willing to accept one another, together with the refinement of the conception of love typical of coeval lyric (love as absence, love as suffering, love as longing for the purity of the lover) was paving the way for a set of ideas which would later eventually converge in the modern conception of romantic love. Yet, by now love is either a game, related to courtly seduction, and in this respect never connected to the marital union, or a pernicious sin and a mistake or, eventually, an ideal.

By trying to trace the evolution of the code of love, Niklas Luhmann connects medieval love to the idealization of the beloved. Love is not yet a form of self-reflexivity of the loving subject. It is, on the contrary, a path to perfection which needs a clear-cut knowledge of the object of love. This conception of love as an ideal is nowhere so visible as in the Italian *Dolce Stil Novo*, a poetic style which evolved in the 13th century, being strongly influenced by Provençal literature, yet assuming the beloved as an object of almost religious worship, with no reference to her physical and bodily nature. This idealizing conception of love is at its best in Dante's *Vita Nova*, a spiritual biography of the perfecting process of the poet's soul through the vision of his beloved, Beatrice.

Vita Nova was probably written in 1294 and is technically a prosimetrum, that is a literary work employing both prose and verses, chiefly sonnets. Although it makes reference to actual episodes of Dante's life, the atmosphere is dreamy and rarefied, with few references to actual reality. Poetry is here the output of the vision of the beloved object and the positive influence it has for the lover and those who are so lucky to behold Beatrice, whose name has a clear reference to heavenly beatitude (Sapegno, 1963). The chief task of love is not, according to Dante, the possession of the loved object but the appraisal of the universal beauty through the contemplation of the beauty of the beloved. Beatrice is, as it were, a miracle of grace, who guarantees salvation to those who have talked to her (Sanguineti, 1977, p. XXXIII). Here the double Medieval conception of women (devil's gate or ideal) is overcome, since the lady of courtly love is transformed into an instrument of moral perfection and religious salvation.

The best-known sonnet in Dante's prosimetrum is *Tanto gentile e tanto onesta pare* (*My lady looks so gentle and so pure*), which may deserve a quotation both in the Italian version and in the translation Dante Gabriele Rossetti made in 1861.

> Tanto gentile e tanto onesta pare
> la donna mia quand'ella altrui saluta,
> ch'ogne lingua deven tremando muta,
> e li occhi non l'ardiscon di guardare.
> Ella si va, sentendosi laudare,
> benignamente d'umiltà vestuta;
> e par che sia una cosa venuta
> da cielo in terra a miracol mostrare.
> Mostrasi sì piacente a chi la mira,
> che dà per li occhi una dolcezza al core,
> che 'ntender no la può chi no la prova:
> e par che de la sua labbia si mova
> un spirito soave pien d'amore,
> che va dicendo a l'anima: sospira

(*Vita Nova*, XXVI)

> My lady looks so gentle and so pure
> When yielding salutation by the way.
> That the tongue trembles and has nought to say.
> And the eyes, which fain would see, may not endure.
> And still, amid the praise she hears secure.
> She walks with humbleness for her array;
> Seeming a creature sent from Heaven to stay
> On earth, and show a miracle made sure.
> She is so pleasant in the eyes of men
> That through the sight the inmost heart doth gain
> A sweetness which needs proof to know it by
> And from between her lips there seems to move

A soothing essence that is full of love,
Saying for ever to the spirit, "Sigh".

> (Dante translated by D.G. Rossetti, 1904, pp. 217–218)

Here the lady is no longer the object of passionate love, sublimated within the elegance of an erotic code. She has achieved a new function, as she connects the lover to a superior reality; love is now an instrument of improvement of the soul, with no apparent link to everyday concerns. Even the suffering of the poet at Beatrice's death is not conceived as a self-reflexive analysis of a loss but as an impulse to further perfection, as the reader may experience in the final sonnet of Dante's spiritual biography (*Oltre la spera che più larga gira.* [*Beyond the sphere which spreads to widest space*]). As Dante anticipates in the final lines of *Vita Nova*, Beatrice, now desubstantialized and made a soul, will be dealt with in a more appropriate context, that is the Reign of Heaven in the *Divine Comedy*.

In Dante, love is an ideal with few relational implications. His relationship with Beatrice is made of encounters, sights, greetings and little more. The visual paradox of distorted sight, which is so typical of Medieval misogyny, is here totally overcome, since the restoring sight of the beloved is an antici-pation of the future vision of God. Dante's approach may be understood as the extreme output of a process which had started in courtly poetry and had been emphasized in the Italian lyric of the 13th century by which the lady, compared to an angel, is deprived of any sensual connotations. Love is taken to its mystical extremes, and the purity of the lady, which grounded the para-dox of perfection in courtly lyrics (how can I love a lady whose purity my love would spoil?) (Bloch, 1991, Chapter 6, *passim*), is not only taken for granted but assumed as an instrument of salvation. In this sublimated form, love has nothing worldly, yet it does confirm its inconsistency with marriage: a married man, Dante finds outside his marital relation (actually in a pseudo-relation made of sights and vision) the appropriate stimuli for his spiritual enhancement.

Dante's *Vita Nova* is, as it were, the final product of a process of idealiza-tion of love. Of course, sexuality is not expunged from literature, as the almost coeval *Decameron* by Boccaccio clearly shows. Yet, to stay in the field of Italian literature, even a precursor of the Renaissance as Petrarch, whose *Canzoniere* is characterized by a stronger sensuality as compared to Dante's *Vita Nova*, may eventually conceive his biographical love experience as a progress towards God. Thus, in its idealized version, worldly love focuses:

> on the difference between loving God and loving a woman [...] Sublime love therefore presents itself to its addressee in a way which incorporates a reli-gious content – and not just as something which allows satisfaction and non-satisfaction to be distinguished from one-another in relation to the addresser own autonomous desire.
>
> (Luhmann, 1982, p. 49)

In such a way, love is both idealized and neutralized. The object of love is hardly conceivable as inferior to the lover. In courtly love, she is the troubadour's lady, hence the unreachable member of a superior class (for the social implications of this asymmetry see Bloch, 1991, Chapter 5, *passim*). In Medieval Italian lyric, the lady is either posed on a superior moral position (Beatrice) or idealized as the aloof lady driving the poet's heart (see, as an instance, Petrarch's sonnet *Pace non trovo e non ho da far guerra*, also in Sir Thomas Wyatt's adaptation *I find no peace, and all my war is done*). At any rate, love does not appear as a destabilizing force, able to transform social hierarchies and structures. It does please and hurt, but, as it were, within the limits of socially defined conventions. The problem of choice, which Eva Illouz (2012, p. 18 ff.) convincingly poses at the core of her reasoning about love (who is my better mate, according to socially shared conventions?), is here inessential because love has to do with a more or less worldly ideal, not with the practical question of choosing a legitimate sexual and life partner.

The question had already been stressed by Luhmann (1982), who considers the possibility of choice as the premise for the development of love as passion. It is, Luhmann writes, the freedom to love someone which transforms love from an ideal into a code for social relations. This relevant shift is to be located in the France of the 17th century, where women are no longer idealized as objects of worship, as they are now conceived as persons who may accept or reject the courtship of a lover. Even here love is, as Luhmann clearly states, neatly separated from marriage. The woman who can accept the courtship of a lover is the married one, not her unmarried daughter, whose virginity is still to be preserved for an arranged marriage (ibid., p. 50). The love code is now a regulator of concrete social relations (for Luhmann systems of interaction) and, in this sense, it implies double contingency, hence the possibility for each partner to comply with or disappoint the expectancy of the other. Double contingency entails that both partners can say yes or no in the game of love; hence the necessity of a code in order to defuse the danger connected to rejection, a danger which is emphasized by the fact that love is now conceived as a passion, that is a sentiment to which the individual is passively subdued but which forces him to act (ibid., p. 60).

A code for love evolves among the upper classes, which eventually ends in a paradox, similar to the paradox of perfection of courtly love: women who accept the lover's advances (*coquette*) lose the esteem of the lover, whereas those who do not (*précieuse*), may bring the relations to an end (Harrison, 1990, p. 235). Yet now, women are supposed to choose, as the destiny of the relation depends on their choice. As Luhmann stresses, love as passion is a step towards the individualization of love, typical of full modernity. Nonetheless, love is part of a complex social game, in which the partners are not yet perceivable as modern individuals, as they are able to choose according to the rules of the game rather than their personal will (Luhmann, 1982, p. 53). Nonetheless this phase (which Luhmann analyzes making reference chiefly to literary works) is relevant. Whereas the Middle Ages had idealized the woman (both positively as an ideal and negatively as the primary source of man's sorrows) woman is now de-idealized, being connected, especially in the 17th century, to sexuality and sexual pleasure. This concreteness of love, together with the idealization of love as such (one begins to love the sentiment of love) would further pave the way for romantic love, the premise of the strong connection between love as passion and the stability of marriage, understood as its logical conclusion.

3 Towards romantic love

Sexuality and love combined may now become an instrument of social upgrading, strategically employable in order to obtain a profitable marriage. Richardson's *Pamela, or the Virtue Rewarded* (1740), is emblematic in this regard. *Pamela* is an epistolary novel, dealing with the misfortune of a girl of poor origins who is sexually harassed by her master. Regardless of the social differences between the aristocrat and the maid, by preserving her virginity, she is eventually able to have her master ask her hand, being thus rewarded for her virtue. The evolution of the character of Pamela may be understood as a shift from virginity to virtue (Harold, 2004): by keeping her body pure, the heroine of the novel may eventually persuade her master of the purity of her soul, which is now conceivable as a solid base for a happy and fruitful marriage. In this sense, *Pamela* betrays the influence of the Puritan milieu in which it was conceived. And indeed, whereas in Catholic culture virginity emphasized the sanctity of a woman – "the martyrdom of a virgin may be noble in Catholicism" (ibid., p. 213) – in a Protestant cultural milieu virginity might be conceived as a step towards further accomplishments, connected with the family as a productive unit. In Pamela's world, sacrifice is quite earthly, as she opts for life and procreation, hence her virginity has to be eventually sacrificed for the reproduction of the social. Yet virtue (and here lies the shifting from the preservation of the body to the morality of the soul) requires that the woman's temper has to be tested: "Pamela's virginity must be 'lost' in the service of procreation and other good works, but it must not be lost prematurely" (ibid.).

It has been stressed that Pamela employs her body and her virginity as an instrument of power, which allows her to eventually "escape her social status, for as a servant, she is the one receiving orders, trapped inside a hierarchy that largely prevents agency" (Kalpakidis, 2008, p. 52). Yet the passage of status is not a matter of fact: in order to make it plausible, Richardson has to endow Pamela with a vast array of qualities which are not common among people of her social position. She can write, a skill which belonged to the higher strata of society; she is pretty, intelligent and well mannered. "Richardson posits his hero above the station of her remarkably poor family […], places her within the skill-context of the educated aristocracy, and allows readers to discern a semblance between the servant and the aristocrats" (ibid., p. 52). Richardson's description of Pamela, from the very beginning of the novel, "helps at once to make her a proper consort for her future husband and keeps her aware of her own individuality" (Folkenflik, 1993, p. 255). Nonetheless, the question of status is posed in several passages in the novel. For instance, in a speech reported by Pamela in one of her numerous letters to her parents, where Mrs. Jervis, the housekeeper and Pamela's best friend, thus describes Mr. B.:

> My master is a fine gentleman; he has a great deal of wit and sense, and is admired, as I know, by half a dozen ladies, who would think themselves happy in his addresses. He has a noble estate; and yet I believe he loves my good maiden, though his servant, better than all the ladies in the land; and he has tried to overcome it, because you are so much his inferior; and 'tis my opinion he finds he can't; and that vexes his proud heart, and makes him resolve you shan't stay; and so he speaks so cross to you, when he sees you by accident.
>
> (Richardson, 1740/1955, p. 28)

Pamela converts the violent passion of her master into admiration for her virtue. She somewhat strategically employs her virginity, understood here as a sort of valuable commodity, in order to force her master into capitulation (Folkenflik, 1993). Virginity is, as it were, an instrument of vindication of Pamela's freedom: she is the *précieuse,* not the *coquette,* in the code of love developed in 17th-century France (Luhmann, 1982), but whereas the code led to the paradox of love (how can I love someone who has surrendered to my courtship?), here it is an instrument for the establishment of virtue and hence of matrimony as a stable institution. Far from being an ideal, Pamela's love is sexualized, thus presenting itself as a symbiotic mechanism, which enables the communicative code to be connected to physiological needs (ibid., p. 27). The sexualization of love is now conceived as a proper base for a happy marriage and, given the freedom to choose imputed to both Pamela, the maid, and her master, marriage becomes gradually, at least in principle, an exogamic institution. In this sense, *Pamela* is the *Bildungsroman* of a maid who is able to convert herself into the wife of a master, marriage being conceived as "the integrator of sexuality" (Folkenflik, 1993, p. 253).

It is here impossible to analyze *Pamela* further. Its success was huge, the protagonist being assumed either as an example to be followed or as a target of stark irony: suffice here to recall Henry Fielding's *An Apology for the life of Mrs Shamela Andrews* (1741) where the protagonist (whose name contains a reference to shame and falsity) is described as an unscrupulous social climber. The idea of a servant's social upgrading through marriage was still unpleasant, as the social structure was still based on hierarchy imagined as a natural, hence unchangeable order. Yet the idea was becoming plausible of marriage as a stable combination of love, tamed sexuality and virtue. The process towards the complete subjectivization of the choice of a marital mate was at any rate still impervious, as is shown in Jane Austen's novels.

***

"It is a truth universally acknowledged, that a single man in possession of a good fortune must be in want of a wife" (Austen, 1833/1913, p. 1). Such a statement, one of the few memorable *incipits* in world literature, sets from the beginning the theme of Jane Austen's *Pride and Prejudice* (1813/1833). The novel promises to be about wealth, marriage and love. In Jane Austen's micro-world, love is a driving force, as it is one of the elements determining her characters' choices. Yet, it is never able alone to determine the selection of a partner, since lovers have to take into account the social structure and to comply with social standards and norms. In Jane Austen's novels, and notably in *Pride and Prejudice*, the plot is triggered by two major concerns: the first is connected to status, and love and marriage opportunities which status may foster or impede; the second is connected to character and the complex interplay between character and the social norms. Class is conceived not only as a social position but also as a set of moral obligations which are to be assumed as a guide for human conduct. Thus, love is not reason enough for marriage, even though Jane Austen seems to think of marriage without love as possible but inconvenient.

Jane Austen's works are sociologically relevant as they combine a mitigated conception of love (no longer imagined as a burning passion) and the requirements of social order. Marriage is socially regulated by a complex set of rules, yet the idea emerges according to which love should be one of the components of a happy matrimony. Since love is only one of the prerequisites of a successful marital union, marriages based on passionate individual choices are with great probability doomed to failure. Let us read, as an example, the characterization of the marital relationship between Mr. Bennet and his wife, through the ironical eyes of Jane Austen:

> Had Elizabeth's opinion been all drawn from her own family, she could not have formed a very pleasing opinion of conjugal felicity or domestic comfort. Her father, captivated by youth and beauty, and that appearance of good humour which youth and beauty generally give, had married a woman whose weak understanding and illiberal mind had very early in their marriage put an end to all real affection for her. Respect, esteem, and confidence had vanished for ever; and all his views of domestic happiness were overthrown [...] To his wife he was very little otherwise indebted, than as her ignorance and folly had contributed to his amusement. This is not the sort of happiness which a man would in general wish to owe to his wife; but where other powers of entertainment are wanting, the true philosopher will derive benefit from such as are given.
>
> (Austen, 1813/1833, pp. 206–207)

The choice of the appropriate life-mate is a matter of importance, which may not be only imputed to sentiments. It is this combination of sense and sensibility which, by making reference to the location one holds in the social structure, may guarantee the social appropriateness of one's feelings and eventually of romantic unions. The choice of the appropriate partner is therefore rationally limited to a restrained number of people, belonging to one's social class or the immediately superior or inferior, who should share similar education and habits. By slightly overemphasizing the relevance of status and rank as a criterion for selection, Eva Illouz writes:

> In the romantic order Austen describes, the romantically successful are those who know their social place and do not aspire to reach above that place, or to go beneath it. In other words, because the criteria to rank people were known and shared and because the decision to marry was explicitly based (at least partially) on social class, being rejected as a marriage prospect did not hinge on the inner essence of the self, only on its position.
>
> (Illouz, 2012, p. 34)

What is at stake here is the relation between the individual and society in connection to important biographical choices. The individual is not left alone in his marital choice, as would later happen in full modernity. In Austen's world, society is both controlling and reassuring the social actor, as it prevents wrong choices and points the right way. And indeed, the way Austen's characters act:

> offer[s] a form of "compromise" between these two forms of action [the one based on rules and the one based on love], and because they offer a good point of entry to understand the cultural system within which early to mid-nineteenth-century English romantic feelings were organized: that is, the rituals, the social rules, and the institutions which constrained the expression and experience of sentiments.
>
> (ibid., p. 22)

When Elizabeth Bennet rejects the marriage proposal from Mr Collins, she does so because of her lack of sentiment towards the character, but also for the social awkwardness of her suitor, his lack of wit and finesse which is reason enough to have the contemporary reader side with her. It is hence no surprise for the reader the perplexity with which Elizabeth Bennet receives the news that her friend, Charlotte Lucas, is going to marry Mr Collins. Love is at least a premise on which to ground a stable union. That is how the narrator comments on Charlotte's decision:

> Mr. Collins, to be sure, was neither sensible nor agreeable; his society was irksome, and his attachment to her must be imaginary. But still he would be her husband. Without thinking highly either of men or matrimony, marriage had always been her object; it was the only provision for well-educated young women of small fortune, and however uncertain of giving happiness, must be their pleasantest preservative from want. This preservative she had now obtained; and at the age of twenty-seven, without having ever been handsome, she felt all the good luck of it.
>
> (Austen, 1813/1833, p. 109)

Thus, marriage is perceived as an instrument to secure young women a position in society. This matter of fact may be unpleasant, yet it is realistically connected to the series of rules (social endogamy in particular) which restrict the possibility of the choice of a mate and have hence little to do with romantic love. Individual choice, which is one of the main features of modern love, is not neglected, but it is, as it were, mitigated by the requirements of the social structure. Let's take another example, now related to a man. Colonel Fitzwilliam, Darcy's cousin, is the younger son of an earl. His social position prevents him from choosing a marriage mate following his sentiments. Inquiring of Colonel Fitzwilliam about his condition as a younger son of an aristocrat, Elizabeth Bennet receives the following answer:

Colonel Fitzwilliam: "[…] But in matters of greater weight, I may suffer from want of money. Younger sons cannot marry where they like.'
Elizabeth: 'Unless where they like women of fortune, which I think they very often do.'
Colonel Fitzwilliam: 'Our habits of expense make us too dependent, and there are not too many in my rank of life who can afford to marry without some attention to money.'

(ibid., pp. 160–161)

Showing self-reflexivity and attention for social relations, Elizabeth Bennet thinks that what Colonel Fitzwilliam is saying of himself is actually meant as a warning to her. Yet what is at stake here is not only the individual destiny of a fictive character but a consolidated social praxis. Individualism as a concept had already established itself both as a topic of philosophical speculation and in the emerging social sciences (economics in particular). Yet in social relations, it was still difficult to conceive the single social actor as an autonomous individual, able to choose for himself regardless of his social environment. Real people were still too compressed by their social circle, hence unable to make their choices (including the choice of a mate) in a complete social void. Society imposed its own rules and those rules implied a balance between the crassness of a marriage for money and the folly of a marriage based only on love (MacAleer, 1989).

Thus, marriage was a compromise between the heart and social and economic needs. And in order to dramatize this compromise, social differences were to be stressed. This is the reason, Elsie B. Michie (2011, p. 40) writes, that the heroines in *Pride and Prejudice* must be perceived by the readers as poor. Both wealth and manners are relevant as a premise for an appropriate marriage. This simple fact gives the author the opportunity to present opposite female characters: those who have wealth (the Bingley sister, Lady Catherine) and estimate it as a factor of social distinction and those who, belonging to the upper middle class (Elizabeth and her sister Jane), contrast wealth with good manner, intelligence and education. The representation of these two modes of being symbolizes the opposition between ostentation and frivolousness on the one side and virtue and social qualities on the other, hence the contrast between the new emerging mercantile society (the Bingleys are after all rich bourgeois), whose social distinction is chiefly based on wealth, and good manners understood as the expression of inner finesse (ibid., pp. 35–36). Thus, the dramatic contrast is less centred on wealth and poverty than on pomposity and social tact.

Jane Austen is, at any rate, too good a novelist to draw a sharp distinction between the better-off and the worse-off. The younger Bennet sisters and Elizabeth's mother are examples of country gentry with little grace and manner. On the other hand, Darcy's sister Georgiana, as well as Darcy himself, as he evolves in the second part of the novel, are clear instances of wealth endowed with dignity and social finesse. The novel may be interpreted as based on a misunderstanding, which affects Elizabeth's perception of the world: the distinction between those who appear as sociable and pleasant (George Wickham being an exemplar in this regard) and those who show pride and selfishness (Darcy in particular) drives Elizabeth's behaviour, and she is eventually compelled to admit that things are different from what they appear (Sherry, 1979). Darcy may so make it manifest in his letter to Jane that his embarrassment with her family was not due to their lack of connections but to their lack of proper manner. He may make thus his marital choice motivating it both with his sentiments and with the compliance of his preference for Elizabeth with what he conceives as proper, hence with the rules of contemporary society. And Elizabeth may follow her heart because Darcy is the appropriate husband, both as for his social rank and his manners and inner feelings.

From a sociological point of view, Darcy and Elizabeth comply with the requirements of society and are hence allowed by the tacit rules of coeval novels to convert attraction into love and love eventually into marriage. They are in this specific sense Parsonsian, that is their personality (and hence their sentiment and the way they express them) is fully integrated into the social context in which they live (Parsons, 1967). It is impossible, as Eva Illouz writes, "to separate the moral from the emotional, because it is the moral dimension that organizes emotional life, which thus has also here a public dimension" (Illouz, 2012, p. 25). The problem is subtle, since the individual actor is able to elude social norms, employing them for his own purposes (think of George Wickham). Or he may reject them altogether, as unfit for his self-fulfilment, particularly when love and biographical choices are concerned (think of Lydia Bennet and her elopement with George Wickham). Yet, when the rules of decency and affection do not combine, the resulting union is doomed to failure. At the stage depicted by Jane Austen, love starts to be understood as both a sentiment and an appropriate social strategy, able as it is to give ground to stable systems of interaction, for example a happy marriage being likely to succeed in so far as it combines moral standards and affection. Yet founding social systems on the sentiment of love would soon prove hardly successful, and literary works would consequently thematize the complications of love chiefly deriving from the inconsistency between personal choices and social demands.

4 The complications of love

The integrative function of love is perceived from the very beginning as transient. The paradox of love being posed as the foundation of a life-long relationship, sanctified in the institution of marriage, is soon evident in high literature, which does not let itself be deceived by the popularity of the happy ending. In Goethe's novel of 1809, *Elective Affinity*, love is an overwhelming force, endowed with a dismantling power: the affinities, which had been perceived as stable, may be directed towards another object, and it is indeed what happens in the novel. Eduard and Charlotte are a couple in their second marriage. They had been both forced to marriages of convenience, although they had been in love with each other in their youth. They meet again, both being widowed, and decide to marry out of love. When two other characters enter the life of the couple, (the Captain, an old friend of Eduard, and Ottilie, Charlotte's niece) new affinities emerge, able to destabilize the equilibrium of the married couple. Charlotte and the Captain, as well as Eduard and Ottilie, discover that they love each other, as a result of an irresistible attraction which is compared, by Goethe, to the chemistry of natural elements. Chemistry, used as a metaphor by the German novelist, symbolizes the imponderability of love, its being strongly individualized, hence its antisocial effect, which results in a tragic ending. In Goethe's novel one may already notice the contradictory idea, which was to become commonplace in serial literature up to recent days, of the stability of authentic love sentiments.

When love, sexuality and marriage begin to be interconnected, the paradox of passion converted into habit becomes explicit. On the one hand, romantic love is conceived as a model, and yet the complications of everyday life may make the model unrealistic. It goes without saying that, love being one of the preferred themes of world literature, it would be impossible even to give an abridged account of all the possible variations on the topic of the paradoxes of romantic love. That is why, in order to show the difficult consolidation of love as a factor of biographical choices, I select three work of Leo Tolstoy (*Family Happiness, Anna Karenina* and *The Kreutzer Sonata*) centred on love, marriage and the contradictory foundation of the bourgeois marriage on love. The selection is due to two motives: the first is linked to the marginal position of Russian culture, and the influence of coeval European literature, which led Russian writers to absorb and redefine European ideas, which allowed in a brief span of time both the acceptance of romantic ideas and the rejection of romantic love. The second motive is connected to the evolution of Tolstoy's approach, from a critique of the new radical ideas spreading in Russia about love and marriage to a complete rejection of marriage as an institution.

In the middle of the 19th century, Russian culture was undergoing a process of strong transformation. Romanticism had affected Russian literature and a new, idealized, conception of love and woman was making its way among intellectuals and the urban educated reading public. Radical circles and writers were legitimizing the idea of free love and adultery. As opposed to this advanced conception of love and woman, both law and popular common sense conceived woman as strongly conditioned by her family in the choice of her partner, arranged marriages being still widely diffuse (Zalambani, 2015).

The first selected work is *Family Happiness* (1859), a juvenile novella, one in which new themes appear (e.g. dissatisfaction with marriage life, extramarital infatuation) which would be fully developed in *Anna Karenina* and in *The Kreutzer Sonata*. Masha, a seventeen-year-old girl, falls in love with a family friend and neighbour, Sergey Mikhaylych, a mature man well in his thirties. Their love story complies with the canon of arranged marriages in the Russian province, an older family friend being often proposed by the parents to the girl. This use had two main reasons: to avoid unexpected surprises, due to the long-established knowledge between the families, and to save the money which would be otherwise necessary for the daughter's debut. Nonetheless, Masha and Sergey love one another; thus their marriage, although traditional, complies with the new ideals of Romanticism. Yet marital life proves to be not what Masha had expected. In order to alleviate her anxiety, Sergey agrees to bring Masha to the city, where she becomes fascinated by St. Petersburg's high society, a world which Sergey detests. She is on the edge of betraying her husband, but she withdraws. The couple eventually return to their country life, Masha's ideal of romantic union being now replaced by new sentiments permeated with resignation: marital friendship, love for the children and domestic routines. Here are Masha's ending words:

> From that day the romance with my husband was over; the old feeling became a dear, irretrievable memory, and a new feeling of love for my children and the father of my children laid the foundation for another, this time completely different, happy life, which I am still living to the present moment.
>
> (Tolstoy, 1859, p. 129)

The paradox of love is here presented as a story of downsized expectations. Love as an intimate exchange of inner worlds may not last. The two characters, who at the beginning seem to dismantle the praxis of arranged marriage, although complying with its rules, discover that the basis of family happiness is a tamed affection and the acceptance of family routines.

Family routine is, on the contrary, sharply rejected by Anna, the protagonist of Tolstoy's second great novel. *Anna Karenina* (1875–1877) is a novel in which the deep crisis of Russian traditional marriage of convenience is ratified. Among the upper strata of society, marriage had been an instrument to strengthen alliances and to preserve social stability. Western influences (particularly Romanticism and social reforms) combined with the access of women to education and the new role of the middle class had, as one of their outputs, the gradual replacement of arranged marriage with marriage of love (Zalambani, 2015, p. 44). *Anna Karenina* shows the crisis of the old traditions, which have not yet been substituted by the new ideas. The novel is not only a psychological study of a tormented lover; it is also an accurate representation of coeval Russian aristocracy at the threshold of radical social changes. By giving voice to moral dilemmas connected to love relations and adultery, Tolstoy was not only able to convey a convincing portrait of Russian upper classes but also to promote changes in the readers' moral values, thus contributing to the dismantlement of the traditional marriage of convenience.

The plot is well known. Anna, married to Count Alexei Karenin, a high bureaucrat twenty years her senior, falls in love with Count Alexei Vronsky. Having a younger lover was not uncommon for a woman of Anna's status in coeval Russia. The scandal blows up because Anna breaks long-established conventions and challenges aristocratic society and its rules and values, as she considers her love for Vronsky reason enough to abandon her marital home. Anna's choice clearly puts the traditional conception of marriage at risk. Marriage of convenience is not based on affectivity but on a set of established rules which allows the partners to lead a pleasant life, provided that the rules are followed.

Love is something which husbands may find outside marriage. That is what Stepan Oblonsky, the incurably unfaithful brother of Anna, says, concerning his sentimental life: "But I don't accept life without love [...], No help for it, that's how I'm made. And really, it brings so little harm to anyone, and so much pleasure for oneself..." (Tolstoy, 1877, p. 119). The unfaithfulness of the husband is taken into account: it does not undermine the moral basis of society and is generally accepted or tolerated. Things are different for Anna. In a conversation with his sister, her indulgent brother so speaks:

> 'Not at all,' he said, 'excuse me. You can't see your situation as I can see it. Allow me to tell you frankly my opinion.' Again he warily smiled his almond–butter smile. 'I'll begin from the beginning: you married a man twenty years older than yourself. You married without love or not knowing what love is. That was a mistake, let's assume.'
> 'A terrible mistake!' said Anna.
> 'But I repeat: it's an accomplished fact. Then you had, let's say, the misfortune to fall in love with someone other than your husband. That is a misfortune, but it's also an accomplished fact. And your husband has accepted and forgiven it.' He paused after each sentence, expecting her to object, but she made no reply. 'That's so. The question now is: can you go on living with your husband? Do you want that? Does he want it?'.
>
> (ibid., p. 294)

Anna's passionate love for Vronsky is to be conceived as a mistake and, as a mistake, it must be amended. Which would mean for Anna to accept the logic of the unsentimental routine of a marriage of convenience. This logic has been definitively rejected by Anna, who may now see her husband under a new, disenchanted, light:

> They say he's a religious, moral, honest, intelligent man; but they don't see what I've seen. They don't know how he has been stifling my life for eight years, stifling everything that was alive in me, that he never once even thought that I was a living woman who needed love. They don't know how he insulted me at every step and remained pleased with himself. Didn't I try as hard as I could to find a justification for my life? Didn't I try to love him, and to love my son when it was no longer possible to love my husband? But

the time has come, I've realized that I can no longer deceive myself, that I am alive, that I am not to blame if God has made me so that I must love and live.

(ibid., p. 205)

It is choosing not to conceal her love which makes Anna both a scandalous and a tragic heroine. Anna's action is characterized both by impudence (her decision to act against consolidated rules) and courage (her acceptance of the social conse-quences of her acts), thus vindicating her passionate love as sufficient legitimation for her outrageous behaviour. Yet her conception of human relations, based as it is on sentiments, clashes with shared moral views, hence her tragic decision to commit suicide.

It has been said that one of the main topics of Tolstoy's reflection is love, and the possibility to ground marital happiness on love (Zalambani, 2015, p. 10). And indeed, the striking *incipit* of *Anna Karenina* – "All happy families are alike; each unhappy family is unhappy in its own way" (Tolstoy, 1877, p. 12) – is a clear reference to the author's interest in love and family life. Whereas in the long novel the impossibility of love and happiness is to be imputed to the pervasive-ness of social convention, *The Kreutzer Sonata* (1889) is an absolute critique of marriage as a social institution. The novella was published in a period of radical changes in the conception of love. By adopting the European model, city mid-dle and upper classes now understood love as the legitimation of the choice of a life partner and, although other more traditional conceptions did coexist, the prevailing model was marriage as based on freedom of choice. As it presents different opinions and ideas about love and marriage (the scene is set in a train coach, where different travellers are engaged in a conversation on the topic), the novella is a plausible presentation of the conflicting arguments on the topic in coeval Russia. Thus, whereas the lady and the lawyer may foster the modern idea of marriage of love, the merchant advocates the traditional conception of marriage, based as it is on the parental sensitive and experienced choice of the appropriate mate for their children. It is when the lady talks of true love as the foundation of marriage – "only love consecrates marriage, and the real marriage is that which is consecrated by love" (Tolstoy, 1889, p. 10) that Pozdnyshev enters the conversation:

"But what is this love that consecrates marriage?" said suddenly the voice of the nervous and taciturn gentleman [Pozdnyshev] who, unnoticed by us, had approached.

He was standing with his arms on the seat, and evidently agitated. His face was red, a vain in his forehead was swollen, and the muscles of his cheeks quivered.

"What is this love that consecrates marriage?" he repeated.

"What love?" said the lady "the ordinary love of husband and wife."

"And how, then, can ordinary love consecrate marriage?" continued the nervous gentleman, still exited and with a displeased air.

(ibid.)

The conception of love, imported from Europe and now become trivial, is openly contested by the protagonist, who takes the scene to recount his personal story, leading to the final rejection of love, marriage and sex. Pozdnyshev's is a bourgeois story of love, marriage and hypothetical betrayal. He meets his wife-to-be, falls in love with her, they get married and have three children. The model (which is both literary and social) of the bourgeois marriage of love seems to have been respected. Yet Pozdnyshev soon becomes dissatisfied with marital life. A suspected betrayal, probably never consummated, leads him to kill his wife and definitively destroy any regard for marriage as an institution. No element of marital life is spared, including sex, which is here conceived as the filthy task at which all romances actually aim.

The representation of love and family life which the novella conveys is so gloomy and hopeless that it is difficult to explain it only as an output of Tolstoy's conversion. It presents a conception of family which irritated most of contemporary readers, both radicals, traditionalists and orthodox. At its core, *The Kreutzer Sonata* is a critical attack against romance and the related idea that true love may ground a solid relationship. It shows the paradoxes of romantic love with a taste for polemic which only an aged, great novelist could allow himself.

5 Late-modern love

Talcott Parsons (1949, 1955) may be understood as the main advocate of an unproblematic conception of romantic love as a means able to give solidity to modern nuclear families. In modern society, the kin-system is no longer able to support the individuals. Thus, the function of making family ties stable is now imputed to love and affectivity among family members. Kin-systems generally repress affectivity, understood as a menace to the stability of well-defined age and gender roles. On the contrary, modern nuclear families ground the very possibility of their success on affective ties and affective attachment among their members (Rusu, 2017, p. 12). Once arranged marriages are replaced by marriages of love, love allows the selection of the appropriate partner; it guarantees the stability of the family system, which may now be isolated from the reassuring connection to the original community; the stability is reinforced by a gendered distinction of roles, the role of bread-winner imputed to the husband while the wife being responsible for affectivity and diffusiveness. In the complex theoretical construction which Parsons bequeathed contemporary sociology, his reflection on love and family appears as disarmingly simplified, a sort of novelette version of romantic love, functional to Parsons' general conception of society but unable to single out the contradictory characters of love and family based on love.

More recent sociological analysis of family relations has shown how the Parsons model is no longer (if ever) adequate to comprehend contemporary processes. Anthony Giddens (1992) has dealt with contemporary transformations, connected to the emergence of new, more complex and often more confused love relations, where gender differences, power relations and roles are no longer pre-defined or predetermined. Love and sexuality become strongly interrelated with the construction of one's identity, in a process of constant redefinition which may result in an ever more tiring process of self-realization. As compared to romantic love, contemporary love (or confluent love, as Giddens defines it) is based on the idea of finitude: love is not absolute, in the sense that it may be replaced by other love experiences, and it is potentially limited, in the sense that it may plausibly end.

> Confluent love – Giddens writes – is active, contingent love, and therefore jars with the 'for-ever', 'one-and-only' qualities of the romantic love complex. The 'separating and divorcing society' of today here appears as an effect of the emergence of confluent love rather than its cause.
>
> (Giddens, 1992, p. 61)

Romantic love is ideally stable, based on power relations and on the predominance of the male partner. Confluent love is egalitarian, experimental both in relational as well as in erotic matters, not predefined as far as gender and gender roles are concerned (as it may include different options, such as polyamory, homosexual relations, open couples, etc.). As it stresses the element of self-realization, the quality of the relation is more important than the quality of the partners. In confluent love, the relation is pure, as it:

> is entered into for its own sake, for what can be derived by each person from a sustained association with another; and which is continued only in so far as it is thought by both parties to deliver enough satisfaction for each individual to stay within it.
>
> (ibid., p. 58)

Such a relation – the model of love engagement in the late modernity – is very different from the model of romantic love, where marriage was conceived as less a place for self-realization than an institution with a set of established rules. Modern marriage is verging – Giddens writes – towards the model of the pure relations, which is producing a series of restructuring processes, including the democratization of sex relations as well as the high instability of family life.

The Unbearable Lightness of Being (1984) is a philosophical novel by Milan Kundera. It is the work of a mature novelist, able to combine philosophical arguments, intermingling plots and deep psychological characterizations against the historical background of the Prague Spring and the subsequent Russian invasion of Czechoslovakia. Love is the main inner motive triggering the action of the protagonists. It is all but traditional romantic love, as it aims at self-fulfilment and the construction of one's identity and, in this sense, may be understood as a plausible literary representation of contemporary sociological analysis on love. At the beginning of the novel, Kundera embarks on a philosophical reflection about lightness and heaviness. Being light as opposed to being heavy has been generally conceived as positive by Western philosophy. Yet lightness has its faults, as the condition of being light may verge into inconsistency:

the absolute absence of a burden causes man to be lighter than air, to soar into the heights, take leave of the earth and his earthly being, and become only half real, his movements as free as they are insignificant.

(Kundera, 1984, p. 5)

Sociologically, the condition of lightness may be put in relation with the loose relationships which are so typical of contemporary sociality, connected to the shifting, multiple identities characterizing the social actor in late modernity. As compared with what Bauman effectively called solid modernity, we are witnessing a general dissolution of social groups guaranteeing individual actors some kind of stability. Social aggregates such as class, status, political parties, trade unions and the likes were strong identity markers which allowed the social actor to acknowledge other social actors as endowed with the same interests and affected by the same problems. Now those groups are no longer able to represent a common place for the construction of social identity (Bauman, 2000). What is left is a sort of nomadic wandering, within unstable social groups (modern tribes, in the jargon of Maffesoli [1988]).

Kundera anticipates the loose subjects of late modernity, incessantly wandering from one social situation to another, unable to settle down, or unsatisfied after he has settled. His interest is not in the solid representation of power in a totalitarian regime, although the Russian occupation of his country functions as an appropriate gloomy background. He is much more interested in dual relationships, which present themselves as pure in the sense Giddens gives to the term, as they depend less on social norms than on the will of the lovers to keep their connection.

Family ties, which were relevant in solid modernity, are rejected by Tomas, the surgeon and one of the protagonists of the novel. When he decides to stop visiting the son he has had from his first wife, he frees himself from family ties altogether, including his parents':

His own parents condemned him roundly: if Tomas refused to take an interest in his son, then they, Tomas's parents, would no longer take an interest in theirs. They made a great show of maintaining good relations with their daughter-in-law and trumpeted their exemplary stance and sense of justice. Thus in practically no time he managed to rid himself of wife, son, mother, and father.

(Kundera, 1984, p. 12)

He thus starts a life as a bachelor and a womanizer who is unwilling to settle down in a stable relationship. Tomas, Kundera writes:

devised what he called "erotic friendship." He would tell his mistresses: the only relationship that can make both partners happy is one in which sentimentality has no place and neither partner makes any claim on the life and freedom of the other.

(ibid., p. 12)

Until he meets Tereza by chance. A waitress in a hotel where Tomas spends a night, she enters Tomas' life with the unplanned strength of love. Love is, as it were, more and more individualized. It does not necessarily comply with social rules (Tereza is after all socially inferior to Tomas) and is as such linked to fate rather than planned social occasions typical of endogamy:

> So fateful a decision resting on so fortuitous a love, a love that would not even have existed had it not been for the chief surgeon's sciatica seven years earlier. And that woman, that personification of absolute fortuity, now again lay asleep beside him, breathing deeply.
>
> (ibid., p. 35)

As love is a strange sentiment to Tomas, he is at a loss. He has, self-reflexively, to investigate his feelings:

> What could it have been if not love declaring itself to him? But was it love? The feeling of wanting to die beside her was clearly exaggerated: he had seen her only once before in his life! Was it simply the hysteria of a man who, aware deep down of his inaptitude for love, felt the self-deluding need to simulate it? His unconscious was so cowardly that the best partner it could choose for its little comedy was this miserable provincial waitress with practically no chance at all to enter his life! Looking out over the courtyard at the dirty walls, he realized he had no idea whether it was hysteria or love.
>
> (ibid., p. 7)

When Tomas becomes aware of his sentiment and marries Tereza, he is not able to stop being unfaithful. Love is conceived by him as intimacy, exemplified in the act of sleeping together, whereas sex is simply connected to copulation:

> Making love with a woman and sleeping with a woman are two separate passions, not merely different but opposite. Love does not make itself felt in the desire for copulation (a desire that extends to an infinite number of women) but in the desire for shared sleep (a desire limited to one woman).
>
> (ibid., p 15)

To Tereza, love overlaps with her need for *Anerkennung*, due to her relation with a selfish and non-affective mother. By escaping from her, Tereza is looking for recognition of herself not as a body but at least as a body endowed with a soul. And this is why Tomas' infidelity is unbearable to her. Yet, regardless of differences, Tomas and Tereza remain together. She tries to escape from Tomas, returning to her country after a brief stay in Zurich:

> In spite of their love, they had made each other's life a hell. The fact that they loved each other was merely proof that the fault lay not in themselves, in their behavior or inconstancy of feeling, but rather in their incompatibility.
>
> (ibid., p. 75)

And indeed, as she leaves, Tomas starts feeling relieved for a while:

> For seven years he had lived bound to her, his every step subject to her scrutiny. She might as well have chained iron balls to his ankles. Suddenly his step was much lighter. He soared. He had entered Parmenides' magic field: he was enjoying the sweet lightness of being.
>
> (ibid., p. 30)

Yet the lightness of being (e.g. the absence of ties and social burdens) proves eventually unbearable, and Tomas returns to Czechoslovakia where, in a process of social downgrading due to both being the suspects of treason to the values of the Communist Party, they end up in a country village where both die in a trivial car accident.

Whereas Tomas does not resist the unbearable lightness of being, Sabina spends her life escaping stable love relations. A dissident painter and Tomas' only stable mistress, she is incapable of settling down. She leaves Franz, a professor in Geneva, when he eventually abandons his wife to establish a common life with Sabina, and keeps on fleeing, by now aware of her constitutive incapacity to cope with stability:

> She had left a man because she felt like leaving him. Had he persecuted her? Had he tried to take revenge on her? No. Her drama was a drama not of heaviness but of lightness. What fell to her lot was not the burden but the unbearable lightness of being.
>
> (ibid., p. 122)

The Unbearable Lightness of Being presents a variety of elements which are typical of love in late modernity. Love is a form of self-fulfilment. It implies authenticity (Illouz, 2012, p. 31) and yet in the very quest for the authentic lies the possibility of infidelity. It implies choice, and yet it contains self-constructed burdens. Love is, as it were, individualized as only the individual choice is what matters. As Illouz puts it:

> The self, thus constituted as unique and individualized, pairs up with another unique person, viewed in possession of unique attributes. The process of choosing a mate becomes defined by the dynamic of taste: that is, becomes the result of the compatibility of two highly differentiated individualities, each looking for specific attributes in a free and unconstrained way.
>
> (ibid., p. 59)

Saying that the individual is what matters in love choices is not denying the relevance of sociality. New forms of families are still striving for cultural and juridical acknowledgement in many Western countries. On the other hand, arranged marriages are the norm in many non-Western areas, as the cultural products (films in particular) of emerging countries (notably India) clearly show, their plots often developing from the contrast between individual love choices and family choices.

Thus, the historical changes as presented above are to be understood as trends, not as universally valid steps of a general evolution of love.

What is evident in Western countries is a tendency toward a further individualization of love, which is the unexpected output of romantic love, hence of the somewhat paradoxical idea that free choices may solidly ground the stability of social intimate relationships. After all, by agreeing with Luhmann, we may still consider love as the code of intimacy. Yet, once intimacy allows the communication of one's individuality, the cultural background is set for the vindication of the right of the individual to differentiate from socially defined standards. This is why a set of once deinstitutionalized variations of love (homosexual, polygamist, polyamorous and the likes) are now asking for recognition. And it is for the selfsame reason that love appears ever more as a form of self-fulfilment (or self-annihilation) rather than the emotional base of a stable social institution.

References

Aguirre, B. E., Wenger, D. and Vigo, G. 1998. A Test of the Emergent Norm Theory of Collective Behavior. *Sociological Forum*, 13(2), pp. 301–320.

Alighieri, D. ca. 1294/1977. *Vita Nuova*. Milano, Italy: Garzanti.

Alighieri, D. ca. 1313/1956. *Purgatorio*. Firenze, Italy: La Nuova Italia Editrice.

Arppe, T. 2014. *Affectivity and the Social Bond: Transcendence, Economy and Violence in French Social Theory*. London, UK: Routledge.

Askew, G. 2005. Envy, Ambivalence, and the Culture of Consumption in Nella Larsen's "Passing". *Soundings: An Interdisciplinary Journal*, 88(3/4), pp. 307–329.

Atkinson, P. and Delamont, S. 2006. Rescuing Narrative from Qualitative Research. *Narrative Inquiry*, 16(1), pp. 164–172.

Austen, J. 1813/1833. *Pride and Prejudice*. London, UK: Richard Bentley.

Austin, J. L. 1975. *How to Do Things with Words*. Cambridge, MA: Harvard University Press.

Baldwin, J. D. 1988. Habit, Emotion, and Self-Conscious Action. *Sociological Perspectives*, 31(1), pp. 35–57.

Banks, J. A. 1968. The Way They Lived Then: Anthony Trollope and the 1870's. *Victorian Studies*, 12(2), pp. 177–200.

Barbalet, J. M. 1992. A Macro Sociology of Emotion: Class Resentment. *Sociological Theory*, 10(2), pp. 150–163.

Barbalet, J. M. 2000. Beruf, Rationality and Emotion in Max Weber's Sociology. *European Journal of Sociology*, 41(2), pp. 329–351.

Barbalet, J. M. 2004. *Emotion, Social Theory, and Social Structure: A Macrosociological Approach*. Cambridge, UK: Cambridge University Press.

Barbalet, J. M. 2008. *Weber, Passion and Profits: 'The Protestant Ethic and the Spirit of Capitalism' in Context*. Cambridge, UK: Cambridge University Press.

Bar-Yosef, E. 2006. 'It's the Old Story'. David and Uriah in II Samuel and "David Copperfield". *The Modern Language Review*, 101(4), pp. 957–965.

Barthes, R. 1966. An Introduction to the Structural Analysis of Narrative. Translated from French by Duisit, L. 1975. *New Literary History*, 6(2), pp. 237–272.

Barthes, R. 1977. *A Lover's Discourse: Fragments*. Translated from French by Howard, R. 1978. New York: Hill & Wang.

Bauman, Z. 2000. *Liquid Modernity*. Cambridge, UK: Polity Press.

Bendelow, G. and Williams, S. J. eds. 1988. *Emotions in Social Life: Critical Themes and Contemporary Issues*. London, UK: Routledge.

Ben-Ze'ev, A. 1992. Envy and Inequality. *The Journal of Philosophy*, 89(11), pp. 551–581.

Berger, M. 1977. *Real and Imagined Worlds: The Novel and the Social Sciences*. Cambridge, MA: Harvard University Press.

Berger, P. and Luckman, T. 1971. *The Social Construction of Reality: A Treatise in the Sociology of Knowledge*. London, UK: Penguin.

Bericat, E. 2016. The Sociology of Emotions: Four Decades of Progress. *Current Sociology*, 64(3), pp. 491–513.

Bianco, A. 2011. Georg Simmel: le forme dell'amore. *Società, Mutamento, Politica*, 2(4), pp. 51–63.

Bierstedt, R. 1981. *American Sociological Theory: A Critical Theory*. New York: Academic Press.

Bloch, R. H. 1987. Medieval Misogyny. Representations, 20. Special Issue: *Misogyny, Misandry, and Misanthropy*, pp. 1–24.

Bloch, R. H. 1991. *Medieval Misogyny and the Invention of Romantic Love*. Chicago, IL: University of Chicago Press.

Blumer, H. 1951. Collective Behaviour. In: McClung, L. A. ed. *New Outline of the Principles of Sociology*. New York: Barnes & Noble Inc., pp. 167–224.

Blumer, H. 1969. *Symbolic Interactionism*. Englewood Cliffs, NJ: Prentice Hill.

Boiger, M. and Mesquita, B. 2012. The Construction of Emotion in Interactions, Relationships, and Cultures. *Emotion Review*, 3(4), pp. 221–229.

Borch, C. 2006. The Exclusion of the Crowd: The Destiny of a Sociological Figure of the Irrational. *European Journal of Social Theory*, 9(1), pp. 83–102.

Borch, C. 2012. *The Politics of Crowd: An Alternative History of Sociology*. Cambridge, UK: Cambridge University Press.

Britton, R. 2008. He Thinks Himself Impaired: The Pathologically Envious Personality. In: Roth, P. and Lemma, A. eds. *Envy and Gratitude Revisited*. London, UK: Karnac, pp. 124–136.

Bruner, J. 1990. *Acts of Meaning*. Cambridge, MA: Harvard University Press.

Burkitt, I. 1997. Social Relationship and Emotions. *Sociology*, 31(1), pp. 37–55.

Burkitt, I. 1999. *Body of Thought: Embodiment, Identity and Modernity*. London, UK: Sage.

Caldarone, F. I. 1987. I "padroni," la proprietà e l'onore da *I Malavoglia* al *Mastro-Don Gesualdo* di Verga. *Forum Italicum*, 21(1), pp. 49–69.

Campbell, C. 1987. *The Romantic Ethic and the Spirit of Modern Consumerism*. Oxford, UK: Blackwell.

Cappetti, C. 1993. *Writing Chicago: Modernism, Ethnography and the Novel*. New York: Columbia University Press.

Carr, D. 2008. Narrative Explanation and Its Malcontents. *History and Theory*, 47(1), pp. 19–30.

Carroll, N. 1990. *The Philosophy of Horror*. London, UK: Routledge.

Ceserani, R. 2007. Pirandello e Simmel. In: Rössner, M., De Michele, F. and Sorrentino, A. eds. *Pirandello e l'identità europea: Atti del Convegno internazionale di studi pirandelliani, Graz, 18-20 ottobre 2007*. Pesaro, Italy: Metauro, pp. 117–132.

Cohen, W. A. 2009. Envy and Victorian Fiction. *Novel*, 42(2), pp. 297–303.

Cohn, D. 1978. *Transparent Minds: Narrative Methods for Presenting Consciousness in Fiction*. Princeton, NJ: Princeton University Press.

Coleridge, S. T. 1817. *Biographia Literaria*. 1834. New York: Levit, Lord & Co.

Coleridge, S. T. 1907. *Essays and Lectures on Shakespeare and Some Other Old Poets and Dramatists*. London, UK: J.M. Dent & Sons.

Collins, R. 1975. *Conflict Theory: Toward an Explanatory Science*. New York: Academic Press.

Collins, R. 1988. *Theoretical Sociology*. New York: Harcourt Brace Jovanovich.

Collins, R. 1990. Stratification, the Emotional Energy, and the Transient Emotion. In: Kemper, T. D. ed. *Research Agendas in the Sociology of Emotions*. Albany, NY: SUNY Press, pp. 27–56.

Comte, A. 1875. *Social Statics & Social Dynamics: The Theory of Order and the Theory of Progress*. 1979. Albuquerque, NM: American Classical College Press.

Cooley, C. H. 1902/1922. *Human Nature and The Social Order*. New York: Charles Scriber's Sons.

Cooley, C. H. 1910. *Social Organization: A Study of the Larger Mind*. New York: Charles Scriber's Sons.

Coser, L. 1963. *Sociology through Literature: An Introductory Reader*. Englewood Cliffs, NJ: Prentice Hall.

Cuin, C. H. 2001. Émotions et rationalité dans la sociologie classique: les cas de Weber et Durkheim. *Revue européenne des sciences sociales*, 120(39), pp. 77–100.

Currie, G. 1990. *The Nature of Fiction*. Cambridge, UK: Cambridge University Press.

Daiches, D. 1969. *A Critical History of English Literature*, Vol. II. London, UK: Secker & Warburg.

Dal Lago, A. 1994. *Il conflitto della modernità. Il pensiero di Georg Simmel*. Bologna, Italy: il Mulino.

Darwin, C. 1872. *The Expression of Emotions in Man and Animals*. London, UK: John Mureay.

Davis, K. and Moore, W. E. 1945. Some Principles of Stratification. *American Sociological Review*, 10(2), pp. 242–249.

De Sousa, R. 1987. *The Rationality of Emotion*. Cambridge, MA: MIT Press.

De Sousa, R. 2015. *A Very Short History of Love*. Oxford, UK: Oxford University Press.

Dickens, C. 1850/1953. *David Copperfield*. London, UK: J.M. Dent & Son.

Dreher, J. 2011. Alfred Schutz. In: Ritzer, G. and Stepniski, J. eds. *The Wiley-Blackwell Companion to Major Social Theorists, Vol. 1: Classical Social Theorists*. Malden, MA: Wiley-Blackwell, pp. 489–510.

Duindam, J. 1995. *Myths of Power: Norbert Elias and the Early Modern European Court*. Amsterdam, the Netherlands: Amsterdam University Press.

Dunn, R. J. 1965. "David Copperfield": All Dickens is There. *The English Journal*, 54(9), pp. 789–794.

Durkheim, É. 1893. *The Division of Labour in Society*. Translated from French by Halls, W. D. 1984. London, UK: MacMillan.

Durkheim, É. 1895. *The Rules of Sociological Methods*. Translated from French by Halls, W. D. 1982. London, UK: MacMillan.

Durkheim, É. 1897. *Suicide: A Study in Sociology*. Translated from French by Spaulding, J. A. and Simpson, G. 1952. London, UK: Routledge and Kegan Paul.

Durkheim, É. 1912. *The Elementary Forms of the Religious Life*. Translated from French by Swain, J. W. 1961. New York: Collier.

Durkheim, É. 1914. The Dualism of Human Nature and Its Social Conditions. Translated from French by Blend, C. 1973. In: Bellah, R. N. ed. *On Morality and Society*. Chicago, IL: University of Chicago Press, pp. 149–165.

Eco, U. 1965. *The Open Work*. 1989. Translated from Italian by Cancogni, A. Cambridge, MA: Harvard University Press.

Eco, U. 1979. *The Role of the Reader: Explorations in the Semiotics of Texts*. Bloomington, IN: Indiana University Press.

Ekman, P. 1984. Expression and the Nature of Emotions. In: Sherer, K. and Ekmann, P. eds. *Approaches to Emotion*. Hillsdale, NJ: Erlbaum, pp. 319–344.

Ekman, P. 1992. An Argument for Basic Emotions. *Cognition and Emotions*, 6(3/4), pp. 169–200.

Elias, N. 1939. *The Civilizing Process: Sociogenetic and Psychogenetic Investigations*. Translated from German by Jephcott, E. 2000. Oxford, UK: Blackwell.

Elias, N. 1969. *The Court Society*. Translated from German by Jephcott, E. 1983. New York: Pantheon Books.

Elias, N. 1970. *What is Sociology?* Translated from German by Morrissey, G., Mennell, S. and Jephcott, E. 1984. New York: Columbia University Press.

Elias, N. 1982. *The Loneliness of the Dying*. 2001. Translated from German by Jephcott, E. 1983. New York: Continuum.

Elias, N. 1987. On Human Beings and Their Emotions. A Process-Sociological Essay. *Theory, Culture and Society*, 4, pp. 339–361.

Elias, N. and Dunning, E. 1986. *Quest for Excitement*. Oxford, UK: Blackwell.

Epstein, J. 2003. *Envy*. Oxford, UK: Oxford University Press.

Falk, C. 1988. Fiction and Reality. *Philosophy*, 63(245), pp. 363–371.

Febvre, L. 1941. Sensibility and History: How to Reconstitute the Emotional Life of the Past. Translated from French by Folca, K. 1973. In: Febvre, L. ed. *A New Kind of History: From the Writings of Febvre*. New York: Harper and Row, pp. 12–26.

Ferguson, F. 2002. Envy Rising. *ELH*, 69(4), pp. 889–905.

Fisher, G. A. and Koo Chon, K. 1989. Durkheim and the Social Construction of Emotions. *Social Psychology Quarterly*, 52(1), Special Issue: *Sentiments, Affect and Emotion*, pp. 1–9.

Flan, H. and King, D. eds. 2005. *Emotions and Social Movements*. London, UK: Routledge.

Folkenflik, R. 1993. Pamela: Domestic Servitude, Marriage and the Novel. *Eighteenth Century Fiction*, 5(3), pp. 253–268.

Frisby, D. 2002. *Georg Simmel*. London, UK: Routledge.

Frye, H. P. 2016. The Relation of Envy to Distributive Justice. *Social Theory and Practice*, 42(3), pp. 501–524.

Garfinkel, H. 1964. Studies of the Routine Grounds of Everyday Activities. *Social Problems*, 11(3), pp. 225–250.

Garfinkel, H. 1967. *Studies in Ethnomethodology*. Englewood Cliffs, NJ: Prentice Hall.

Gerhards, J. 1986. Georg Simmel's Contribution to a Theory of Emotions. *Social Science Information*, 25(4), pp. 901–924.

Giddens, A. 1976. *New Rules of Sociological Method*. London, UK: Hutchinson.

Giddens, A. 1984. *The Constitution of Society*. London, UK: Polity Press.

Giddens, A. 1992. *The Transformation of Intimacy: Sexuality, Love and Eroticism in Modern Societies*. Stanford, CA: Stanford University Press.

Gilmour, R. 2004. The Novel in the Age of Equipoise: Wilkie Collins, Trollope, George Eliot. In: Bloom, H. ed. *The Victorian Novel*. New York: Chelsea House, pp. 147–170.

Goethe, J. W. 1809. *Elective Affinities*. Translated by Constantine, D. 1883. New York: Henry Holt and Co.

Goffman, E. 1959. *The Presentation of Self in Everyday Life*. Garden City, NY: Doubleday.

Goldie, P. 2000. *Emotions: A Philosophical Exploration*. Oxford, UK: Oxford University Press.

Goodwin, J., Jasper, J. M. and Polletta, F. eds. 2001. *Passionate Politics: Emotions and Social Movements*. Chicago, IL: University of Chicago Press.

Grauso, G. 2010. Envy and Gratitude Revisited. *International Journal of Psychoanalysis*, 91, pp. 231–236.

Greimas, A. J. and Fontanille, J. 1991. *The Semiotics of Passion: From States of Affairs to States of Feelings*. Translated from French by Perron, P. 1999. Minneapolis, MN: Minnesota University Press.

Habermas, J. 1984. *Theory of Communicative Action, Vol. 1: Reason and the Rationalization of Society*. Translated from German by McCarthy, T. Boston, MA: Beacon Press.

Habermas, J. 1987. *Theory of Communicative Action, Vol. 2: Life-World and System: A Critique of Functionalist Reason*. Translated from German by McCarthy, T. Boston, MA: Beacon Press.

Halas, E. 2010. *Towards the World Culture Society: Florian Znaniecki Culturalism*. Frankfurt am Main, Germany: Peter Lang.

Hammond, M. 1983. The Sociology of Emotions and the History of Social Differentiation. *Sociological Theory*, 1, pp. 90–119.

Hammond, M. 1990. Affective Maximization: A New Macro-Theory in the Sociology of Emotions. In: Kemper, T. D. ed. *Research Agendas in the Sociology of Emotions*. Albany, NY: SUNY Press, pp. 58–81.

Harold, C. 2004. Faking It: Female Virginity and Pamela's Virtue. *Eighteenth Century Fiction*, 16(2), pp. 197–216.

Harrison, P. 1990. Niklas Luhmann, Love as Passion. *Thesis Eleven*, 27(1), pp. 234–239.

Harvey, D. 1990. *The Condition of Postmodernity: An Enquiry into the Origins of Cultural Change*. Cambridge, UK: Blackwell.

Hewitt, M. 1963. Anthony Trollope: Historian and Sociologist. *The British Journal of Sociology*, 14(3), pp. 226–239.

Hill, M. J. 1995. *Social Policy: A Comparative Analysis*. Hemel Hempstead, UK: Prentice Hall/Harvaster Wheatsheaf.

Hochshild, A. R. 1975. The Sociology of Feeling and Emotion: Selected Possibilities. *Sociological Inquiry*, 45(2–3), pp. 280–307.

Hochshild, A. R. 1979. Emotion Work, Feeling Rules and Social Structure. *The America Journal of Sociology*, 85(3), pp. 551–575.

Hochschild, A. R. 1983a/2012. *The Managed Heart: Commercialization of Human Feelings*. Berkeley, CA: University of California Press.

Hochshild, A. R. 1983b. Comment on Kemper's "Social Constructionist and Positivist Approaches to the Sociology of Emotions". *The American Journal of Sociology*, 89(2), pp. 432–434.

Hochshild, A. R. 1990. Ideology and Emotion Management: Perspective and Path for Future Research. In: Kemper, T. D. ed. *Research Agendas in the Sociology of Emotions*. Albany, NY: SUNY Press, pp. 117–142.

Hogan, P. C. 2003. *The Mind and Its Stories: Narrative Universals and Human Emotion*. Cambridge, UK: Cambridge University Press.

Hogan, P. C. 2011. *What Literature Teaches Us about Emotion*. Cambridge, UK: Cambridge University Press.

Holland, N. N. 2004. The Power(?) of Literature: A Neuropsychological View. *New Literary History*, 35(3), pp. 395–410.

Homans, G. C. 1964. Bringing Man Back in. *American Sociological Review*, 29(6), pp. 809–818.

Homans, G. C. 1974. *Social Behavior: Its Elementary Forms*. New York: Harcourt Brace Jovanovich.

Huizinga, J. 1924. *The Waning of the Middle Age: A Study of the Forms of Life, Thought and Art in France and the Netherlands in the Dawn of the Renaissance*. Garden City, NY: Doubleday.

Hunsacker, D. 1983. The Social Construction of Emotion: Comment on Kemper. *American Journal of Sociology*, 89(2), pp. 434–439.

Iagulli, P. 2011. *La sociologia delle emozioni. Un'introduzione*. Milano, Italy: Franco Angeli.

Illouz, E. 2012. *Why Love Hurts: A Sociological Explanation*. Cambridge, UK: Polity Press.

Jasper, J. M. 1998. The Emotions of Protest: Affective and Reactive Emotions in and around Social Movements. *Sociological Forum*, 2(13), pp. 397–424.

Jasper, J. M. 2011. Emotions and Social Movements: Twenty Years of Theory and Research. *Annual Review of Sociology*, 37, pp. 285–304.

Jensen, T. W. and Pedersen, S. B. 2016. Affect and Affordances – The Role of Action and Emotion in Social Interaction. *Cognitive Semiotics*, 9(1), pp. 79–103.

Kalpakidis, C. 2008. The Power of Sex: Pamela and the Genealogy of a New Tool to Power. メディア·コミュニケーション研究 *(Media and Communication Studies)*, 54, pp. 47–59.

Kemper, T. D. 1978. Toward a Sociology of Emotions: Some Problems and Some Solutions. *The American Sociologist*, 1(13), pp. 30–41.

Kemper, T. D. 1981. Social Constructionist and Positivist Approaches to the Sociology of Emotions. *American Journal of Sociology*, 87(2), pp. 336–362.

Kemper, T. D. 1990. Themes and Variations in the Sociology of Emotions. In: Kemper, T. D. ed. *Research Agendas in the Sociology of Emotions*. Albany, NY: SUNY Press, pp. 3–23.

Kemper, T. D. 2000. Emotions. In: Borgatta, E. F. and Montgomery, R. J. V. eds. *Encyclopedia of Sociology*. New York: Macmillan Reference USA, pp. 772–788.

Kuhn, T. 1962. *The Structure of Scientific Revolutions*. Chicago, IL: University of Chicago Press.

Kundera, M. 1984. *The Unbearable Lightness of Being*. Translated from Czech by Heim, M. R. 1984. New York: Harper and Son.

Lamarque, P. 1981. How Can We Fear and Pity Fictions? *British Journal of Aesthetics*, 21(4), pp. 291–304.

Larsen, N. 1929/2004. *Passing*. Mineola, NY: Dover Publications Inc.

Lawler, E. J. and Thye, S. R. 1999. Bringing Emotions into Social Exchange Theory. *Annual Review of Sociology*, 25, pp. 217–244.

Le Bon, G. 1895. *The Crowd: A Study of the Popular Mind*. Translated from French. 1896. New York: The MacMillan Co.

Lemmings, D. and Brooks, A. 2014. The Emotional Turn in the Humanities and Social Sciences. In: Lemmings, D. and Brooks, A. eds. *Emotions and Social Change: Historical and Sociological Perspectives*. London, UK: Routledge, pp. 3–18.

Lepenies, W. 1985. *Between Literature and Science: The Rise of Sociology*. Translated from German by Hollingdale, R. J. 1988. Cambridge, UK: Cambridge University Press.

Levinson, J. 2006. *Contemplating Art: Essays in Aesthetics*. Oxford, UK: Clarendon Press.

Litvak, J. 2012. Unctuous: Resentment in *David Copperfield*. *Qui Parle*, 20(2), pp. 127–150.

Lofland, J. 1981. Collective Behavior: The Elementary Forms. In: Rosenberg, M. and Turner, R. H. eds. *Social Psychology: Sociological Perspectives*. New York: Basic Books, pp. 411–446.

Logan, S. 2004. Domestic Disturbance and the Disordered State in Shakespeare's *Othello*. *Textual Practice*, 18(3), pp. 351–375.

Longo, M. 2001. *Struttura della società e semantica del soggetto*. Lecce, Italy: Pensa Multimedia.

Longo, M. 2005. *L'ambivalenza della modernità. La sociologia tra disincanto e reincanto*. San Cesareo di Lecce, Italy: Manni.

Longo, M. 2015. *Fiction and Social Reality: Literature and Narratives as Sociological Resources*. Farnham, UK: Ashgate.

Longo, M. 2018. Mozart and the Concept of Equality. In: Annunziata, F. and Colombo, G. F. eds. *Law and Opera*. Cham, Switzerland: Springer International Publishing, pp. 195–208.

Luhmann, N. 1980. *Gesellschaftsstruktur und Semantik*. Frankfurt am Main, Germany: Surkamp.

Luhmann, N. 1982. *Love as Passion*. Translated from German by Gaines, J. and Jones, D. L. 1986. Cambridge, UK: Polity Press.

Luhmann, N. 1984. *Social Systems*. Translated from German by Bednarz, J. with Baeker, D. 1995. Stanford, CA: Stanford University Press.

Luhmann, N. 1997. *Die Gesellschaft der Gesellschaft*. Frankfurt am Main, Germany: Suhrkamp.

Lukács, G. 1971. *Prolegomeni a un'estetica marxista: Sulla categoria della particolarità*. Rome, Italy: Editori Riuniti.

Luperini, R. 1982. *Pessimismo e Verismo in Giovanni Verga*. Torino, Italy: UTET.

MacAleer, J. 1989. The Comedy of Distinction in *Pride and Prejudice*. *Persuasion*, 16(11), pp. 70–76.

Maffesoli, M. 1988. *The Time of Tribe: The Decline of Individualism in Mass Society*. Translated from French by Smith, D. 1996. London, UK: Sage.

Manzoni, A. 1842. *I Promessi Sposi. The Betrothed*. Translated from Italian by Colquhoun, A. 1909. New York: Collier and Son.

Mason, J. 2002. *Qualitative Researching*. London, UK: Sage.

Matt, S. J. 2009. *Keeping Up with the Jones: Envy in American Consumer Society, 1890–1930*. Philadelphia, PA: University of Pennsylvania Press.

Matt, S. J. 2014. Methods for the Historical Study of the Emotions. In: Matt, S. J. and Stearns, P. N. eds. *Doing Emotions History*. Urbana, Chicago and Springfield: University of Illinois Press, pp. 41–56.

Matt, S. J. and Stearns, P. N. 2014. Introduction. In: Matt, S. J. and Stearns, P. N. eds. *Doing Emotions History*. Urbana, Chicago and Springfield: University of Illinois Press, pp. 1–16.

McCarthy, E. D. 1989. Emotions are Social Things: An Essay in the Sociology of Emotions. In: Franks, D. D. and McCarthy, E. D. eds. *The Sociology of Emotions*. Original Essays and Research Papers. Greenwich, CT: Jai Press Inc., pp. 51–72.

McCarthy, E. D. 1994. The Social Construction of Emotions: New Directions from Culture Theory. In: Wentworth, W. M. and Ryan, J. eds. *Social Perspectives on Emotion*. Greenwich, CT: Jai Press Inc., pp. 267–279.

McPhail, C. 1991/2017. *The Myth of the Madding Crowd*. London, UK: Routledge.

McWilliam, G. H. 1961. Verga and 'verismo'. *Hermathena*, 95, pp. 3–20.

Michie, E. B. 2011. *The Vulgar Question of Money: Heiress, Materialism and the Novel of Manners from Jane Austen to Henry James*. Baltimore, MD: Johns Hopkins University Press.

Miller, D. L. 2011. *Introduction to Collective Behavior and Collective Action*, 3rd ed. Springfield, IL: Waveland Press.

Milton, J. 1667/1800. *Paradise Lost*. New York: Cassell, Petter, Galpin and Co.

Moran, R. 1994. The Expression of Feeling in Imagination. *The Philosophical Review*, 103(1), pp. 75–106.

Myrdal, G. 1944. *An American Dilemma: The Negro Problem and Democracy*. New York: Harper & Bros.

Nisbet, R. A. 1976. *Sociology as an Art Form*. New Brunswick, NJ: Transaction.

Nussbaum, M. 2001. *Upheavals of Thought: The Intelligence of Emotions*. New York: Cambridge University Press.

Nussbaum, M. 2013. *Political Emotions: Why Love Matters for Justice*. Cambridge, MA: Harvard University Press.

Oatley, K. 2004. *Emotions: A Brief History*. Malden, MA, Oxford, UK and Victoria, Australia: Wiley Blackwell.

Oatley, K. 2011. *Such Stuff as Dreams: The Psychology of Fiction*. Oxford, UK: Wiley-Blackwell.

Oatley, K. and Johnson-Laird, P. N. 1987. Towards a Cognitive Theory of Emotions. *Cognition & Emotion*, 1(1), pp. 29–50.

Park, R. E. 1921. The Crowd Defined. In: Park, R. E. and Burgess, E. W. eds. *Introduction to the Science of Sociology*. Chicago, IL: University of Chicago Press, pp. 893–895.

Park, R. E. 1928. Human Migration and the Marginal Man. *American Journal of Sociology*, 33(6), pp. 881–893.

Park, R. E. and Burgess, E. W. eds. 1921. *Introduction to the Science of Sociology*. Chicago, IL: University of Chicago Press.

Parrish, T. L. 2000. The End of Identity: Philip Roth American Pastoral. *Shofar: An Interdisciplinary Journal of Jewish Studies*, 19(1), pp. 84–99.

Parsons, T. 1940. An Analytical Approach to the Theory of Social Stratification. *American Journal of Sociology*, 45(6), pp. 841–862.

Parsons, T. 1949. The Social Structure of the Family. In: Anshen, R. N. ed. *The Family: Its Function and Destiny*. Oxford, UK: Harper, pp. 173–201.

Parsons, T. 1951. *The Social System*. Glencoe, IL: The Free Press.

Parsons, T. 1955. The American Family: Its Relations to Personality and to the Social Structure. In: Parsons, T. and Bales, R. F. eds. *Family, Socialization and Interaction Process*. New York: The Free Press, pp. 3 33.

Parsons, T. 1965. Full Citizenship for the Negro American? A Sociological Problem. *Daedalus*, 94(4), pp. 1009–1054.

Parsons, T. 1966. *Societies: Evolutionary and Comparative Perspective*. Prentice-Hall, NJ: Englewood Cliffs.

Parsons, T. 1967. Durkheim's Contribution to the Theory of Integration of the Social System. In: Parsons, T. ed. *Sociological Theory and Modernity*. Glencoe, IL: The Free Press, pp. 3–34.

Parsons, T. 1970. *Social Structure and Personality*. Glencoe, IL: The Free Press.

Parsons, T. 1991. A Tentative Outline of American Values. In: Robertson, R. and Turner, B. S. eds. *Talcott Parsons: Theorist of Modernity*. London, UK: Sage, pp. 37–65.

Parsons, T. and Smelser, N. J. 1956. *Economy and Society*. Glencoe, IL: The Free Press.

Perus, F. 1976. El concepto de realismo en Lukacs. *Revista Mexicana de Sociología*, 38(1), pp. 111–126.

Pirandello, L. 1937. *Maschere Nude*, Vol. 1. Milano, Italy: Mondadori.

Pismenny, A. and Prinz, J. 2017. Is Love an Emotion? In: Grau, C. and Smuts, A. eds. *The Oxford Handbook of Philosophy of Love*. Oxford, UK: Oxford University Press. Online: www.oxfordhandbooks.com/view/10.1093/oxfordhb/9780199395729.001.0001/oxfordhb-9780199395729-e-10.

Radford, C. 1977. Tears and Fiction. *Philosophy*, 52(200), pp. 208–213.

Radford, C. 2001. Review: Paradoxes of Emotions and Fiction by Robert J. Yanal. *The Philosophical Review*, 110(4), pp. 617–620.

Radford, C. and Weston, M. 1975. How Can We Be Moved by the Fate of Anna Karenina? *Proceedings of the Aristotelian Society*, 49, pp. 67–93.

Reddy, W. M. 1997. Against Constructionism: The Historical Ethnography of Emotions. *Current Anthropology*, 38, pp. 327–351.

Reddy, W. M. 2001. *The Navigation of Feeling: A Framework for the History of Emotions*. Cambridge, UK: Cambridge University Press.

Richardson, S. 1740/1955. *Pamela*. London, UK: J.M. Dent and Son Ltd.

Ricoeur, P. 1983. *Time and Narrative*, Vol. 1. Translated from French by Blamey, K. and Pellauer, D. 1984. Chicago, IL: University of Chicago Press.

Ricoeur, P. 1984. *Time and Narrative*, Vol. 2. Translated from French by Blamey, K. and Pellauer, D. 1985. Chicago, IL: University of Chicago Press.

Rodman, H. 1965. Talcott Parsons's View of the Changing American Family. *Merrill-Palmer Quarterly of Behavior and Development*, 3(11), pp. 209–227.

Rosenwein, B. H. 2010. Problems and Methods in the History of Emotions. *Passion in Context: International Journal for the History and Theory of Emotions*, I(1), pp. 1–33.

Rossetti, D. G. ed. 1904. *Early Italian Poets*. London, UK: George Newnes Lmt.

Roth, P. 1997. *An American Pastoral*. New York: Vintage Books.

Russell, J. A. 1991. Culture and the Categorization of Emotions. *Psychological Bulletin*, 110(3), pp. 426–450.

Rusu, M. S. 2017. Theorising Love in Sociological Thought: Classical Contributions to a Sociology of Love. *Journal of Classical Sociology*, 18(1), pp. 3–20.

Sanguineti, E. 1977. Per una lettura della "Vita nuova". Introduction to D. Alighieri. *Vita Nuova*. Milano, Italy: Garzanti, pp. XV–XLIII.

Sapegno, N. 1963. *Storia della letteratura italiana*, Vol. 1. Firenze, Italy: La Nuova Italia.

Schimank, U. 1999. Funktionale Differenzierung und Systemintegration der modernen Gesellschaft. *Koelner Zeitschrift fuer Soziologie und Sozialpsychologie*. Sonderheft, 39, pp. 47–65.

Schoeck, H. 1966. *Envy: A Theory of Social Behaviour*. Translated from German by Glenny, M. and Ross, R. 1987. Indianapolis, IN: Liberty Fund.

Schutz, A. 1962. Common-Sense and Scientific Interpretation of Human Action. In: Schutz, A. ed. *Collected Papers I. The Problem of Social Reality*. The Hague, the Netherlands: Martinus Nijhoff, pp. 3–47.

Schutz, A. 1964. Don Quixote and the Problem of Reality. In: Schutz, A. ed. *Collected Papers II. Studies in Social Theory*. The Hague, the Netherlands: Martinus Nijhoff, pp. 135–158.

Scribano, A. and Mattar, G. V. 2009. Feos, sucios y malos: la regulación de los cuerpos y las emociones en Norbert Elías. *Cad. CRH*, 22(56), pp. 411–422. Online: www.scielo.br/scielo.php?script=sci_arttext&pid=S0103-49792009000200014&lng=en&nrm=iso.

Searle, J. R. 1989. How Performatives Work. *Linguistics and Philosophy*, 12, pp. 535–558.

Shakespeare, W. 1604/1873. *Othello*. New York: George F. Nesbitt & Co.

Sheff, T. J. 2000. Shame and the Social Bond: A Sociological Theory. *Sociological Theory*, 18(1), pp. 84–99.

Sherry, J. 1979. *Pride and Prejudice*: The Limits of Society. *Studies in English Literature, 1500–1900*, 19(4), pp. 609–622.

Shilling, C. 1993. *The Body and the Social Theory*. London, UK: Sage.

Shilling, C. 2002. The Two Traditions in the Sociology of Emotions. *The Sociological Review*, 50(2), pp. 10–32.

Shott, S. 1979. Emotion and Social Life: A Symbolic Interactionist Analysis. *American Journal of Sociology*, 84(6), pp. 1317–1334.

Simmel, G. 1903. The Metropolis and Mental Life. Translated from German by Wolff, K. H. 1950. In: Wolff, K. H. ed. *The Sociology of Georg Simmel*. Glencoe, IL: The Free Press, pp. 409–424.

Simmel, G. 1904. The Sociology of Conflict I. *American Journal of Sociology*, 9(4), pp. 490–525.

Simmel, G. 1911. Flirtation. Translated from German by Oakes, G. 1984. In: Simmel, G. ed. *On Woman, Sexuality and Love*. New Haven, CT and London, UK: Yale University Press, pp. 133–152.

Simmel, G. 1917. Fundamental Problems of Sociology. Individual and Society. Translated from German by Wolff, K. H. 1950. In: Wolff, K. H. ed. *The Sociology of Georg Simmel*. Glencoe, IL: The Free Press, pp. 1–84.

Simmel, G. 1919. Fragment on Love. Translated from German by Oakes, G. 1984. In: Simmel, G. ed. *On Woman, Sexuality and Love*. New Haven, CT and London, UK: Yale University Press, pp. 153–192.

Smelser, N. 1962. *Theory of Collective Behaviour*. New York: The Free Press.

Snævarr, S. 2010. *Metaphors, Narratives, Emotions: Their Interplay and Impact*. Amsterdam and New York: Rodopi.

Sottong, H. R. 2012. The Crowd and Manzoni's Conception of Cultural Unification. *Carte Italiane*, 2(8), pp. 29–39.

Sperduti, M., et al. 2016. The Paradox of Fiction: Emotional Response toward Fiction and the Modulatory Role of Self-Relevance. *Acta Psychologica*, 165, pp. 53–59.

Stearns, P. N. 2008. History of Emotions. In: Lewis, M., Haviland-Jones, J. M. and Feldman Barrett, L. eds. *Handbook of Emotions*. New Haven, CT and London, UK: Guilford Press, pp. 17–31.

Stearns, P. N. 2014. Modern Patterns in Emotions History. In: Matt, S. J. and Stearns, P. N. eds. *Doing Emotions History*. Urbana, Chicago and Springfield: University of Illinois Press, pp. 17–40.

Stets, J. E. and Turner, J. H. 2004. Introduction. In: Stets, J. E. and Turner, J. H. eds. *Handbook of the Sociology of Emotions*. Cham, Switzerland: Springer International Publishing, pp. 1–7.

Stets, J. E. and Turner, J. H. 2014. Introduction. In: Stets, J. E. and Turner, J. H. eds. *Handbook of the Sociology of Emotions*, Vol. 2. Cham, Switzerland: Springer International Publishing, pp. 1–7.

Stevenson, L. 2004. The Modern Value of Victorian Fiction. In: Bloom, H. ed. *The Victorian Novel*. New York: Infobase Publishing, pp. 47–52.

Stichweh, R. 1998. Differenz und Integrazion in der Weltgesellschaft. In: Giegel, H. J. ed. *Konflikt in modernen Gesellschaften*. Frankfurt, Germany: Suhrkamp, pp. 173–189.

Sullivan, N. 1998. Nella Larsen's Passing and the Fading Subject. *African American Review*, 3(32), pp. 373–368.

Tabboni, S. 1993. *Norbert Elias. Un ritratto intellettuale*. Bologna, Italy: il Mulino.

Terry, R. C. 1977. *Anthony Trollope: The Artist in Hiding*. London and Basingstoke: The MacMillan Press Inc.

Thois, P. A. 1985. Self-Labeling Processes in Mental Illness: The Role of Emotional Deviance. *American Journal of Sociology*, 91(2), pp. 221–249.

Thois, P. A. 1990. Emotional Deviance: Research Agenda. In: Kemper T. D. ed. *Research Agendas in the Sociology of Emotions*. Albany, NY: SUNY Press, pp. 180–203.

Thomas, W. I. and Znaniecki, F. 1918. *The Polish Peasant in Europe and America: Monograph of an Immigrant Group, Vol. 1–2: Primary Group Organization*. Chicago, IL: Chicago University Press.

Thomas, W. I. and Znaniecki, F. 1919. *The Polish Peasant in Europe and America: Monograph of an Immigrant Group, Vol. 3: Life Record of an Immigrant*. Boston, MA: Badger.

Titolo, M. 2003. The Clerks' Tale: Liberalism, Accountability, and Mimesis in "David Copperfield". *ELH*, 70(1), pp. 171–195.

Tolstoy, L. 1859. Family Happiness. Translated from Russian by Fitz Lyon, A. 1913. In: Tolstoy, L. ed. *The Devil and Family Happiness*. London, UK: Spearman and Calder.

Tolstoy, L. 1877. *Anna Karenina*. Translated from Russian by Pevear, R. and Volokhonsky, L. 2002. London, UK: Penguin Books.

Tolstoy, L. 1889. *The Kreuzer Sonata*. Translated from Russian by Florence, I. 2007. New York: Clap Publishing.

Trollope, A. 1875/1941. *The Way We Live Now*. London, UK: Oxford University Press.

Tullmann, K. 2012. HOT Emotions: Dissolving the Paradox of Fiction. *Contemporary Aesthetics*, 10. Online: http://hdl.handle.net/2027/spo.7523862.0010.009.

Tullmann, K. and Buckwalter, W. 2014. Does the Paradox of Fiction Exist? *Erkenntnis*, 79(4), pp. 779–796.

Turner, R. H. and Killian, L. M. 1957. *Collective Behavior*. Englewood Cliffs, NJ: Prentice-Hall.

Van Krieken, R. 2014. Norbert Elias and Emotions in History. In: Lemmings, D. and Brooks, A. eds. *Emotions and Social Changes: Historical and Sociological Perspectives*. London, UK: Routledge, pp. 19–41.

Verga, G. 1890. *Mastro Don Gesualdo*. Translated from Italian by Cecchetti, G. 1979. Berkeley, CA: University of California Press.

Vester, H. G. 1999. Emotions in Postemotional Culture. In: Schlaeger, J. and Stedman, G. eds. *Representations of Emotions*. Tübingen, Germany: Gunter Narr Verlag, pp. 19–28.

Vidaillet, B. 2008. *Workplace Envy*. London, UK: Palgrave Macmillan.

von Scheve, C. and Ismer, S. 2013. Towards a Theory of Collective Emotions. *Emotion Review*, 5, pp. 406–413.

Walker, P. 1984. *Germinal and Zola's Philosophical and Religious Thought*. Amsterdam, the Netherlands and Philadelphia, PA: John Benjamins Publishing Company.

Walton, K. L. 1978. Fearing Fictions. *The Journal of Philosophy*, 75(1), pp. 5–27.

Weber, M. 1905. *The Protestant Ethic and the Spirit of Capitalism*. Translated from German by Parsons, T. 2005. London, UK: Routledge.

Weber, M. 1915. *Economy and Society*. Edited by Roth, G. and Wittich, C. 1978. Berkeley, CA: University of California Press.

Weber, M. 1946. *The Methodology of the Social Sciences*. Translated from German and Edited by Shils, E. A. and Finch, H. A. Glencoe, IL: The Free Press.

Weber, M. 1958. *From Max Weber*. Translated and Edited by Gerth, H. H. and Wright, Mills C. New York: Oxford University Press.

Wells Slights, C. 1997. Slaves and Subjects in *Othello*. *Shakespeare Quarterly*, 48(4), pp. 377–390.

Wesling, D. 2008. *Joys and Sorrows of Imaginary Persons: (On Literary Emotions)*. Amsterdam and New York: Rodopi.

White, H. 1980. The Value of Narrativity in the Representation of Reality. *Critical Inquiry*, 7(1), pp. 5–27.

Williams, R. 1977. *Marxism and Literature*. Oxford, UK: Oxford University Press.

Williams, S. J. and Bendelow, G. 1998. Introduction: Emotions in Social Life. Mapping the Sociological Terrain. In: Bendelow, G. and Williams, S. J. eds. *Emotions in Social Life: Critical Themes and Contemporary Issues*. London, UK: Routledge, pp. XII–XXVII.

Wolff, K. H. 1950. Introduction. In: Wolff K. H. ed. *The Sociology of Georg Simmel*. Glencoe, IL: The Free Press, pp. XVII–LXIV.

Wrong, D. H. 1961. The Oversocialized Conception of Man in Modern Sociology. *American Sociological Review*, 26(2), pp. 183–193.

Yanal, R. 1991. Hume and Others on the Paradox of Tragedy. *The Journal of Aesthetics and Art Criticism*, 49(1), pp. 75–76.

Young, J. 1999. *The Exclusive Society: Social Exclusion, Crime and Differences in Late Modernity*. London, UK: Sage.

Zalambani, M. 2015. *L'istituzione del matrimonio in Tolstoj. Felicità familiare, Anna Karenina, La sonata a Kreutzer*. Firenze, Italy: Firenze University Press.

Znaniecky, F. 1925. *The Laws of Social Psychology*. Chicago, IL: University of Chicago Press.

Znaniecky, F. 1936. *Social Action*. New York: Farrar and Rinehart.

Zola, É. 1880. *The Experimental Novel and Other Essays*. Translated from French by Sherman, B. M. 1893. New York: The Cassel Publishing Co.

Zola, É. 1885. *Germinal*. Translated from French by Ellis, H. 1894. Online: www.ibiblio.org/eldritch/ez/germinal.html.

Index